The Financialized Economy

Social science theorists from various scholarly disciplines have contributed to a recent literature that examines how the finance industry has expanded and now wields increasing influence across a variety of economic fields and industries. In some cases, this tendency towards a more sizeable and influential finance industry has been referred to as "the financialization" of the economy. This book explains how what is referred to as the finance-led economy (arguably a more neutral and less emotionally charged term than financialization) is premised on a number of conditions, institutional relations, and theoretical propositions and assumptions, and indicates what the real economic consequences are for market actors and households.

The book provides a theoretically condensed but empirically grounded account of the contemporary finance-led economy, in many cases too complicated in its design and rich in detail to be understood equally by insiders—empirical research indicates—and lay audiences. It summarizes the relevant literature and points at two empirical cases, the construction industry and life science venturing, to better illustrate how the expansion of the finance industry has contributed to the capital formation process, and how the sovereign state has actively assisted this process. It offers a credible, yet accessible overview of the economic conditions that will arguably shape economic affairs for the foreseeable future.

The book will find an audience amongst a variety of readers, including graduate students, management scholars, policymakers, and management consultants.

Alexander Styhre is chair of Organizational Theory and Management, Department of Business Administration, School of Business, Economics and Law, University of Gothenburg, Sweden.

Routledge International Studies in Money and Banking

The Financialized Economy

Theoretical Views and Empirical Cases

Alexander Styhre

Routledge
Taylor & Francis Group

LONDON AND NEW YORK

First published 2021
by Routledge
2 Park Square, Milton Park, Abingdon, Oxon OX14 4RN

and by Routledge
52 Vanderbilt Avenue, New York, NY 10017

Routledge is an imprint of the Taylor & Francis Group, an informa business

British Library Cataloguing-in-Publication Data
A catalogue record for this book is available from the British Library

Library of Congress Cataloging-in-Publication Data
Names: Styhre, Alexander, author.
Title: The financialized economy: theoretical views and empirical cases / Alexander Styhre.
Description: Abingdon, Oxon; New York, NY: Routledge, 2021. |
Series: Routledge international studies in money and banking |
Includes bibliographical references and index.
Subjects: LCSH: Financialization. | Economics.
Classification: LCC HG173 .S8359 2021 (print) |
LCC HG173 (ebook) | DDC 332/.0415–dc23
LC record available at https://lccn.loc.gov/2020047629
LC ebook record available at https://lccn.loc.gov/2020047630

ISBN: 978-0-367-90272-8 (hbk)
ISBN: 978-0-367-75456-3 (pbk)
ISBN: 978-1-003-02350-0 (ebk)

Typeset in Sabon
by Newgen Publishing UK

Contents

Preface

One of the noteworthy features of the Trump presidential campaign and the following presidency is that the Trump team targeted the coal mining community and made promises that coal mining activities should be resumed to restore economic growth in these quarters of the American society.[1] This declaration upset sustainability experts and the environmental protection movement as coals are widely regarded as one of the dirtiest energy sources in terms of its CO_2 footprint and a most inefficient way to generate energy. Consequently, coal mining has been heavily disputed in various parts of the world. After all, one may suspect that this targeting of coal mining was part of the Trump campaign's tactics to maximize media attention and to provoke the mainstream, preferably liberal political communities that Trump's campaign advisers regarded as their principal adversaries. Nevertheless, in addition to being widely criticized for being an unsustainable source of energy, the American coal mining industry faces a perhaps even larger challenge: technological shifts and falling market demand. According to a 2015 McKinsey & Company report, the coal industry's production capacity has "vastly outpaced demand," Maccy and Salovaara (2019: 911) write. When demand falls, prices and revenues follow suit, and a business becomes obsolete, not only in terms of its lack of technical sophistication and lack of institutional support, but in terms of its economic return. Curiously enough, Macey and Salovaara (2019) show, large American coal mining companies have managed to remain in business *despite* such price drops, but only on the basis of their manipulation of their assets and liabilities through the use of American bankruptcy law. By moving the costs for retirement funds, healthcare benefits for former miners, and the cost to restore lands degraded by extractive activities to subsidiaries, eventually declared bankrupt under the so-called Chapter 11 bankruptcy legislation, coal companies can remain in business. "[P]arent companies repeatedly spin off subsidiaries comprised of depleted mining assets and significant liabilities, either through divestiture or liquidation," Macey and Salovaara (2019: 934) write, and go on to say, "When a successor company inevitably liquidates, the company that originally incurred these liabilities is shielded from the obligations."

Furthermore, to make bankruptcy judges prescribe Chapter 11 reorganization activities, coal mining companies "[e]ngage in financial gimmickry by overvaluing assets, undervaluing liabilities, or pushing liabilities off balance sheet in order to appear solvent and continue operating" (Macey and Salovaara, 2019: 934). The immediate consequence is that billions of dollars of contracted costs are externalized to the miners, local farmers, taxpayers, and other constituencies: "Taxpayers, regulators, and retired miners have been left to foot the bill for reclaiming degraded mines; cleaning up polluted water and farmland; and treating black lung disease, damaged appendages, and other ailments borne of careers in the mines" (Macey and Salovaara, 2019: 884). Chapter 11 bankruptcies prescribe that defaulting companies should be "reorganized" so that the total value of the corporation and employment opportunities is maximized. In contrast, Chapter 7 bankruptcies result in the liquidation of the business charter. Courts can therefore permit Chapter 11 reorganizations in cases where there is a reasonable prospect for future business activities. Unfortunately, Macey and Salovaara (2019) argue, American coal mining companies instrumentally use the Chapter 11 clause as a bailout mechanism that externalize all the social costs that the coal mining companies assumed as part of their original business licenses (Macey and Salovaara use the legal theory term "executory contracts" to denote such bundles of rights and liabilities): "[W]e posit that bankruptcy law can be manipulated in a manner that allows corporations to ignore federal environmental and labor laws even when those companies are solvent" (2019: 885). By transferring pension and healthcare costs and the costs related to the harm inflicted on the local environment that the coal mining companies have agreed to cover to subsidiaries, coal mining companies use bankruptcy legislation to undermine federal and state-based regulation, and to externalize costs on an industrial scale. Macey and Salovaara (2019: 888) believe such practices are inconsistent with policymakers' and legislators' intentions, and therefore such possibilities to externalize costs should be blocked: "[A] company should not be able to use bankruptcy to dispose of obligations whose purpose is to force corporations, shareholders, and creditors to bear the social costs of corporate activities" (Macey and Salovaara, 2019: 888).

This case is of relevance for the issue at hand being addressed in the current volume. The legal theory of finance advocated by, for example, Pistor (2013) understands the finance industry and its various assets, transactions, and contracts and agreements as ultimately being a matter of legal rights (see also Listokin, 2019; Listokin and Murphy, 2019). Without the sovereign state passing laws and imposing regulatory control that generates operable and functional markets, there would be no finance market, nor any finance industry. Financial affairs is a matter of generating credit and credit relations (i.e., an asset on the balance sheet for the creditor, and debt as liability for the borrower), and such abstract relations demand a solid legal framework and a legal system that monitors finance market activities and enforces the rule of law in cases of disputes. The coal mining industry case is similarly rendered intelligible within a legal–financial framework: without the possibility of Chapter 11 bankruptcies, leading to a restructuring of the corporation, coal mining activities would not be possible as they are widely criticized in terms of their impact on global warming and the destruction of land resources, and in the face of declining profits. The question at hand is rather *why* legislators and courts are supportive of a business activity that externalizes all the social costs originally included in the business model, but that is another question, essentially being political in nature and presumably to be explained on basis of the idiosyncrasies of the American polity.

The finance industry and global finance markets are immensely complex in their details and all the asset pricing activities, and is almost impenetrable for a lay audience. Yet, finance industry activities immediately affect the everyday life of billions of people. News reporting is filled with finance industry-related dispatches regarding, for example, changes in interest rates, stock market evaluations, and similar indications of the state of the market, at times changing by the hour or even by the minute or second during episodes of market turbulence. Furthermore, today, in a highly differentiated society characterized by the integration of various economic activities on different levels of aggregation, it is virtually impossible to escape the influence of the finance industry. Similar to the medieval man or women who believed they lived their lives under the gaze of God, who would not fail to detect sinful behaviour or other acts that violated the rules of scripture, which imposed an ethics of prudence as each individual was deemed to be held responsible for his or her actions when entering the afterlife, the modern man or woman endures a situation wherein most everyday activities have a more or less close connection to global finance. The belief in divine supervision has been largely abandoned in a secular age, whereas the modern legal–institutional system, mutatis mutandis, takes its place. This formulation is not intended to indicate a conspiracy, nor to suggest that such institutional conditions are inevitable facts of nature. On the contrary, like in the case of all institutional conditions, these are man-made and social structures that have the benefit of creating unprecedented levels of economic and social welfare, but also generate unintended consequences. The finance industry is no conspiracy against mankind, the working class, or developing economies, and so on, but is a highly sophisticated legal–economic activity that is populated by professional men and women who can be reasonably assumed to wish to do good and to make the world a better place. This does not mean that the finance industry cannot display dysfunctions or result in unintended consequences (e.g., financial crises, bank runs, asset price drops, fire sales, and a number of other, well-documented finance market events). On the contrary, the very complexity of the business activities at hand, to assess risk, uncertainty, and creditworthiness within the horizon of an uncertain future and under the influence of a profit motive, may result in outcomes that are disappointing for some parts. In addition to that, the presence of speculators, naive investors, and fly-by-night and non-prudent lenders in finance markets add to the complexity.

This volume seeks to provide some insights into the mechanisms and devices that are employed to generate credit relations that result in increased venturing activities and economic welfare more generally. It does not attempt to provide a comprehensive or conclusive view of finance industry activities, but it aims to connect the abstract scholarly literature on law and finance with the more day-to-day activities that are commonly understood to be the subject of management studies. In order to bridge what is abstract (and oftentimes either expressed in a legal theory vocabulary, or in mathematical formulae and statistical data) with what is reasonably concrete (e.g., life science venturing activities, or home ownership conditions), practical examples are used throughout the volume. While the tone of the volume may at times indicate a certain scepticism towards finance industry activities (largely the effect of dysfunctional cases being more illustrative of theoretical propositions, and consequently used, than its opposite, the smooth and mutually rewarding finance market transaction), the finance industry is in fact understood as a constitutional creation within the realm of the sovereign state's jurisdiction and the work of transnational governance agencies. That is, at the end of the day, the finance industry exists because policymakers and legislators believe an advanced and differentiated finance industry benefits non-financial activities and results in increased economic welfare. However, it should be recognized that once a finance industry is established, it may itself execute agency in ways that policymakers and legislators failed to anticipate to a full degree. That is still another issue, an epiphenomenon following from the original accomplishments made to generate credit supply in an economic system. Under all conditions, the volume is intended to serve the purpose of providing an integrated overview of the recent literature on the finance-led economy, a literature that spans the disciplinary boundaries between management studies, economics, legal theory, and economic sociology (and a number of additional, yet more marginal disciplines). This work reported in this volume hopefully inspires further scholarly studies of the finance-led economies and all its possibilities and dysfunctions.

Note

1 It should be noticed that studies indicate that Trump voters have fared badly in the Great Recession that followed from the 2008 finance industry crisis. Research shows that the counties that voted for Hillary Clinton in 2016 accounted for 64 per cent of the nation's economic activity; the counties that voted for Donald Trump accounted for 36 per cent. In comparison, when Al Gore lost to George W. Bush in the 2000 Presidential election, the counties Gore won accounted for 54 per cent of total national economic activity (Blanchflower, 2019: 24–25). Furthermore, Levitin and Wachter (2020: 228) suggest that a decline in housing

prices raised fear among American voters, which had repercussions throughout the political system. A study found that negative equity rates increased in the 2015–2016 period in "over a third of the countries that had voted for Barack Obama in 2012 but for Donald Trump in 2016" (Levitin and Wachter, 2020: 229). Households in economic distress were thus more susceptible to populist statements regarding, for example, the rehabilitation of the moribund American coal mining industry.

Acknowledgements

I would like to thank Kristina Abbotts, Senior Editor, Economics, Finance and Accounting, and Terry Clague, Senior Publisher and Commissioning Editor, Taylor & Francis/Routledge, for providing me with the opportunity to write this volume. The work is the outgrowth from empirical and theoretical work I have been occupied with over the last few years, and is largely a systematic overview of some of the most interesting aspects of the financed-led economy that we are all dependent on in our day-to-day life, before, during, and after the Covid-19 pandemic that served to define the annus horribilis of 2020. In this context, I would like to thank my colleagues at my home department, the Management & Organization Section at the Department of Business Administration, School of Business, Economics, and Law, University of Gothenburg, and in particular a number of persons with whom I have recently collaborated more closely: Kajsa Lindberg, Björn Remneland-Wikhamn, Sara Brorström, Ola Bergström, Maria Norbäck, and Jonas Fasth. As always, the possibility to engage in academic work under a considerable degree of analytical freedom is a wonderful benefit, yet it demands much concentration and self-discipline, and not the least to persistently engage in oftentimes quite painful self-correcting activities when reading and rereading passages and chapters for the nth time. Nevertheless, these not so appealing elements of the academic work (or even the academic "lifestyle," for some) need to be weighed against all the other benefits that come with the work. Having said that, even though I rely on extensive citing of secondary scholarly literature, all the flaws and concerns regarding the content of the text are the outcome from my own limitations, and no one else should be blamed for these shortcomings of the text.

Introduction

Vignette: the civilizing effects of commerce argument

The history of the liberal economy, based on the private business venture incorporated by the sovereign state and operating outside of the monarchy's realm of influence and interest, is remarkably short, lasting no more than 270 years, from the middle of the eighteenth century. One of the first scholarly volumes that actually addressed the benefit of the "liberal economy" is Charles-Louis de Secondat Montesquieu's (1748) *De l'esprit des loix*, published two and a half decades before Adam Smith's much-praised thesis *The Wealth of Nations* (1776). By and large, Montesquieu (who published his treatise anonymously) argued that economies that were subordinate to monarchic powers were less productive and venturesome in comparison to that of "une nation libre."[1] This idea was also endorsed by David Hume, the Scottish philosopher and "man of letters" (in his own account), who declared in the bold spirit of Enlightenment thinking that "the poverty of the common people is a natural, if not an infallible effect of absolute monarchy" (1996: 165). Furthermore, Montesquieu argued (1788a: 141) *le commerce*, trade and other industrious activities generated several differences in a specific society, for example, a broader variety of people are engaged in trade, new conventions and practices are established, and new ways of accumulating wealth are developed.[2] This is again a thesis that Hume endorses, saying that "[i]ndusty, knowledge, and humanity are linked together" (1996: 169–170. Original emphasis omitted). Hume explicates this position and points at how trade generates many benefits in a society:

> [T]his is perhaps the chief advantage which arises from a commerce with strangers. It rouses men from their indolence […] [and] raises them a desire of a more splendid way of life than what their ancestors enjoyed.
> (1996: 163)

In the end and over time, commercial activities grow together with the sovereign state so that commerce and policy are essentially co-produced activities that equally contribute to economic welfare: "The greatness of a state, and the happiness of its subjects, how independent soever they may be supposed in some respects, are commonly allowed to be inseparable with regard to commerce," Hume (1996: 154) contends.

Montesquieu's (1748) account of the value of commerce, later enshrined in Smith's seminal treatise *The Wealth of Nations* (1776), especially held in esteem in the Anglo-American cultural sphere, portrayed trade outside of the direct rent-seeking activities of the monarchy as a tool for the leverage of economic welfare. What was known among French intellectuals such as the proponents of the physiocratic school of economic theory as *doux commerce* was thus an emphatic defence of trade as a liberal approach to the modernization of society. Not only did *doux commerce* add to aggregated welfare, but it institutes discipline among actors involved in trade as they are increasingly incentivized to honour their part of the contract they initiate, Fourcade (2017) writes:

> Adam Smith thought that being involved in economic exchange made people more punctual, polite, prudent and cordial. The French went further, seeing the market as an agent of political emancipation against the special privileges of social orders and corporations.
>
> (2017: 665)

For this new generation of proponents of the free market (with "free" as in the absence of rent-seeking monarchies, intervening in the contractual relations among business partners and their subcontractors), the market was a key institutional and legal innovation. Unsurprisingly, given the prediction of Montesquieu and Hume regarding the adverse effects of monarchical rent-seeking, it was the Dutch, who had abjured their Habsburg ruler in 1581 and subsequently "established themselves as a republic with a federal structure and a limited central power responsive to commercial interests" (Dari-Mattiacci et al., 2017: 198), that became the leading economic power in Europe in the seventeenth century. Between 1598 and 1608, the investors in Amsterdam's early companies earned an "average annual return of 27%," Dari-Mattiacci et al. (2017: 206) report. Furthermore, the Dutch invented what is arguably the first private business corporation operating outside of monarchial protection when the Dutch East Asian Company (Vereenigde Oost-Indische Compagnie) was established. During the coming period in the early 1600s, several European countries, including France, Britain, Sweden, and Denmark, followed suit and "moved to grant monopoly rights to trade companies" (Dari-Mattiacci et al., 2017: 195; see also Wezel and Ruef, 2017: 1012). By the time of the publication of Montesquieu's major work in 1748, the advantage had started to move towards Great Britain, which developed as a major seafaring nation (Allen, 2012: 108) to compete with the venturesome, fiercely competitive, and religiously liberal Dutch Republic (the Netherlands hosted, e.g., a sizeable Jewish population). The new private business venture embodied all of the bourgeois qualities and virtues that defined the coming centuries of economic expansion: risk-taking, self-discipline, thrift, a trust in business partners, being accompanied by new legal devices such as contracts, and the reinvestment in earnings in new economic ventures rather than to squander them—as the aristocracy was prone to do—on lavish expenses and conspicuous luxury consumption, which further propelled the virtuous cycle of economic growth.

Regardless of the overall efficiency of existing and new businesses, for example, Hume was concerned with rentiers who could reap benefit from the work conducted by the venturesome merchant class. Oddly, given today's strong emphasis on the alleged virtues shareholder welfare, Hume addressed "stockholders" as one such category of rentier investors who were given the opportunity to passively await a return on investment:

> In this unnatural state of society, the only persons who possess any revenue beyond immediate effects of their industry, are the stockholders, who draw almost all the customs and excises. These are men who have no connection with the state, who can enjoy their revenue in any part of the globe in which they choose to reside, who will naturally bury themselves in the capital, or in great cities, and who will sink into the lethargy of a stupid or papered luxury, without spirit, ambition, or enjoyment. Adieu to all ideas of nobility, ambition, and family.
>
> (1996: 209)

In Hume's view, the rentier is a form of ersatz aristocrat who benefits from a growing economy and, similar to the aristocrat, who relied primarily on a rural economy and could maintain control over that production, well into the end of the nineteenth century in backward economies such as Russia, add little value to the business operations as such (apparently, Hume did not regard the risk-taking that all investments include as a form of contribution to the economy). This statement by Hume is indicative of the concern that early proponents of private business ventures and a liberal market economy paid to the issue of rentier investors, a theme that needs to be examined in more detail when discussing the mechanisms and devices determining the contemporary, finance-led economy. Even during the *doux commerce* era, the prospects of a liberal economy were overshadowed by concerns regarding rentiers free-riding and thus compromising the overarching ideology wherein economic returns is a function of the risk being taken in the business venture, the *primus motor* of the bourgeois merchant economy and the liberal trade of the seventeenth and eighteenth centuries.

This introduction provides the basis for a number of questions to be discussed. First of all, the assumption that commerce both shapes human societies and more specifically refines social practices and human behaviour more generally was firmly established in the early modern period among proponents of the *doux commerce* thesis. Second, at an early stage, there were concerns that the species of the rentier would be able to reap economic benefits on the basis of investing in ventures so that the risk was minimized despite making a considerable return on investment. At the same time, the rentier is not harmful to the economic system as long as finance capital is invested in ways that generate net economic welfare, preferably to optimize the efficiency of the economic system. These two elementary ideas— commerce has civilizing qualities but commerce per se cannot always ensure that opportunistic behaviour is ruled out—are of great relevance for this volume. Rather than sorting out these two propositions and trying to answer the questions either affirmatively or negatively here and now, history can be fast-forwarded to the current situation, wherein financial trade has shifted gear, and wherein, for example, algorithm trade measures transactions in micro-seconds (Mackenzie, 2018).

Commerce in the new millennium: business deals made in microseconds

On May 6, 2010, what would eventually be known as "the Flash Crash" occurred in the global finance market. During a short period of time, lasting only a few minutes, automatic finance trading (so-called robot trade), governed by algorithms instructing the trading system to buy, hold, or sell stocks under certain predefined conditions, eliminated "one trillion U.S. dollars in value from U.S. equity and derivatives markets" (Johnson, 2017: 836–837). Linton and Mahmoodzadeh (2018: 250) define flash crashes more generally as "[s]hort and relatively deep price movements that are not apparently driven by fundamentals, or rather, they are movements in prices that are in excess of what would be warranted based on fundamentals, at least according to hindsight." When finance trading runs amok, the conventional wisdom suggests that such events are indicative of either some exogenous factor including the introduction of new information (say, a change in fiscal policy) that affects trade activities or, alternatively, some actors changing their investment strategies, or otherwise assessing the market data differently than they did previously. In the aftermath of the 2010 Flash Crash, it was instead revealed that "algorithmic bias" caused the spike in finance trading, a finding that has important implications for the finance industry (Vives, 2019). First of all, as a practical industry matter, the resilience and predictability of automatic trading activities were questioned. As the finance industry has historically been at pain to distance its activities from mere speculation, or even "gambling" (Banner, 2017; Goede, 2005), such adverse events tend to cast a shadow of doubt over the legitimacy of the finance industry. The question is then how the algorithms are designed in the first place, and to what end they serve: to generate net economic welfare on the basis of more efficient price-discovery processes, or, to be a mere automatic "money-machine" for the benefit of a small minority of elite speculators, at low cost skimming off economic value generated elsewhere in the economy? Second, the very presence of these non-human actors, de facto being a complex mathematical model, generated a debate regarding legal issues pertaining to its use in finance trading (Crawford and Schultz, 2014). If algorithms fail, who is then to be held legally accountable? Is it the firm using the algorithm (algorithms often travel across the finance industry to harmonize the price-discovery process among heterogeneous actors; MacKenzie and Spears, 2014: 437), the individual trader using the algorithm, the firm that originally developed it, the original designer of the algorithm (a so-called quant), or perhaps even the regulatory authority that permitted the use of the algorithm (and eo ipso making the failure of algorithms a matter of force majeur in the legal sense of the term)? These legal issues are more convoluted than one may believe at first sight. For instance, within the Delaware corporate legislation (the state of choice for incorporating business ventures in the United States), an algorithm and its software code is a trade secret, and finance institutions do not therefore have to disclose algorithms to third parties (Kroll et al., 2017: 704). It is also equally unclear whether clients can take to court cases wherein they are dissatisfied with the return on their investment on the basis of the use of suboptimal algorithms within the current legislation. "[T]he accountability mechanisms and legal standards that govern decision processes have not kept pace with technology. The tools currently available to policymakers, legislators, and courts were developed primarily to oversee human decision makers" (Kroll et al., 2017: 636) summarize.

Leaving these issues aside for now, positive reviews of the uses of algorithm trade suggest that the presence of "algorithmic traders" in the market causes "both a reduction in the frequency of arbitrage opportunities and a decrease in high-frequency excess volatility" (Chaboud et al., 2014: 2075). Expressed in less technical terms, Chaboud et al. (2014) suggest that algorithm traders contribute to net economic welfare. At the same time, Chaboud et al. (2014) cannot rule out that so-called "model risks," which denotes the situations wherein algorithms per se create systemic risks as the models may be biased in ways so that they underrate certain market conditions, cannot cause the effects being revealed by the 2010 Flash Crash event. During such episodes, so-called herd behaviour (e.g., Froot, Scharfstein, and Stein, 1992) results in a downward spiral of market prices (resulting in asset price drops), beyond the stipulated "fundamental value" of the assets (see, e.g., Bryan and Rafferty, 2013; Ferrillo, Dunbar, and Tabak, 2004). For instance, algorithm trade may work impeccably in the upward movement of the economic cycle, when the supply of finance capital is abundant and when the liquidity of the market is satisfying, whereas it may work less smoothly during a downward movement in the economic cycle. For instance, a study issued by the US Securities and Exchange Commission (SEC) and the Commodity Futures Trading Commission (CFTC) indicated that "a large number of high frequency traders [i.e., algorithm traders] exacerbated market volatilities by rapidly leaving the market when conditions became stressed unexpectedly" (Yadav, 2015: 1614). When unexpected information was introduced on the market, traders displayed a tendency towards herd behaviour. Furthermore, there are auxiliary effects of algorithm trading, for instance, the lowered costs for participating in finance trade easily result in a situation wherein weakly capitalized, fly-by-night finance traders initiate activities under favourable conditions, but withdraw from the market or even declare bankruptcy as soon as the situation turns dire (Yadav, 2015: 1624). These forms of undesirable behaviour (from the clients' and regulators' perspectives) are not considered by, for example, Chaboud et al. (2014).

The 2010 Flash Crash is an illustrative case of how far the advanced economic system has taken the basic idea that regional and local differences in production factor costs can be fruitfully exploited on the basis of trade and the legal device of contracting. Finance trade is no longer so much a matter of carefully assessing the risks and calculated returns of economic ventures as it is a matter of orchestrating advanced technological systems to reap the benefits of being able to trade differentiated derivative assets at the speed of a fraction of the blink of an eye. Whether this line of work contributes to social welfare and refinement is an open question, but it is nevertheless an empirical condition that is qualified for extended scholarly inquiry. On the basis of this proposition, the purpose of the thesis can be formulated.

The purpose of the thesis

All economic systems are founded on institutional conditions, which include political decision-making, legislation, law enforcement, and social norms. In addition, various "market devices" (Callon, Millo, and Muniesa, 2007), that is, the technologies, tools, and algorithms that reduce transaction costs, are introduced to make economic activities more efficient. This volume will examine the various institutional conditions that have paved the way for the finance-led economy, and provide practical examples for how different economic activities (say, life science innovation work or housing production) to a varying degree access finance capital on the basis of idiosyncratic combinations of laws, rules, regulatory control, and calculative practices. In the following, the term "the finance-led economy" will be used, a term that is tangential to the concept of *financialization* but introduced to escape the social theory connotations of the latter term. The finance-led economy includes the creation of legislative practices, that is, legal conditions determine how, for example, credit is issued in the economy, and therefore neither economic theory (which overstates rationalist and instrumental explanations) nor economic sociology theory (which stresses the role of social norms and political processes and beliefs) provides any comprehensive and plausible explanation for the unprecedented expansion of the finance industry in advanced economies.

Drawing on the work of Pistor (2013), who advocates a "legal theory of finance," this volume has two purposes: (1) to provide a review of the transdisciplinary literature that addresses the growth and expansion of the global finance industry, and (2) to point at the implications for two distinct industries (life science ventures and housing production and the mortgage lending industry), being at the end points of a continuum, being thickly and thinly capitalized economic activities, respectively. In the end, the purpose of this volume is to indicate the degree of theoretical and practical complexity of the finance industry that increasingly determines what business ventures and social activities are worthy of being bestowed with credit. Much of the conventional wisdom, say, things being taught at business schools, for instance, that financial institutions act as intermediaries between mature industries and entrepreneurial ventures, is an inadequate description, which calls for a revision of the image of the economy. The new economic order, grounded in legislative reforms, and supported by political ideas and convictions, is arguably yet in its infancy, but a proper understanding of the new conditions is arguably of great importance for the capacity to anticipate its unintended consequences and the long-term effects on economic welfare and social stability. As Auguste Comte (1975: 88), the founder of positivism, once declared, "From science comes prevision; from prevision comes action." In order to act and to anticipate things in the making, science, and more specifically scientific methodologies and scientific concepts and theories, are tools, devices, and heuristics that render a world overwhelmingly complex and rich in details understandable and manageable. Whether such perceived possibilities for agency are overstated on the basis of such resources is of secondary interest only—a question that needs to be answered in the light of the value of having at least *some* theoretical mapping of the economic reality wherein the subject operates. In other words, the risk of failing to provide a comprehensive overview of a field is tolerable as the potential benefits of this venture are estimated to be higher than the costs of not making this effort. The scholarly project is pursued on the basis of this proposition.

Outline of the volume

This book is structured into five chapters. The first chapter reviews the literature on the so-called financialization of the global and regional economic system, and pays specific attention to financial innovations such as securitization and the role of shadow banking in the contemporary financial economy. The second chapter more explicitly discusses the capital formation process, which includes the involvement of the sovereign state inasmuch as insurances generate so-called safe assets that play a key role for the credit supply. The third chapter shifts the focus to a thickly financialized domain of the economy, that of housing and real estate production. The credit formation process demands qualitative collateral to enable also private-backed safe assets. Housing facilities have a comparably stable market value over the business cycle, and home ownership is a political priority in many welfare states that host advanced economies. Housing facilities therefore serve as the collateral *par préférence* in the credit formation process. As a consequence, soaring housing prices that burden household budgets are therefore not primarily explained on the basis of mismatches between supply and demand, but derive from the capacity of mortgage lenders to securitize such financial assets, a business practice that is supported by insurances from the sovereign state that render, for example., mortgage-based securities safe assets.

In contrast, in Chapter 4, life science ventures are examined as an exemplary thinly capitalized business activity, also explained on the basis of the broader socio-economic conditions that shape the production of new drugs, medical technologies, and medical visualization devices. Whereas housing production is assisted by political objectives and insurances that render, for example., mortgage lending lucrative, investment in knowledge-intensive, yet uncertain innovation work includes considerable difficulties from presumptive investors' perspective. In, for example, new drug development work, there are both epistemic risks in clinical trials as it is, for instance, complicated to extrapolate results from in vivo studies in the laboratory to studies in humans, and market risks inasmuch as a new therapy needs to be both approved by the US Food and Drug Administration (FDA) and thereafter procured by hospitals and healthcare companies. Current risk management models can calculate levels of tolerable risk, but non-parametric risk, that is, uncertainty, is more complicated to deal with. The primary consequence is that, for example, life science ventures are either thinly capitalized and need to raise new funds on a short-term basis, which means that life science ventures commit a significant proportion of their resources to refinance themselves, or are financed by state-governed agencies such as investment funds or incubators, which per se is a deviation from the market-based investment model that most mainstream commentators take to be the standard model. In the end, the differences between, for example, housing production and life science venturing—despite their equally central role in terms of their capacity to generate economic and social welfare—result in a biased allocation of financial capital that arguably results in excessive housing price growth and the undercapitalization of, for example, life science ventures.

Given these concerns regarding the financial economy's ability to self-regulate or to operate on the basis of private ordering models, the final chapter of the volume summarizes the basic arguments and points at some future challenges pertaining to the governance and monitoring of the economic system. For instance, how should the sovereign state and transnational governance organization seek to balance rentier interests and investment in entrepreneurial activities? Scholarly research indicates that entrepreneurial activities are in decline in the United States, and the limited supply of credit to uncertain development work appears to be one explanatory factor. Another issue is whether the sovereign state should actively assist the creation of new markets for finance capital investors, for instance, within the realm of welfare state activities. One such example is how so-called social impact bonds (SIBs) have been used as a financial services device to fund the rehabilitation work of former prisoners in, for example, the United Kingdom, a financial innovation in the domain of the civic society that is controversial inasmuch as much of the downside risk is still carried by the sovereign state, whereas the financial institutions that issue SIBs as an investment asset benefit from the upside risk. The final chapter more broadly sketches a financial economy wherein policymakers and regulatory agencies need to carefully consider both the benefits and the costs of various finance industry reforms and the financial innovations that follow from such reforms but also serve to justify such changes in policy in the first place. In the postscript to the volume, yet another financial phenomenon appearing on the horizon but otherwise not addressed in detail in the volume is briefly discussed, that of the issuance of digital media-based cryptocurrencies, which will possibly further complicate the work of policymakers and finance industry regulators for the rest of the century. But that is, as is oftentimes said, quite another story to be told.

Summary and conclusion

The financial economy certainly has its roots in early modern thought regarding the many benefits of free trade and venturing uninhibited by, for example, the interests of monarchs or the church. Yet the contemporary financial economy measures business transactions in the realm of microseconds (as in the case of high-frequency trading), and this high degree of technical and legal sophistication renders a more common-sense view of financial services somewhat antiquated. Rather than playing a traditional intermediary role between, for example, finance capital owners and business promoters in demand of finance capital, a role once played by banks granted the licence from the sovereign state to issue credit on the basis of risk-averse calculations, the finance industry now transcends this stricter role and instead actively intervenes in all domains of economic affairs. Furthermore, the sheer complexity of the entire finance industry and its intricate relations to what is at times referred to as the real economy preclude any full mapping of the activities, and also insiders claim that they cannot fully oversee the industry (Jacobides, 2005; Souleles, 2019). Based on these propositions, this volume does not provide any attempts to comprehensively map the financial industry in full. What the volume intends to do is instead point at the complexities of the financial economy and examine some of the unintended consequences of purposeful action, for example, in the domain of policy-making supportive of home ownership and in industry policy intended to assist innovation-led growth. Already in these two cases, a considerable degree of complexity can be reported.

Notes

1 "Régle génerale: dans une nation qui est dans la servitude, on travaille plus à conserver qu'à acquérir. dans une nation libre, on travaille plus a acquérir qu'à conserver," Montesquieu (1788a: 127) writes.
2 "Le commerce introduit dans le même pays différantes sortes de peuples, un grand nombre de conventions, d'éspèces de biens, et de manières d'acquérir" (Montesquieu, 1788a: 141).

1 The financial economy
A review of the literature

Introduction: the business franchise to issue credit

The purpose of the financial system is to provide credit, that is, to ensure the circulation of money in the economic system. While the term *credit* may be regarded as a technical term, the word *money* is better aligned with everyday practices and a common-sense outlook, but still the concept of money is fairly complex. Without delving into all the details regarding the various classes of money (e.g. as currency, fiat money, as managed money, e.g. assets holdings), money can be practically defined as the monetary supply in an economy, defined accordingly:

> [W]e can define the money supply *(M)* as consisting of currency *(C)*, checkable bank deposits *(D)*, shadow-banking instruments *(S)*, and government obligations *(G)*. Thus, $M = C + D + S + G$.
>
> (Levitin, 2016: 433)

For most non-expert readers, this definition introduces more questions than it answers, and it includes many technical terms. At this point, it may be simply concluded that money is more than currency, the bills and coins that people carry around in their purses and pockets and that they retrieve from their bank accounts when they need to make a purchase (if paying in cash, that is). Currency, money used in everyday practices is something similar to the tip of the iceberg in the well-known metaphor: it is the money people see and practically deal with in day-to-day transactions. In addition to such money, there are a variety of classes of money in the money supply stock.

By the end of the day, the supply of money, for example, in the form of credit, is a "constitutional project," Levitin (2016: 446) says: "Control over the monetary system is a fundamental part of the sovereign condition." That is, it is the sovereign state (say, the state of Denmark or Chile) that is the principal-agent relations of the finance industry being granted the right to issue credit de novo and ex nihilo. To better explain the rationale and the implications of Levitin's (2016) statement, what Pistor (2013) calls the legal theory of finance is helpful. In this theoretical perspective, Pistor

(2013: 315) writes, "finance is legally constructed; it does not stand outside the law." Consequently, financial assets are issued on the finance market and traded as contracts whose value "depends in large part on their legal vindication" (Pistor, 2013: 315). In this view, finance assets are contracts, which per se are legal devices constituted by legislation monitored by the sovereign state, and it is therefore not fully meaningful to speak of financial assets outside of the context of their legal constitution, ultimately backed by the legislative authority of the sovereign state. Hockett and Omarova (2016) speak explicitly about the credit supply provided by the finance industry as a "franchise arrangement," a "public-private partnership" initiated to assist credit formation in the economy, and ultimately intended to lower the cost of capital so that market participants, both businesses and households, can access credit in a safe and efficient manner (see also Braun, 2016; Sgambati, 2016). Boy and Gabor (2019: 304) regard this "franchise arrangement" as a form of "social contract" formulated in the nineteenth century:

> [T]he nineteenth century saw the state enter into a "social contract" with banks, agreeing to support bank money parity to state money and thereby removing convertibility risk from bank money creation. States guaranteed banks' pledges to their depositors through deposit insurance and access to central bank liquidity during times of crisis as lender of last resort. In exchange for underwriting financial and monetary stability, states demanded control over money creation through regulation and monetary policy. Yet as this systemic insurance comes at a cost, private actors continually seek to circumvent the state's balance sheet and create pledges that credibly pledge moneyness.

Hockett and Omarova (2016: 147) argue that the finance industry acts on the basis of a licence issued by the sovereign state: "Pursuant to this arrangement, the sovereign public, as franchisor, effectively licenses private financial institutions, as franchisees, to dispense a vital and indefinitely extensible public resource: the sovereign's full faith and credit."

More specifically, this franchise arrangement stipulates at least three activities that finance institutions actively participate in: (1) "credit-*intermediation*"; (2) "credit-*multiplication*"; and (3) "credit *generation*" (Hockett and Omarova, 2016: 1148; emphasis in the original). In addition, Bai, Philippon, and Savov (2016: 627) identify five key activities that the finance industry and the finance market are held responsible for in the economy: (1) generating information about "investment opportunities and allocation of capital," (2) handling the "mobilization and pooling of household savings," (3) monitoring investments and performance, (4) financing trade and consumption, and, finally (5) handling a series of financial services pertaining to the "provision of liquidity, facilitation of secondary market trading, diversification, and risk management." The implication from the close relation between the state and the finance industry is that the state, acting through its political entities, legislative bodies, and regulatory agencies (e.g. the central bank), "ultimately generates and underwrites capital flows in a modern financial system" (Hockett and Omarova, 2016: 1149). Ricks (2018: 758–759) refers to this view as the "the money paradigm," wherein banks are not only seen as intermediaries, being in the "business of 'taking funds' from depositors and then 'lending them out'" (Ricks, 2018: 758), but also being "distinctly monetary institutions" inasmuch as the claims on banks are, in a real sense, money. This means that banks "augment the money supply" (Ricks, 2018. 758–759). Rather than seeing bank money creation as "a legitimate private activity," the money paradigm view regards "money creation as an intrinsically public activity that is then outsourced" (Ricks, 2018: 765–766). For instance, if the finance industry is in distress, for instance on the basis of a too high level of systemic risk that makes it complicated to borrow and lend money on the money market[1] as it is difficult (i.e., costly) to determine which market actors that are at risk to default, the sovereign state needs to serve as the lender of last resort and actively implement resolution system activities so that the faith in the market is restored, and the credit supply activities can be maintained. Critics have argued that such insurances, which result in rescue activities whenever they are needed, generate moral hazard, that is, invite opportunistic behaviour and excessive risk-taking as the finance industry de facto (but not necessarily de jure) is insured against default. Under all conditions, the franchise model for credit supply renders the line of demarcation between the state and market actors fluid and permeable, Pistor (2013: 322) proposes: "Financial systems are not state or market, private or public, but always and necessarily both." She continues:

> [D]escribing finance as a system of private/private commitments subject to some (external) constraints that may enhance market efficiency [...] misses much of what is unique to contemporary finance: It is based on money as the legal tender, relies on the legal enforceability of private/ private commitments and in the last instance depends on backstopping by a sovereign.
>
> (Pistor, 2013: 323)

At the same time as the state and the finance industry are intimately connected through the legislative foundation of the finance industry and the credit formation process, this does not of necessity translate into a harmonious coexistence as finance industry actors are incentivized to extract returns and economic compensation for their work, and whenever the state imposes regulations such as disclosure rules or prohibitions against the trading of certain classes of assets (say, collateralized debt obligations (CDOs), a complex "second-level" derivative instrument that is complicated to price and therefore essentially illiquid; see, e.g., Bluhm and Wagner, 2011), finance industry actors tend to circumvent regulatory rules by creating financial innovations or new investment vehicles (Funk and Hirschman, 2014). "[L]aw and finance are locked into a dynamic process in which the rules that establish the game are continuously challenged by new contractual devices, which in turn seek legal vindication," Pistor (2013: 315) says. In the end, the credit supply is a concern of the sovereign state, but it is practically accomplished by granting business charters to finance institutions such as banks to issue credit as part of their business operations. The complexity that follows from this elementary relation are considerable, and at times even complicated to anticipate or understand for centrally located agents, which makes the finance industry protean and vulnerable to disturbances, not the least from the inside of the industry, wherein, for example, speculation on prices may distort the market pricing of assets.

Finance industry expansion

A sizeable scholarly literature indicates that the finance industry turnover has expanded considerably over the last four decades since the early 1980s. In 2003, Rajan and Zingales (2003: 17) reported that "the average ratio of deposits to GDP increased by 35%, [while] the average ratio of stock market capitalization to GDP increased four times," which are indicators of how the finance market both deepened (i.e., included a larger variety of asset classes) and thickened (i.e., increased its turnover). Stockhammer (2013: 513) reports that this tendency has continued more or less unabatedly since 2003:

> From 1997 stock-market capitalization exceeds GDP [in the United States], rising from 58 percent of GDP in 1988 to 163 percent in 1999 (and flattering out thereafter). The rise of stock-market turnover is even more spectacular in the period from 33 percent in 1988 to 383 percent in 2008.

The perhaps most remarkable change in the industry is the expansion of the securities trade, wherein the estimated value of total derivatives in 2007 (just prior to the 2008 finance industry collapse) was "600 trillion according to United Nations—964 percent of world GDP" (Levitt, 2013: 166). This figure indicates that the total output of securities is today valued at more than 9.5 times the global gross domestic product (GDP), a mind-boggling figure to consider and apprehend.

Another indication of the consolidation of the finance industry and its more central role in the global economy is the concentration of economic power in the finance industry. In the United States, the total asset share of the ten largest banks grew from approximately 28 per cent in 1990 to 68 per cent in 2010 (Strahan, 2013: 53, figure 2). Expressed differently, the ten largest US banks increased their relative share of total assets holding by 2.5 times in two decades. In the United Kingdom and in the measure of asset holdings as a share of GDP, a similar tendency has been reported: by the beginning of the twentieth century, the largest three banks had asset holdings that corresponded to 7 per cent of GDP, and by the mid-century the figure had reached 27 per cent. In 2007, this figure stood at 2,000 per cent of the GDP. That is, three banks alone held assets worth 20 times the United Kingdom GDP (Dodd, 2014: 114). Statistics that indicate a growing finance industry have prompted increased scholarly interest, also among non-finance theory-oriented disciplines (e.g. economic sociology and management studies) regarding finance industry business practices and their role in the contemporary economy (see e.g. Lépinay, 2011; Mackenzie, 2006; Jacobides, 2005). Critical scholars use the term *financialization* to denote how the finance industry not only serves an intermediary function in the globalized economy but actively shapes how non-financial industries act and make business decisions (e.g. Carruthers, 2015; Davis and Kim, 2015; Dore, 2008; Epstein, 2005).

The concept of financialization

"Many analysts see financialization as the defining characteristic of the world economy of the last twenty-five years," Milberg (2008: 423) argues, and thereby underlines the centrality of the finance economy in the contemporary period of time (say, after the turn of the millennium). To define financialization is no trivial issue as there are a variety of perspectives and underlying disciplinary frameworks that are deemed to shape economic conditions. Dore (2008: 1097–1098) provides a definition of the term and says it denotes "[t]he increasing role of financial motives, financial markets, financial actors and financial institutions in the operation of domestic and operational economies." Onaran, Stockhammer, and Grant (2011: 637) recognize a variety of implications of the finance-led economy:

> The notion of financialization covers a wide range of phenomenon: the deregulation of the financial sector and the proliferation of new financial instruments, the increase in household debt, the development of the originate-and-distribute model of banking, the emergence of institutional investors as major player on financial markets, the boom (and bust) in asset markets, shareholder value orientation and changes in corporate governance (of non-financial business), and a spectacular rise of income in the financial sector and of financial investments.

In this account, financialization may cover most things under the sun, which by default may render it inoperable as a scholarly term, critics may contend. To examine the consequences of finance-led economic activities on a more manageable scale, Van der Zwan (2014: 118) introduces what she refers to as a "varieties of financialization" view (inspired by the "varieties of capitalism" literature; Hall and Thelen, 2009). Furthermore, in addition to the examination of finance-led economic activities in local and regional settings, the term can be discriminated along theoretical categories. Wansleben (2018: 775) associates financialization with institutional conditions and changes thereof, and defines the term as "[a] structural process and institutional transformation in capitalist democratic states." One such example is the management studies view that the finance industry-led growth has been assisted or even made possible on the basis of changes in corporate governance practices, and more specifically with what is referred to as shareholder value governance, the policy of transferring the residual cash generated by a corporation—the money that remains when all other costs are covered—to the owners of the stock (Tomaskovic-Devey, Lin, and Meyers, 2015; Lazonick and O'Sullivan, 2000). "Financialization is understood here as a finance-led regime of accumulation and as a process based on a strategy of shareholder value maximization," Darcillon (2015: 499) writes.

Other commentators, who do not necessarily reject this view but may regard it as being more of several implications of a finance-led economy, point at financialization as an explicitly "techno-political project, which both professional, political and economic actors promote" (Livne and Yonay, 2016: 340). In this view, the finance industry is merely one of many devices in the hands of activists and policy entrepreneurs who actively seek to downplay the role of the welfare state and its legislative entities and regulatory agencies. Finally, financialization has been understood as a new set of rules of the game that have equally behavioural roots and create a demand for behavioural changes. This may sound tendentious, but Tori and Onaran (2018: 1394–1395) propose that "'financialization' is a self-reinforcing socio-economic process, which manifests itself in the growing prominence of behaviours derived from the functioning of the financial sector." For instance, to substantiate the point made, in a society wherein the access to credit at reasonable costs (to enable, e.g., home mortgage borrowing as part of a house purchase), individuals need to pay attention to their creditworthiness, being a most complicated term, in the United States operationalized as a so-called FICO score, which is a standardized method to estimate the parametric risk regarding a presumptive client would default within a two years' time horizon. In this view, the finance-led economy may be a legal creation at the level of the constitutional rights of the sovereign state, but the consequences of this legal-political system inevitably trickle down to behavioural practices and regulations, and not least the social norms, such as the valuing of prudence and calculated risk-taking, derived therefrom. The "substantial meaning of financialization," Bryan and Raffery (2014: 891) write, is "not (or not just) that the finance sector is getting bigger but that financial ways of calculating are becoming more pervasive socially." In this view, all subjects are incentivized and encouraged to consider themselves and the assets and resources they hold as a form of finance asset portfolio on which they can yield rents or returns, per se a form of reification of human skills, competencies, and relations, but is nevertheless one of the foremost consequences of the finance-led economy, critics repeatedly remark (Rona-Tas, 2017; Baradaran, 2015; Fourcade and Healy, 2013; Karger, 2005).

A more critical view of financialization, regardless of the underlying theoretical interests of analytical models, is to consider it as what is unambiguously related to forms of policy failure. Hockett and Omarova (2016: 1213–1214) speak explicitly about financialization as "a dysfunctional mode of interaction between the financial system and the real (i.e., non-financial) economy, in which a disproportionate share of the flow of the monetized full faith and credit of the sovereign is continuously re-absorbed by the former rather than flowing to the latter." More explicitly, Hockett and Omarova (2016: 1214) argue, financialization denotes the situation wherein rentier interests overshadow and are prioritized over the entrepreneurial need for credit to finance the development that would be supportive of a new generation of businesses and corporations:

> [A]t its most fundamental, systemic level, financialization is a manifestation of the failure of the finance franchise arrangement to deliver its intended result: effective modulation and allocation of credit that ensures full utilization of the economy's productive capacity.

In this situation, the finance industry no longer serves an intermediary role at all, that is, to transfer credit from mature industries and risk-tolerant investors to emerging industries and start-up ventures. This is thus a situation wherein the finance-led economy becomes dysfunctional as it eats its own tail, investing considerable resources in illiquid high-risk/high-return assets such as hedge funds or in second-level securities such as CDOs or credit default swaps (CDSs). In that situation, Müller (2014: 548) says, "financialization does not entail close institutional interconnections between banks and industry, but rather their dissolution and a widening of the distance between them."

Regardless of this critique, the finance-led economy provides many benefits, including a more sizeable credit supply, which lower the costs to borrow money. This in turn justifies a series of changes in legislation and regulatory control, each allegedly serving to expand the economy and to generate net economic welfare effects. Still, one of the consequences of the finance-led economy is that in economies with progressive taxation schemes (e.g. in Scandinavia), the taxation of labour income is markedly higher than for capital returns income, which makes it more lucrative to trade in finance markets, all things equal, than to factually work to make material contributions to social welfare. This is one of the major conundrums in transnational governance, why the various insurances and tax exemptions granted to the finance industry, including not the least generous so-called ex post resolution systems that insure finance institutions against default, are complemented by most generous capital income taxes.

Firm-level financialization

Given the changes in the capital structure of corporations and their gradual movement towards more pronounced finance industry-oriented activities—that is, non-financial corporations are increasingly managed like portfolios of financial and non-financial assets—the legal theory of finance is of relevance also for non-financial companies. Roe (2018: 107) argues that the contemporary economy is characterized by the central role of intangible assets:

> The world's wealthiest economies are shifting from hard asset manufacturing to information-based economies. That shift predicts more R&D and less spending on manufacturing assets, both of which we see in this article's data. In retailing, brick-and-mortar physical stores are disappearing; instead, online distribution is growing.

In 1970, Roe (2018: 107) says, only one-tenth of the average public firm's assets were intangible (e.g. brand, patents, know-how, etc.), whereas today, Dallas (2011: 324) writes, "[o]nly twenty-five percent of a company's market value can be attributed to accounting book value, with the remaining seventy-five percent based on an assessment of value created by intangibles, such as strategy, product innovation, people and customer loyalty" (for more detail, see Pagano and Rossi, 2009: 670. figure 2.). Corporate governance scholars such as Roe (2018) tend to regard the increased proportion of intangibles as prima facie evidence of a differentiated and highly efficient economy, but scholars generally tend to treat intangible assets as an economic and not the least accounting-based phenomenon that itself needs to be explained and located within the broader framework of legal, regulatory, and institutional changes over the last half century, beginning in the early 1970s. Orhangazi (2019: 1255) examines two trends over the 1952–2016 period. The first is that capital accumulation, measured as investment in production capital, is slowing down:

> The downward trend in the rate of capital accumulation begins in the 1980s but this is reversed in the mid-1990s with a significant expansion in investment. After 2000 though, the rate of capital accumulation displays a sharp decline and collapses after the 2008 crisis.

This secular decline in capital accumulation coincides or is co-produced with the second major trend, the increased level of reported profits in public companies: "[D]espite a short-lived decline after the financial crisis, by 2014, the rate of profit reaches record levels, highest during the entire neoliberal period," Orhangazi (2019: 1256) writes. Sissoko (2019: 330) addresses the issue of "secular stagnation" in the economy—defined as "economic underperformance that is enduring and impervious to the forces that would normally generate a cyclical improvement" (2019: 337, footnote 23)[2]—and refers to the net saving of US corporations since 2001 (with the 2007–2008 period as an exception for reasons explained in detail elsewhere) as not only indicative of secular stagnation but also a change in corporate governance practice that is "unnatural" and remains largely "unexplained":[3]

> [N]et savings of US corporations which have been positive since 2001 [...] This change in behaviour is both unprecedented and "unnatural," as corporations should be best positioned to find investment opportunities and to be "natural" borrowers when they exploit these opportunities. Because this shift has taken place across most of the high-income countries, a general explanation of this corporate behaviour is needed.

The traditional view of industrial production and return on investment stipulates that investment in, for example, R&D results in above-normal industry profit, but in this case, finance capital investment and profit levels diverge. To provide one example, between 2002 and 2005, the American sports goods company Nike experienced an 82 per cent increase in profitability (which amounted to US$1.2 billion in net income) (Soener, 2015: 549). In the same period, Nike's rate of real investment declined by 12 per cent. It is conceivable that the 2002–2005 upsurge in revenues and profits was the effect of previous investments, but the level of profits reported is puzzling nonetheless. Empirical evidence indicates that Nike was engaged in various financial activities: despite generating US$1.2 billion in net income, the company spent "nearly US$1.4 billion on stock repurchases and US$837 million on short-term financial investments" (Soener, 2015: 549). On top of that expenditure, the income Nike received from "interest and dividends" increased by 470 per cent in the period (Soener, 2015: 549–550). By any standard, Nike is exemplary of a financialized corporation that relies on intangible assets to boost returns but without making investments in production capital. Orhangazi (2019) argues that the economic and accounting concept of the *intangible asset* and its widespread use and enforcement is part of the explanation for how investment-free profits are soaring in the US economy and elsewhere. By 2006, the market value of intangible assets "exceeded the value of tangible assets in the USA," Orhangazi (2019: 1258) writes, and in industries such as high technology and pharmaceuticals, intangible assets now represent "over 90% of corporate value." As Pagano (2014) remarks, in an economic regime where intangible assets are the primary production factor, monopoly or oligopoly is no longer based on the market power generated on the basis of the capacity to organize machines, production technology, and skills in efficient ways so that the unit costs or the market price cannot be surpassed by any existing or presumptive competitor. On the contrary, monopoly or oligopoly becomes a matter of the legal protection of intangible assets.

The legal theory view

In Pistor's (2013) legal theory of finance, the finance industry operates on the basis of a business charter from the sovereign state, and under a governance model that includes considerable insurances, subsidies, and tax exemptions that enable a credit supply that is conducive of economic growth and welfare. This legal constitution of the credit formation process is based on agreements and contracts, and in the situation wherein certain industries run a large-scale and profitable operation on the basis of up to 90 per cent intangible assets, there is no de facto difference between the finance industry and the non-financial sector. In both cases, it is legislation, legal contracts, regulatory practices, and packages of insurances, subsidies, and tax exemptions that define finance and non-financial industries and that influence how they operate. Expressed differently, in an economic regime characterized by a majority of intangible assets that serve as the primary driver of revenues and reported profits, it is the legal system and the legal protection of assets, contracts, and entrenched positions that define the nature of industrial production. "Intangibles are coded in law and are backed by the coercive powers of the state. They come in the form of intellectual property rights, as financial assets, or as a combination of both," Pistor (2020: 165) writes. The law of contract and property is combined with additional protection that comes from trust, corporate, or bankruptcy law, and to understand how law and legal practices are constitutive of the creation and distribution of assets is critical, in Pistor's (2020: 166) account. In this context, it should be noted that to participate in this legal business is highly lucrative.

Smith, Yagan, Zidar, and Zwick (2019: 1691) examine how the top 1 per cent income group in the United States make their earnings, and they report that fewer than "one in six people" in the 99.9th percentile derive most of their income from "interest, rents, and other capital income." That is, high net-worth households are not primarily rentiers (which does not suggest that revenues from financial asset holdings are marginal for this income group), but are working people who own businesses that generate revenues: "In 2014, over 69% of the top 1% and over 84% of the top 0.1% earn some pass-through business income," Smith, Yagan, Zidar, and Zwick (2019: 1677) write. In this category of the five largest so-called pass-through businesses, industries that are part of legal-financial activities account for the absolute majority of the aggregated profit: "The five largest industries for millionaire-owned pass-through profits are legal services ($28.6B), other financial investment activity ($28.2B), other professional and technical services ($8.2B), offices of physicians ($8.0B), and auto dealers ($6.7B)" (Smith, Yagan, Zidar, and Zwick, 2019: 1699, 1703).

Importantly, the question regarding how economic wealth can be generated on the basis of intangible assets, examined by, for example., Orhangazi (2019) and Pagano (2014), is to be sought within the realm of law and legal practices. Pistor (2020: 183) argues that legislation serves to "mint wealth," and that there are consequences, at least in theory but arguably also in practice, for the concept of scarcity, being a key concept in economic theory:

> If law can be used to mint wealth, it can be produced ad infinitum, at least in theory. What happens to scarcity under such conditions? Scarcity does not disappear entirely, because the law cannot guarantee actual returns at all times, but scarcity does not prevent the creation of assets that can produce a lot of monetary value in the meantime [...] In short, legal coding moves the boundaries of scarcity outwards.

In such a situation, monopolies and oligopolies are no longer the outcome from the superior capacity to combine and manage physical production capital, supply chains, and distribution and marketing channels, but is a matter of advocating legal rights in the court of law or vis-à-vis policymakers, regulatory agencies, or transnational governance organizations (Pollman and Barry, 2017; Eichenseht, 2019). The entire sphere of economic affairs and venturing drifts towards becoming a legal concern, a question of the capacity to enforce abstract contractual rights within and between jurisdictions (as in the case of globalized value chains). Ultimately, the growth in intangibles underlines that the legal theory of finance has a broader application to include virtually all industries that operate on the basis of assets and know-how that are complicated to capture in conventional accounting.

In addition, the question whether certain intangible assets are worth as much as market actors believe they are (as in the case of brands, often-times valued in astronomical measures, in billions of US dollars of worth; Willmott, 2010), or if such markups of the book value of intangible assets is a key mechanism in a financialized economy is still disputed. Unfortunately, what counts as an asset, intangible or not, is not a fact of nature but is determined by corporate law, accounting standards and procedures, and regulatory practices. For instance, an individual can rarely argue that a person's alleged credibility is a legitimate source for getting a loan at reduced interest (i.e., below the current market rate, all things being equal), but corporations can make the claim that they control intangible assets such as a brand being worth billions of dollars (oftentimes a claim substantiated by market research, conducted either by the corporation itself or business partners, formally acting with integrity vis-à-vis their contractor). The claim of such asset ownership can thereafter reduce the cost of lending in financial markets as credit rating agencies regard intangible assets as evidence of a portfolio of assets with a defined market value. In such situations, a legal theory of finance converges towards a legal theory of business, with significant practical and theoretical implications following. In addition, the contemporary financialized capitalist economic system is premised on the recognition of assets, know-how, and skills that investors and others cannot practically lay their hands on.

Entangled financial conditions: foreign direct investment (FDI) and corporate offshoring

Ivanova (2019) pays attention to the fact that the US economy has been run on a current account deficit (CAD) in the United States since 1982. That is, the US budget deficit over close to four decades needs to be explained on the basis of the specific advantages the US economy has over its competitors as the US dollar remains the currency of choice in international trade. The United States is the world's largest exporter of capital and the largest importer of foreign goods, but also the largest recipient of foreign investment. This combination has resulted in rising corporate profits, but at the expense of weak domestic investment and a lower share of labour compensation (measured in terms of real wage growth, and complementary economic welfare indicators). In October 2000, the US Congress passed legislation that granted China a Permanent Normal Trade Relations (PNTR) contract (Pierce and Schott, 2016: 1632). This political decision has strongly shaped the American labour market, Pierce and Schott (2016: 1632) argue: "US manufacturing employment fluctuated around 18 million workers between 1965 and 2000 before plunging 18 percent from March 2001 to March 2007." The Chinese PNTR agreement arguably represents a major policy change as it puts further pressure on, for example, blue-collar worker job creation through a number of mechanisms:

> Eliminating the possibility of sudden tariff spikes on Chinese imports may have affected US employment through several channels. First, it increased the incentive for US firms to incur the sunk costs associated with shifting operations to China or establishing a relationship with an existing Chinese producer. Second, it similarly provided Chinese producers with greater incentives to invest in entering or expanding into the US market, increasing competition for US producers. Finally, for US producers, it boosted the attractiveness of investments in capital- or skill-intensive production technologies or less labor-intensive mixes of products that are more consistent with US comparative advantage.
>
> (Pierce and Schott, 2016: 1633)

Instead of investing in human resources, R&D, and production capital, the consequences of a more effective allocation of productive resources, US corporations have committed their residual cash to more generous dividend payments and share buybacks, which puts pressure on American wage earners and results in soaring economic inequality. Ivanova (2019) is particularly concerned with the relation between the offshoring of the so-called stable-technology industries (STIs), which include automobiles, oil, rubber, nonelectrical machinery, and metal. In comparison to the high-tech industries (e.g. aerospace, chemicals, pharmaceuticals, computers, and electrical and electronic equipment), the STIs rely to a lesser extent on R&D investment and new-product development, and instead target process improvement and cost reduction to increase their competitiveness. As opposed to the high-tech industries (which largely maintain their operations in the United States), STIs have been thoroughly shaped by the new managerial practices that were developed in the 1970s and 1980s, which include intense merger and acquisition activities and take-over bids, shareholder primacy governance, and short-termism more generally. Unsurprisingly, the STIs have generated few job opportunities in the United States as offshoring and outsourcing have been favoured approaches to boost corporate profits.

Based on these conditions, Ivanova (2019: 708) argues that financialization is not, as has been argued at times, "decoupled" from production. On the contrary, Ivanova proposes, the relation between finance and production has undoubtedly changed since the 1970s, but the relation is best characterized as a form of "codependence." To substantiate this claim, Ivanova (2019: 715) accounts for the "relative slowdown of domestic capital accumulation," and the simultaneous "surging capital exports" in the US economy. In the 2007–2017 period, US outward foreign direct investment (FDI) averaged $316.1 billion per annum. In the 1999–2006, period, the comparable figure was $212.6 billion per annum. In the same period, US FDI income averaged $420 billion per annum, versus $181.6 billion per annum, a figure that indicates that US outward FDI as a percentage of gross fixed capital formation grew from 1.77 per cent in 1980 to 9.65 per cent in 2010–2016, a more than fivefold increase in proportion. This substantial increase in finance capital investment is indicative of how financialization is co-produced with what is referred to as "globalization," a conspicuously amorphous term that nevertheless indicates how national borders are increasingly crossed when corporate returns are maximized.

Soener (2015) and Auvray and Rabinovich (2019) operationalize globalization as the overarching trend to offshore production activities to overseas jurisdictions. Soener (2015: 550) examines "the US apparel and footwear industry" in the 1991–2005 period, and finds strong support for the proposition that "supply chain types are strong predictors of financialization" (2015: 566). Financialization is here defined as a marked growth of financial payments, defined as interest payments, dividend payouts and stock repurchases combined, in comparison to investment in production capital and human resources. Companies that were closely tied to a global value chain (GVC) were more likely to use offshoring and to increase their financial payments at the expense of investment and job creation in the home market. Auvray and Rabinovich (2019) use a considerably larger sample of companies that include US non-financial corporations' (NFCs) investments between 1995 and 2011. Their result reveals a negative correlation between "payouts and investment in capital expenditures" in industries with a high offshoring rate (Auvray and Rabinovich, 2019: 1185). The mechanism at work is that corporations that own "less productive facilities due to off-shoring" do not reinvest their residual cash in plants, equipment, and human resources (e.g., training and job creation), but rather use profits to purchase financial assets and to increase financial payments to raise the market price of the corporations' stock (Auvray and Rabinovich, 2019: 1192). This result is consistent with the empirical data reported by Ivanova (2019). The residual cash generated from offshoring and outsourcing overseas has not been committed to investment in the United States.[4] Instead, Ivanova (2019: 715) accounts for "the spectacular amounts that have flown into share buybacks": "[F]rom 2003 to 2012, the 449 publicly listed companies in the S&P 500 index chose to use 54% of their earnings—a total of $2.4 trillion—to buy back their own stock." Furthermore, the so-called "internal funds," the cash-holdings of corporations, are substantial, and stood at "$1.8 trillion in 2013 and $1.9 trillion in 2016" (Ivanova, 2019: 715). On balance, these results suggest that "financialisation and offshoring are related phenomena," Auvray and Rabinovich (2019: 1185) contend.

The empirical data reported by Soener (2015) and Auvray and Rabinovich (2019) substantiate the stipulated causality between a number of conditions: financialization, measured in terms of the aggregated growth of financial payments, is co-produced with globalization, which is in turn operationalized as the magnitude of offshoring activities in primarily stable-technology industries. In the next step, offshoring activities have implications for the corporate structure and its position in the global value chain. Therefore, Soener (2015: 551) deduces, the corporation's organizational type or supply chain type has "high explanatory power." In the same vein, Auvray and Rabinovich (2019: 1215) argue that corporations that make the strategic choice to "distribute financial payouts at the expense of their capital accumulation," the "real source" of the cash distributed, should be found in global value chains. Based on such evidence, Soener (2015: 550) instructs scholars and policymakers to not only accept empirical evidence that indicates increased financialization but to actively examine firm- and industry-level data to be able to theorize "*why* firms financialize and *where* divergent financialization behaviour occurs" (emphasis in the original). "Without unpacking where and when financialization occurs, it is difficult to engage in theory building," Soener (2015: 550) contends.

What Ivanova (2019: 716) refers to as "the global reorganization of production" has apparently been a lucrative affair for US corporations. The concern is that the economic wealth primarily benefits certain segments of the American domestic economy. According to elementary economic theory, a shortage of supply results in high prices under the influence of market competition, all things being equal. In the labour market, a shortage of qualified salaried workers results in increased compensation, measured in, for example, real wage growth or other benefits. However, in the United States, since the late 1970s, real wage growth for the majority of American workers has "been modest to nonexistent," Ivanova (2019: 716) writes. Even in the period following the financial crisis of 2008–2009, referred to as the Great Recession, which lingered on for more than ten years in many economies, "wage growth remains subpar despite one of the lowest levels of unemployment in US history" (Ivanova, 2019: 716). Between 2001 and 2017, the wage share of national income declined from 54 per cent to circa 50 per cent. In the same period, the profit share of national income increased from 9 to 14 per cent (Ivanova, 2019: 716). This shift from income from salaried work to financial rents has resulted in growing economic inequality, a condition that becomes particularly salient when the population is separated into income quintiles:

> [F]or households in the second income quintile the value of the primary residence represents over 91% of total net worth, while the share of direct and indirect stock holdings is only 1.2%. For households in the top income quintile, the shares of total stock holdings and housing in total net worth are, respectively, 29.7% and 54.5%. By boosting equity prices more than house prices, unconventional monetary policy has tended to significantly increase wealth inequality. In particular, the net wealth of richer households in the US has grown four times as fast as that of poorer ones.
>
> (Ivanova, 2019: 716–717)

Ivanova (2019: 719) is sceptical regarding the ability of policymakers or market actors to slow down this rising income inequality in the US population as this condition is "[i]nextricably linked to the transformation of the occupational and wage structure, which is being reshaped and restructured along the demands of globalized production driven by MNCs [multinational corporations]." Consequently, proposed reforms within the existing system of taxes and transfers, Ivanova (2019: 719) continues, are "unlikely to have any significant impact on the growing inequality in the distribution of income and wealth in the US." The regime of shareholder primacy governance would not compromise its fundamental proposition—that maximized shareholder wealth benefits long-term growth and optimizes the efficiency of the economic system—which precludes new policies regarding the economic compensation of salaried workers. Second, despite receiving considerable FDIs, jobs created in the American economy in the 1990–2008 period were primarily in the "nontradable sector" (around 26.7 million jobs out of a total stock of 27.3 million new jobs, corresponding to 98 per cent of all new jobs), which include government, healthcare, retail, hospitality, and construction (Ivanova, 2019: 721). "While unemployment has been substantially reduced, the US economy seems doomed to create low-wage jobs. Unsurprisingly, wage growth has been weak, while the labor share of national income does not show any signs of recovery," Ivanova (2019: 721) summarizes.

Even if growing economic inequality can be tolerated, as it is in the eyes of neoconservative and neoliberal policymakers, advisers, pundits, and academics, Ivanova is concerned about the sustainability of the current economic regime, structured around substantial corporate profit: "Once profits start falling, a major realignment is likely to ensue," Ivanova (2019: 721) writes. Financialization is a socio-economic and legal process that has been successful in restoring corporate profitability on the basis of offshoring production activities to low-cost economies, especially in stable-technology industries, and resolute shareholder primacy governance principles, but the viability of the economic model is questioned, not the least because the economic wealth generated primarily benefits a smaller proportion of the American population. "It may be appropriate to conclude with a warning that the days of this success could be numbered," Ivanova (2019: 722) contends.

Additional financialization activities and their relations

The historical trajectories that preceded the finance-led economy run deep and are diverse. Haiven (2014: 1) dates the origin of the finance-led economy to the retirement of the Bretton Woods system in 1971, which rendered capital formation a process separated from any underlying material condition (such as the supply of gold). The 1970s was a remarkably shaky decade in terms of economic performance, stock market valuation, and economic growth, but in the 1980s, the first attempts to remove capital control rules and to deregulate finance markets were made in the United States and Europe (Deeg, 2009: 554). Deeg (2009) described financialization as a "self-reinforcing process" wherein market actors used the "new freedom" to expand financial markets and to create new financial product markets. As finance markets expanded, new actors such as institutional investors, hedge funds managers, and so on emerged and further reinforced the process towards finance market deepening and thickening (Deeg, 2009: 554). Wansleben (2018: 778) pays specific attention to what he characterizes as "a symbiotic relationship" between "accelerated financialization" and "growing central bank power" in the United States. This intimate relationship between the Federal Reserve, construed as an "independent agency" in the otherwise dense regulatory milieu of the finance industry, and the finance industry itself, is indicative of the structural changes in the economy that shifted the focus of economic accumulation "from labor and consumption to financial markets," Wansleben (2018: 778) says. Over the period of the two centuries (1780–1980), Western capitalism increased its economic output fiftyfold, and the population increased sevenfold, which indicates remarkable and historically unprecedented growth in economic welfare.

After circa 1980, this hugely successful economic system shifted gears as the finance industry gradually advanced its position on the basis of changes in doctrines (e.g. the shareholder primacy governance model, advocated from the mid-1970s by economists such as Michael C. Jensen, supported by pro-business industrialists and financiers; Chabrak, 2012), the active enforcement of free-market ideology, legislative reform, regulatory liberalization, extensive finance industry innovations, and not the least a solid belief at the apex of the political and regulatory system in the efficacy of the new regime of capital formation.

Of particular interest in this setting are the financial innovations that have served to actively circumvent and undermine the regulatory efforts that have been made by political entities such as the US Congress after the most recent finance industry crisis (Funk and Hirschman, 2014; Murdock, 2012; Frame and White, 2004). Arthur Stinchcombe (1965) once spoke of "the liability of newness" regarding the difficulties involved when starting new ventures and businesses, and this term may be applicable also for finance market actors who trade assets with incomplete market pricing data series, especially if the data does not cover the full business cycle (Adrian and Shin, 2010). Fortunately for finance market actors, unlike the new entrepreneurial ventures that Stinchcombe talked about, these actors can rely on insurances from the sovereign state if financial innovations prove difficult to price accurately (i.e., systemic market risks are either excluded altogether or underpriced). This creates a situation wherein traders of financial innovations and new asset classes can reap the benefits of the upside risk while they pass on the potential cost for mispricing downside risks, which in many other situations would be treated as a bona fide example of moral hazard created on the basis of insurances that distort the price formation process (at times euphemistically referred to as the "price discovery" process, derived from the doctrine that assets may have a "fundamental value" from which market prices may diverge).

Financial innovations: the case of asset securitization

Awrey (2013) is sceptical regarding the concept of "financial innovation" inasmuch as the original term *innovation* denotes some idea, product, and process that "somehow made the world a better place."[5] Prior to the global financial crisis of 2008, this term was widely accepted within the finance industry and among its proponents as it was univocally stated that new financial assets would fall within this class, that is, what reduces costs in the credit formation process, distributes and evens out risks, or creates new markets that benefit net economic welfare. Recent financial innovations such as over-the-counter (OTC) derivatives, swaps, structured finance, and structured investment products, all being highly idiosyncratic and specific finance market devices, are not of necessity conducive to net economic welfare gains, Awrey (2013: 401–402) argues. Consistent with Pistor's (2013) legal theory of finance, Awrey (2013: 402) points at two critiques of finance market innovations. The first emphasizes that financial innovations assume a demand-side view wherein finance market intermediaries simply cater for emerging market demands. That is, intermediaries act strictly as suppliers of innovations on the basis of exogenous conditions. That is not the case, Awrey states, as most finance innovations are, like Miller (1986: 460) remarked already in the mid-1980s on the verge of the finance industry expansion, devices that help finance industry traders escape either regulation or taxes (or combinations thereof). Therefore, in an institutional perspective, financial innovations are not a species of finance market devices being introduced to primarily generate net economic welfare, but rather serve to benefit finance market actors themselves so that they can avoid regulatory control and/or bypass fiscal policies. Awrey (2013: 410) argues that the "diffusion rates" of many financial innovations are "exceptionally high," which is indicative of the individual innovating finance institution's quickly diminishing comparative advantage vis-à-vis its competitors. In mainstream innovation theory, this observed pattern would reduce the incentives to innovate as innovations do not translate into sustainable competitive advantages if innovations diffuse quickly. Yet this is precisely the opposite of what has been observed in finance markets, which suggests other incentives for innovation than to generate firm-specific competitive advantages.

Second, Awrey (2013: 402) argues that the information economics theory (see, e.g., Akerlof, 1970; Grossman and Stiglitz, 1980; Greenwald and Stiglitz, 1986) concepts of *informational asymmetry* and *adverse selection* have been underrated inasmuch as finance market innovators always know how to capitalize on complex financial asset classes long before the regulators learn how to push down the systemic risk and other externalities such innovations generate. Furthermore, genuine uncertainty is present in all trade with assets that seeks to project future returns, which also makes finance innovations an implausible candidate as a vehicle for the generation of economic welfare. For instance, Awrey examines the case of the OTC derivatives market, which is now so structurally complex and complicated to overview also for insiders that the market microstructure now "looks less like the atomized (i.e., flat) markets of conventional financial theory," and more like "an informational hierarchy with a relatively small, close-knit group of derivatives dealers residing at the apex" (2013: 408). OTC assets are thus not innovations in the regular sense of the term, but are advanced packages of contracts that generate a variety of benefits for specific market participants.

In the end, Awrey (2013) argues, financial innovations are a species of market devices that cannot automatically be associated with the benign connotations of the term *innovation*, which by definition makes welfare contributions. "Financial innovation" is therefore a misnomer and a euphemism as the primary beneficiary of the newly introduced innovation is oftentimes the finance industry itself. One such case are CDSs, a form of "secured lending whereby one counterparty transfers relatively liquid assets to another in exchange for less liquid collateral" (Awrey, 2013: 413).[6] The primary purpose of collateral swaps, Awrey (2013: 413) writes, is to arbitrage "the differences in the regulatory capital regimes applicable to banks, on the one hand, and pension funds and insurers, on the other." Newly introduced liquidity rules determined by the Basel III regulation, being a consequence of the 2008 events, is therefore actively circumvented. The use of collateral swaps can therefore be expected to contribute to "the build-up and crystallization of systemic risk" (Awrey, 2013: 413), that is, precisely the type of risk that, for example, the Basel III framework intends to reduce on the basis of stricter regulatory rules. Ultimately, Awrey (2013: 413) writes, the use of collateral swaps can be viewed as evidence of the "legal construction of markets." That is, finance market operations cannot be considered outside of the legal framework that determines financial products and transactions. This does not suggest that finance innovations always and of necessity are questionable, but the medium- to long-term consequences must be assessed and carefully monitored by regulatory agencies prior to any conclusions regarding the welfare-inducing capacities of the new asset class can be made (Posner and Weyl, 2012).

One hotly debated (after 2008) but also widespread finance innovation is the securitization of assets, which is one of the drivers of the finance industry expansion over four decades. Levitin (2016: 396) writes that securitization is a "financing technique" that involves "the issuance of debt securities against an isolated pool of cash flow generating assets." Such assets can be a home mortgage loan, a contract that stipulates interest payment and the repayment of the loan, and that consequently generates a predictable cash flow. Gorton (2017: 564) explains how the securitization of financial assets serves to make illiquid holdings such as mortgage loans, with a long maturation period, in many cases in a range of 30 years, mobile, that is, tradable:

> Securitization is the private production of safe debt. It takes bank loans as inputs and produces bonds (asset-backed securities) as outputs. Bank loans are mostly immobile; they cannot be traded or used for collateral. They sit on the banks' balance sheets. But when used to produce ABS/MBS [asset-backed securities/mortgage-backed securities], the resulting bonds, backed by these same loans, become mobile: That is, they can be traded, used as collateral, rehypothecated, and held to store value.

Seen in this view, securitization does the job to render illiquid holdings more attractive as they can be restructured in securities to be sold on the global financial market. This in turn increases the credit supply as structured finance instruments make, for example, home mortgage lending more lucrative as securitization increases the liquidity of capital markets, Caverzasi, Botta, and Capelli (2019: 1030) argue:

> [S]ecuritisation has opened the opportunity for standard banking institutions to expand their business and widen the pool of potential creditworthy borrowers, and—perhaps more relevantly—it has also provided the financial system with the 'raw materials', i.e., the securitised assets necessary for the manufacturing of complex structured financial products satisfying the increasing demand for financial assets of financial institutions, seeking either remuneration for intermediated funds or collaterals for the repo market.

The concern is that the quality of the underlying collateral (e.g. a house that is associated with the home mortgage loan) needs to be qualitative inasmuch as its actual market price is stable (and not subject to what is called "negative equity" or being "below the waterline," as in the case of the local and regional housing market prices drops), and the home mortgage borrower is capable of holding the contract during the entire stipulated contract period (i.e., the borrower will not default). Shin (2009) examines the situation, as it happened in the 2003–2006 period, until the US subprime market collapsed, wherein non-prudential mortgage lenders enter the market to take advantage of the securitization process. Shin (2009: 310) emphasizes the systemic risk generated within the banking system as a whole when securities with poor collateral (e.g. sub-prime mortgage loans) are mixed with securities with more robust collateral (e.g. prime mortgage loans):

> Although securitisation may facilitate greater credit supply to ultimate borrowers at the aggregate level, the choice to supply credit is taken by the constituents of the banking system taken as a whole. For a financial intermediary, its return on equity is magnified by leverage. To the extent that it wishes to maximise its return on equity, it will attempt to maintain the highest level of leverage consistent with limits set by creditors (for instance, through the "haircuts" on repurchase agreements) or self-imposed risk constraints.

Expressed differently, financial institutions are eager to maximize the return-on-equity and therefore leverage their liabilities-to-assets ratios, but higher leverage also means that the risk of default rises as even smaller depreciations of underlying collateral (i.e., the housing stock) may render financial institutions insolvent. The combination of securitization, leverage, and increasingly less robust collateral is an explosive combination, Shin (2009) indicates. If mortgage lenders is optimistic regarding the value of collateral, they tend to expand their portfolio of mortgage loans to increase the return-on-equity:

> In benign financial market conditions when measured risks are low, financial intermediaries expand balance sheets as they increase leverage. Although the intermediary could increase leverage in other ways—for

instance, returning equity to shareholders, buying back equity by issuing long-term debt—the evidence suggests that they tend to keep equity intact and adjust the size of total assets.

(Shin, 2009: 310)

Unfortunately, Caverzasi, Botta, and Capelli (2019: 1047) argue, securitization was not originally developed to benefit households and the mortgage loan industry, but emerged as a response to increased demand for new financial assets in the non-financial industry:

[S]ecuritisation has led to the "financialisation of the everyday" by allowing for the extension of credit to a much larger audience. Such expansion in bank credit was not intended to address the needs of common people, but was rather driven by the increasing demand for financial commodities to be used in the manufacturing of complex financial products remunerating financial investments done by wealthy rentiers and financialised non-financial firms.

In a situation wherein securitization become the primus motor of home mortgage lending as it provides these opportunities for leverage and a higher return-on-equity, the mortgage lender may easily downshift the credit rating standards (as happened in 2003–2006; Mian and Sufi, 2014) so that the asset stock on the balance sheet can be expanded. At this stage, also subprime borrowers are granted home mortgage loans as they can ensure that the balance sheets can expand. At this stage, lenders primarily participate in what Bubb and Prasad (2014: 1556) refer to as "asset-based lending," wherein mortgage lenders increasingly "look to the value of the house rather than the creditworthiness of the borrower to ensure repayment."

One indication of this tendency is the growing proportion of shadow banking-based home mortgage origination, which nearly doubled from roughly 30 per cent in 2007 to 50 per cent in 2015 (Buchak, Matvos, Piskorski, and Seru, 2018: 454). This growth was particularly robust in the so-called US Federal Housing Administration (FHA) market, which serves less creditworthy borrowers, and wherein shadow banks held 75 per cent of the market share in 2015. In contrast, Fuster et al. (2019: 1858) found "little evidence" that fintech lenders "disproportionately target marginal borrowers with low access to finance." Buchak, Matvos, Piskorski, and Seru (2018: 455) report that what they refer to as fintech shadow banks "[c]harge significantly higher interest rates than both non-fintech shadow banks and traditional banks." Furthermore, the variation in the fintech shadow banks' interest rates in comparison to non-fintech lenders cannot be explained on the basis of "standard variables" such as FICO scores or loan-to-value ratio (LTV). Buchak, Matvos, Piskorski, and Seru (2018: 456) argue that "technology-based lending" uses different information, potentially based on big data, "in addition to standard pricing variables." If this proposition is correct, it contradicts the asset-based lending hypothesis as a superior method of processing public information, and the higher interest rates being charged protect fintech shadow banks against losses. For instance, Fuster et al.'s (2019: 1871) data reveal that loans originated by fintech lenders are "35% less likely to default than comparable loans from non-FinTech lenders." Furthermore, there are consumer benefits as fintech lenders reduce processing time by about ten days, which corresponds to about 20 per cent of the average processing time (Fuster et al., 2019: 1856).

Regardless whether fintech shadow banks have more effective methods for calculating the creditworthiness of presumptive borrowers, Buchak, Matvos, Piskorski, and Seru (2018: 465) propose that the increased regulatory control imposed on traditional banks creates possibilities for regulatory arbitrage that fintech shadow banks exploit: "As a consumer segment, economically disadvantaged and minority borrowers have seen more mortgage-related lawsuits, and therefore we interpret these findings as shadow banks focusing on segments in which traditional banks face greater regulatory scrutiny." That is, Buchak, Matvos, Piskorski, and Seru (2018: 473) report findings that are consistent with the proposition that traditional banks retreated from markets with a larger regulatory burden, and that shadow banks "filled this gap." Vives (2019: 264) calculates that the increased regulatory burden on traditional banks can explain "approximately 55% of shadow banking growth," whereas the "remaining 35% can be attributed to the use of FinTech." De la Mano, and Padilla (2018: 495) list a number of competitive and regulatory advantages of fintech lenders, including their leaner business organizations, their use of state-of-the-art technology, and their selective targeting of banking business segments with higher return-on-equity. Based on these premises, De la Mano and Padilla (2018: 498) are concerned that "within a few years," Big Tech companies may succeed in "monopolizing the origination and distribution of loans to consumers and SMEs, forcing traditional banks to become 'low cost manufacturers,' which merely fund the loans intermediated by the Big Techs." This may in turn harm competition, which reduces consumer welfare in the next stage, and increases financial instability in the medium term (De la Mano and Padilla, 2018 498). Regardless of such concerns, in Fuster et al.'s (2019: 1894–1895) account, the long-term consequences of fintech lending are largely still to be determined:

> In the long run, it is unclear whether technology-based lending will remain dominated by nonbanks or whether commercial banks will be able to use technology to regain market share in the mortgage market. Banks are likely to be less nimble than specialist nonbank mortgage lenders, because they are more highly regulated and organizationally complex, and often have complex legacy processes and information systems. On the other hand, banks also have significant competitive advantages, including access to low-cost deposit funding, cross-selling

opportunities, and the availability of branches for those borrowers preferring a mix of online and face-to-face interactions.

Under all conditions, when low-quality collateral loans are included in the pool of mortgage loans to be securitized, "the seeds of the subsequent downturn in the credit cycle are thus sown," Shin (2009: 310) contends. Later in this article, Shin also says:

> Once all the prime borrowers in the population have a mortgage, the banks must find new borrowers in order to expand their balance sheets. The only way they can do this is to lower their lending standards. Subprime borrowers will then start to receive funding.
>
> (325–326)

In this situation, home mortgage lenders are either naive regarding the future of housing prices, and estimate that prices will be on the rise for a considerable period of time,[7] or cynical regarding their lower lending standards as they assume that "there is always a greater fool in the chain who will buy the bad loan" (Shin, 2009: 312).

The possibility to securitize assets with low-quality collateral in a pool of assets backed by more qualitative collateral thus demands that the principle of prudent lending needs to be enforced so naive investors (Bubb and Prasad, 2014) are not buying securities with the result that the systemic risk inflates as it did in the 2003–2006 period. The period after 2008–2009 has been a long process of reflection on the accuracy of the various over-optimistic ideas portraying the finance industry being able to self-regulate, and this despite the enormous possibilities to extract rents on the basis of finance asset issuance and trade. The catchphrase has been "macroprudential regulation" (Adelino, Schoar, and Severino, 2018; Gorton, 2017; Hockett, 2015), which is proposed as a package of regulatory principles and practices that make systemic risk a key target for regulatory agencies. With the benefit of hindsight and a historical record, it is easier to understand what in fact caused the major debacle of failed self-regulation, but there are also scholars who early on pointed out that the securitization of asset holdings contained the possibility to inflate systemic risks but without carrying the full cost of this externality, especially in the case of imprudent lenders (e.g. so-called *predatory lenders* that entered the industry at its later, speculation-driven stage; Agarwal et al., 2014; Peterson, 2007; Engel and McCoy, 2001, 2007). The work of LoPucki (1996) discusses such concerns, but as what Turner (2015: 169) referred to as "the Greenspan doctrine," that is, the belief that securities and other forms of structured finance instruments reduced and distributed risk rather than inflated systemic risk, the conventional wisdom in the free-market doctrine, the observations of LoPucki (1996) and other critics of new financial assets were largely declared to be a heresy or, alternatively, simply ignored. In hindsight, if only the policymakers and decision makers at the apex of the global (and especially the American) finance market system would have cared to pay attention and respond to dissenting views and discordant information (regarding, e.g., the unprecedented growth of housing prices, widely treated as an evidence of an economic system in full bloom, and supported by what authorities such as the Federal Reserve chairman declared to be sound "economic fundamentals"), some of the social and economic costs of the Great Recession may have been avoided. But sceptical commentators were alone in the wilderness and few cared to listen to a dissenting storyline, inconsistent with neoclassical economic doctrines regarding the informational efficiency of the market pricing process and allegedly "rational actors" that were better positioned to assess market risks than any external actor.

Securitization and the escape from liability

LoPucki (1996: 3) argues that liability is a central mechanism for the government and the state that enforce law. Liability is therefore central to civil law, and operates through its association between contracts and the payment of money. This is a central principle of civil law enforcement: "To hold a defendant liable is to enter a money judgment against the defendant. Unless that judgment can be enforced, liability is merely symbolic," LoPucki (1996: 4) says. Yet, securitization represent a form of "avoidance of liability," LoPucki (1996: 6) suggests. As opposed to stock and bonds being issued by a business, wherein the holder of such assets (in legal terms, a contract) thus has a claim against an entire business, that is, the incorporated business venture that operates as an autonomous legal entity, the holder of a security associated with an asset with a defined cash flow and an underlying collateral is a claim against the asset—and not the entire business that holds the asset in the first place (LoPucki, 1996: 29). In this way, a finance trader can choose between holding contracts which include claims against a business (stock, bonds, etc.), or a specific asset (say, an MBS, with an underlying mortgage loan and a physical asset, a house, as collateral). Empirical evidence indicates that finance traders are willing to pay a premium for the latter category of assets, that is, securities (LoPucki, 1996: 28), but the question is *why* this is the case, given that finance theory (see, e.g., Modigliani and Miller, 1958) stipulates that the capital structure of the firm does not affect its valuation:

> Finance theory tells us that selling securities that allocate the risks and returns from a business enterprise does not change the total risks and returns. Slicing the rights in different ways may add to the value of one type of security, but only by detracting from the value of another [...] But that cannot explain why *asset securitization* would be chosen over *business securitization*.
>
> (LoPucki, 1996: 29. Emphasis in the original)

LoPucki (1996: 30) argues that the benefit for the finance trader is that "third-party ownership of assets" provides a "priority over liability claims" that mere stock ownership does not. That is, to hold securities means to escape some of the liabilities associated with share ownership. Seen in this view, the securitization of assets denotes a circumvention of liability as it is defined in civil law and, more specifically, in corporate legislation. LoPucki (1996: 30) states this point explicitly:

> Asset securitization may be the silver bullet capable of killing liability [...] Liability is in disrepute. Asset securitization, by contrast, is widely regarded as an engine of the U.S. economy. Commentators all seem to agree that the savings available through asset securitization depend on the insulation of the securitized asset from bankruptcy—in essence, from liability.

LoPucki (1996) argues that the securitization of corporate assets is part of a tendency to "de-entify" the firm, and to enact it as bundle of contracts that individually carry specified liabilities but little else. For a legal scholar such as LoPucki (1996), this is an attempt to overstate contract theory within the constitutional law of corporate legislation. The driver of this contract theory-based model of the corporate entity is to avoid regulatory control: "Corporate financiers routinely employ strategies to escape limitations imposed by regulation," LoPucki (1996: 47) says. As the corporate charter is in the first place based on stipulated insurances, tax exemptions, and other benefits that the sovereign state bestows upon the incorporated business, to construct additional benefits or to identify new ways to escape liabilities is a violation of the legislators' intention with the business charter: "De-entification will deprive the system of a fundamental concept for ordering and specifying liability," LoPucki (1996: 69) argues. In the end, securitization was at an early stage (i.e., prior to the expansion of the securities market in 2003–2006, triggered by a liberalization of US finance industry regulation in 1999 and 2000) claimed to represent a tendency towards downplaying liability as a law enforcement mechanism of central importance for the regulatory control of markets. In the more recent wake of macroprudential regulatory control (Adelino, Schoar, and Severino, 2018; Hockett, 2015; Dell'Ariccia, Laeven, and Marquez, 2014), these ideas have been dusted off to better explain the unintended consequences of purposeful action in the domain of securities issuance and regulation.

Securities regulation to uphold the liability law enforcement mechanism

After 2008, the regulatory pendulum swung back and the Dodd-Frank Act was passed by the US Congress in July 2010 to better monitor systemic risk and to ensure macroprudent business practices among finance market actors. What Bubb and Prasad (2014: 1542) describe as the "landmark

Dodd-Frank Act" imposes a variety of new rules, including "higher capital requirements on banks," a new resolution regime to "safely wind down
insolvent financial institutions," and the establishment of the Financial
Stability Oversight Council (FSOC) being assigned the role to identify and
address "emerging systemic risks." Speaking more specifically about securities regulation, Goshen and Parchomovsky (2006) identify three broad categories of securities regulation: (1) "disclosure duties," (2) "restrictions on
fraud and manipulation," and (3) "restrictions on insider trading." The role
of these three categories is explained accordingly:

> Disclosure duties reduce their information gathering costs. Restrictions
> on fraud and manipulation simultaneously lower information traders'
> cost of verifying the credibility of information, and improve their ability
> to make accurate predictions. Finally, restrictions on insider trading
> protect information traders from competition from insiders that would
> undercut the ability of information traders to recoup their investment in
> information, driving information traders out of the market.
>
> (Goshen and Parchomovsky, 2006: 716)

The Dodd-Frank Act includes elements from these categories, and yet it has
been subject to scorching criticism from several scholars in terms of being
incapable of monitoring and pushing down systemic risks (Richardson,
Schoenholtz, and White, 2015; Wilmarth, 2013; Krawiec, 2013; Tillman,
2012; Coffee, 2012, 2011).[8] For instance, Bubb and Prasad (2014: 1546)
propose a *naive-investors theory* that potentially explains why also allegedly
informed finance market traders acted in ways that in hindsight appear as
irresponsible or overoptimistic. The issue this theoretical model addresses is
that, unlike the Dodd-Frank Act, it not only recognizes "first-order market
failure" such as moral hazard but also includes second-order market failure,
that is, the failure that derives from the inability to effectively recognize
and respond to first-order market failures. To express it differently, finance
traders were perhaps not aware of the moral hazard they exploited, and
this ignorance—grounded in cognitive and behavioural limitations such as
positive asymmetry, herd behaviour, and the inability to process discordant
information—precluded a more elaborate view of, for example, systemic
risk, which ultimately resulted in the situation that the Dodd-Frank Act now
seeks to correct. Similar to several other commentators, Bubb and Prasad
(2014) do not express their faith in the Dodd-Frank Act's ability to reduce
either first- or second-order regulatory failures in the finance market. To further complicate the issues at hand, *even if* the Dodd-Frank Act and its implementation and law enforcement would be able to discipline finance market
traders to act prudently, it would not per se be able to reach the substantial share of finance market trading that is located to the so-called shadow
banking sector, that is, the financial business that is located outside of the
protection of the sovereign state and its legislative and regulatory activities.

To fully examine the scope of the regulatory challenges that the sovereign state and transnational governance agencies are now set to handle, a review of the shadow banking literature is presented.

Shadow banking and its role in the credit formation process

Greenwood and Scharfstein (2013: 21) stress that the growth of the securitization of assets was co-developed with what is called the shadow banking system, that is, the finance market transacting outside of the regulated banking sector and operating on the basis of "non-bank financial entities." Adrian and Ashcraft (2012: 100) emphasize that shadow banks "conduct credit and maturity transformation similar to traditional banks," but do so without "the direct and explicit public sources of liquidity and tail risk insurance via the Federal Reserve's discount window and the Federal Deposit Insurance Corporation (FDIC) insurance." Despite its nocturnal connotations, the shadow banking system is a well-known feature of the global finance industry. Greenwood and Scharfstein (2013: 21) define shadow banks as "financial intermediaries that conduct maturity, credit, and liquidity transformation without explicit access to central bank liquidity or public sector credit guarantees." Fernandez and Wigger (2016: 408) use terms such as "non-banks" or "quasi-banks" to define shadow banking as the "borrowing and lending by non-depository financial institutions." Fernandez and Wigger (2016: 413) explicate the use of the term, and point at the diverse set of services offered by non-depository financial institutions:

> Shadow banking comprises a system of non-banks, such as non-depository or investment banks, asset management firms, hedge and private equity funds or financial holding corporations that interconnect across various jurisdictions, making use of a broad range of products and markets. Shadow banking involve maturity or liquidity transformations without having to comply with regulatory requirements such as capital reserves and other (trading) rules.

The purpose of the shadow banking system is to further expand the spreadsheets of financial institutions so that they can avoid regulatory rules that delimit the leverage of banks. Shadow banking devices and activities thus represent a straightforward circumvention of regulatory control. These activities are tolerated by regulatory agencies and ultimately the political and legislative entities as a sizeable shadow banking system, Dow (2017: 1544) says, acts as an "alternative source of credit on a massive scale." In many cases, these financial engineering activities are technically complex and complicated to price for non-expert traders as, for instance, "various debt instruments can be re-used multiple times as collateral" (Fernandez and Wigger, 2016: 409). Critical commentators claim that the increased credit supply is associated with heightened systemic risks, which is an indication of the increased fragility of the financial system:

> [T]he shadow banking system that facilitated this expansion [of mortgage credit] made the financial system more fragile. This runs counter to the traditional "functional" view of finance, which suggests that a primary function of the financial sector is to dampen the effects of risk by reallocating its efficiently to parties that can bear risks the most easily.
>
> (Greenwood and Scharfstein, 2013: 26)

The sheer size of the non-depository financial institutions makes this issue "[o]ne of the most pressing issues in financial regulation today," Judge (2017: 415) argues. Estimates made by the Financial Stability Board (FSB), a transnational regulatory agency, suggested that in 2002, the total holdings of the shadow banking sector amounted to US$26 trillion (Fernandez and Wigger, 2016: 408). By 2012, this figure had grown to US$71 trillion, which is equivalent to "almost half of the size of the regular banking system" (Fernandez and Wigger, 2016: 408). Judge (2017: 415) argues that the shadow banking system—that stands at US$75 trillion in the most recent estimate (Judge, 2017: 437)—is "poised for further growth," and suggests that one of the key drivers of the shadow banking sector expansion is that companies and institutional investors "currently hold massive amounts of cash that they want to store for future use," whereas regular banks are "not suited to accept deposits in such large amounts."

As a matter of elementary statistics, the growth of the shadow banking sector in comparison to traditional banking (a so-called retronym as the prefix "traditional" now needs to be added for clarification) is shrinking in relative proportion: in 1970, commercial banks, savings institutions, and credit unions collectively "held 54.41% of the assets in the financial sector," being more or less the same amount they held a decade earlier, but by 2005, this share had fallen to 24.22 per cent (Judge, 2017: 437). Consistent with Pistor's (2013) legal theory of finance framework, Judge (2017) argues that the expansion of the shadow banking sector remains "incompletely understood" inasmuch as the information asymmetry and informational costs in finance market transacting are understated, especially given the continuous introduction of new financial innovations that cannot be accurately priced on the basis of data time series generated over only one business cycle, or even less. In other words, financial innovations are in most cases introduced to avoid regulatory control (mostly measured as costs), but the difficulties involved in pricing new asset classes may generate systemic risks or other forms of uncertainty in the financial system that ultimately lower the net economic welfare as only a few finance institutions can reap the benefits, whereas other actors or stakeholders carry the cost for such externalities. Under all conditions, Judge (2017: 437) argues, "it is clear that this system could not exist but for an array of legal and financial innovations that enabled new methods of pooling and the issuance of new types of financial claims."

The most significant concern for finance institutions that trade new asset classes is that these transactions induce informational costs. Theoretically speaking, the orthodox efficient market hypothesis stipulates that all public information available is accommodated in the market pricing of the asset, but there is no robust evidence that suggests that the question regarding considerable information costs can be buried. Instead, empirical evidence indicates that market pricing show "anomalies" and that the analytical model as such is based on "debatable assumptions" (Ferrillo, Dunbar, and Tabak, 2004: 83). "Consequently," Ferrillo, Dunbar, and Tabak (2004: 83) write, "rather than being supportive, recent research into the efficient capital markets hypothesis has been critical at best":

> Scholars have pointed to many holes in both the theory and its predictions, including a lack of correlation in the price movements of individual stocks to public announcements, "noise trading," irrational investors, and the limits of arbitrage, and have concluded, like the thesis of this article, that the efficient capital markets hypothesis is sometimes less than efficient for a given security.

If information costs is a factual condition, as suggested by substantial scholarly research, also being a plausible condition in a market wherein it is well documented that traders are granted astronomical economic compensation, which indicates a considerable degree of illiquidity in the assets being traded as these assets demand professional expertise and skills to be bought and sold, then the nature of the shadow banking system needs to be examined in more detail than to simply be assumed to be some rational solution to market demand. If nothing else, the asymmetrical access to information and informational cost would explain the fragility of the shadow banking system, at times being on the verge of tipping over if new and unfavourable information is introduced.

This tendency, to be prone to crises and breakdowns, speaks against the idea that advanced structured finance instruments would make the finance system more resilient. Fernandez and Wigger (2016: 412) emphasize the protean quality of the shadow banking system, and stress the need for many different conditions to be synchronized and in harmony: "[W]henever the accumulation of capital and the accumulation of debt get too out of sync, a capitalist crisis emerges." Judge's (2017) explanation for this susceptibility to disturbances is that the various entities included in the highly integrated financial system respond to all sorts of changes within the system, and new system-relevant information is particularly prone to generating a crisis. For instance, "[w]hen money claimants make large-scale withdrawals from shadow banks, the effects are felt throughout the shadow banking system, and widespread market dysfunction often follows," Judge (2017: 437) argues. Expressed in theoretical terms, herd behaviour is always an issue as rumours regarding distressed or insolvent institutions may easily become a self-fulfilling prophecy as market actors are concerned to minimize their own losses whenever a financial crisis unfolds. As Judge (2017: 441) remarks, the ability to access credit on the basis of short-term contracts in the money market "is a mixed blessing" as such business partners may quickly withdraw at any sign of liquidity or solidity concerns. Therefore, the risk of herd behaviour that generates social and economic costs in excess of actual and measurable risks needs to be counteracted by a combination of market discipline and insurances from the sovereign state to avoid bank runs[9] (being the final and full-blown herd behaviour stage of an episode wherein rumours circulate; Martin, Skeie, and von Thadden, 2014; Diamond and Dybvig, 1983).

Under all conditions, the shadow banking system is inherently unstable and contains "information gaps" (Judge, 2017) that need to be, if not closed, at least marginalized as a form of concern or distraction among finance market actors. The issue is therefore how the sovereign state and its regulatory agencies can effectively control the shadow banking system that already from the outset is construed as a regulation cost avoidance activity. This is an issue that a considerable scholarly literature addresses and with a variety of proposals being presented, oftentimes being indicative of underlying theoretical assumptions regarding the efficacy of finance market activities. When all factors are considered, it is unlikely that the already extensive regulatory system would be able to fully control the shadow banking system anytime soon.[10] Already at this stage, there are a large number of federal regulatory agencies in place, carrying their own responsibilities, and new legislation (such as the Dodd-Frank Act) oftentimes adds new agencies, a condition that Awrey (2012: 256) emphasizes:

> In the U.S. […] federal responsibility for financial regulation is currently divided between a cacophony of regulators including the Federal Reserve Board, Financial Stability Oversight Council (FSOC), Securities and Exchange Commission (SEC), Commodity Futures Trading Commission (CFTC), Federal Deposit Insurance Corporation (FDIC), Financial Industry Regulatory Authority (FINRA), Office of the Comptroller of the Currency (OCC), Federal Housing Financing Agency (FHFA), and Consumer Financial Protection Bureau (CFPB).

This expansion of the arsenal of regulatory activities occurs despite the suspicion that the current financial system has rendered the Federal Reserve's traditional monetary policies inefficient in monitoring systemic risks, largely an effect of the structural changes in the finance industry, wherein the role of the traditional banks has been marginalized, Min (2018: 935) proposes:

> The shift from traditional banks, which are directly affected by the Federal Reserve's Fed Funds rate changes, to shadow banks, which are

only indirectly affected by these rate changes, has led to distortions in how monetary policy is actually transmitted into the real economy. Many economists have found that monetary policy transmission has been dampened by the growth of shadow banking [...] It appears clear that the shift from traditional banking to shadow banking has disrupted the traditional monetary policy levers used by the Federal Reserve.

Given these conditions, it is unlikely that the incidence of finance industry crises will be reduced. On the contrary, the fragmentation and specialization of the securities-driven finance industry reduce the possibilities for robust regulatory control of the capital formation process.

Systemic risk: the ghost in the finance machinery

To use an astrophysics metaphor, systemic risk in the finance industry is like gravity: it is largely ignored as an elementary fact of the matter, and it can be temporarily be overcome by skilled and professional actions (think of the pole vaulter, throwing herself over the bar as a graceful act that boldly and temporarily defies gravity), but in the end it cannot be defeated: it will always already be there, to be handled in one way or the other. According to contemporary finance theory, a branch of neoclassical economic theory, much of the risk in a portfolio of asset holdings can be diversified. That is, the portfolio manager can choose to hold assets that converge towards the index of the specific stock exchange. In contrast, systemic risk is *relational risk* that cannot be reduced on the basis of diversification as informational gaps and uncertainty (i.e., non-parametric risk) cannot be monitored by either the market actors themselves or regulators. For instance, Coval, Jurek, and Stafford (2009: 4) say that securities is one class of finance assets that are associated with systemic risk inasmuch as so-called structured finance assets that separate securities into what is referred to as *tranches* that carry different levels of risk, are to a varying degree susceptible to exogenous chocks, that is, new information introduced into the market (say, new regulatory principles, or some political event, say election results):

> [A] neglected feature of the securitization process is that it substitutes risks that are largely diversifiable for risks that are highly systematic. As a result, securities produced by structured finance activities have far less chance of surviving a severe economic downturn than traditional corporate securities of equal rating.

Sceptical commentators who are not convinced that systemic risk is an actual construct as it is complicated to measure, may consider empirical evidence that can be established ex post facto. For instance, during the 2008 finance crisis, credit rating agencies, which were assigned the role to act as the gatekeepers in the essentially self-regulating finance industry, underestimated the default rates for CDOs (a particularly difficult asset to price over the full business cycle) by 20,155 per cent on average (Lockwood, 2015: 727). That is, even the most sophisticated and best equipped professional service organizations in the entire finance industry apparently had not even the faintest idea regarding how to rate CDOs. If incompetence or ignorance factors are excluded from the explanation, the considerable residual is explained on the basis of the systemic risk that remained at this stage of the business cycle, when all other factors have been discounted.

Another approach to measuring systemic risk is to compare, for example, LIBOR, the interest rate that finance institutions used to pay when they initiated short-term contracts on the money market (i.e., a finance industry reference rate) and the interest rate on so-called overnight interest swaps (OIS) (Gorton and Metrick, 2012). "[T]he LIB-OIS spread acts primarily as a proxy for counterparty risk in the banking system," Gorton and Metrick (2012: 428) argue. In practical terms, when the LIB-OIS spread grows, this indicates that finance market actors cannot be sure whether the financial institution with which they initiate contracts is fully solvent, which results in a demand for a higher compensation in terms of a higher interest rate vis-à-vis LIBOR (the industry reference rate). Therefore, Gorton and Metrick (2012: 434) say, the LIB-OIS spread is a "proxy for fears about bank solvency." In other words, the LIB-OIS spread is low during the upward movement in the business cycle, whereas systemic risk grows as the market expands and the LIB-OIS spread grows as an indication of inflated systemic risk, which suggests a growing concern regarding the presence of potentially insolvent actors in the finance industry (say, late-coming speculators, thinly capitalized fly-by-night companies, imprudent mortgage loan lenders, etc.). Under all conditions, systemic risk is a key construct when it comes to understanding finance industry crises and breakdowns, an increasingly frequently occurring event.

Allen (2018: 718) discriminates between "financial stability" and "systemic risk" inasmuch as the two constructs cannot be construed as "two sides of the same coin." Allen (2018: 719) proposes that systemic risk is a finance market-specific construct, whereas financial stability can only be determined when looking beyond the finance industry as such and the wider real economy is included. Allen (2018: 719) provides a quite lengthy and technically detailed definition of financial stability, which can be cited in toto:

> [Financial stability is] a state of affairs wherein (i) financial institutions and markets are able to facilitate capital intermediation, risk management and payment services in a way that enables sustainable economic growth; (ii) there is no disruption to the ability of financial institutions or markets to carry out such functions that might cause harm to persons (wherever they may be resident) who are not customers or counterparties of those financial institutions, nor participants in those financial markets; and (iii) financial institutions and markets are able to withstand

economic shocks (such as the failure of other markets and institutions, or a chain of significant loses at financial institutions) so that (x) there will be no disruption to the performance of the functions set forth in (i) and (y) no harm will be caused to the persons set forth in (ii).

This is a fairly strict definition of financial stability risk, and if it is to be honoured by, for example, regulatory agencies, a quite steadfast approach to such a regulatory assignment would be needed. Formal definitions of systemic risk are indeed needed to initiate robust governance and regulatory control, but the larger empirical questions are, what triggers the growth of systemic risk and what measures can be taken to avoid the disastrous consequences of, for example, a global finance industry meltdown?

One key explanation for soaring systemic risk is that many asset classes are informationally sensitive. That is, they are not associated with high-quality collateral (as in, e.g., the case of prime home mortgage loans, with an actual house being the underlying referent), which means that new information being introduced on the market (say, a "Fed speech" declaration that anticipates rising interest rates, or a slowdown of economic activities) is interpreted in ways so that the economic value of the specific asset is downgraded. When the finance industry trades a majority of assets that are equally weakly collateralized, the systemic risks grows, which makes the entire system vulnerable to exogenous shocks (these so-called "shocks" do not really need to be overwhelming as also most moderate predictions regarding the near future of economic affairs can serve as the tipping point for a system-wide downgrading of asset prices), a so-called asset price drop follows (Acharya and Viswanathanm, 2011; Bell and Quiggin, 2006; Allen and Gale, 1994). "Because the market is dominated by investors with low liquidity preference, holding small reserves of cash, even small variations in the proportion of liquidity traders can cause a significant variation in prices," Allen and Gale (1994: 934) write. The more complex in design a finance asset class is, the lower the degree of historical pricing records that are available, in combination with the quality of the underlying collateral, the greater the risk of that specific asset classes for asset price drops whenever new information is introduced. It is important to notice that this kind of "informational sensitivity" is normally accommodated by the finance industry, and is therefore not a decisive issue as such, as Morris and Shin (2012: 18) write:

> The opaqueness of the asset-backed securities market and the attendant potential for adverse selection has frequently been blamed for the sudden drying up of liquidity. Yet, there is a puzzle at the heart of the crisis. Uncertainty about the true value of an asset should not invariably lead to the breakdown of trade. The stock market is a good illustration of how financial markets are normally well adapted to aggregating the diverse information of traders and arriving at a market-clearing price.

Instead, information-sensitive assets constitute one specific class of assets, and their role is likely to be particularly pronounced during the peak of the economic cycle, a situation wherein finance trader behaviour displays a growing "flight to quality," or "flight to liquidity assets," so that traders can secure their returns from the asset holdings following the previous upward turn of the business cycle (Guerrieri and Shimer, 2014). At this point, increasingly nervous finance traders become "more sensitive to private information and the asymmetric information begins to exert an influence in the trading decisions" (Morris and Shin, 2012: 19).

In the end, systemic risk is a structural, yet undesirable feature of the credit formation process, which needs to be weighed against the benefits of an ample supply of credit in the economic system. This is the reason why political entities and regulatory agencies demonstrate a fairly lenient attitude towards inflated systemic risks and the projected costs to restabilize a finance system in distress, and to recreate faith in the robustness of the finance market: they anticipate that the cost to rebalance wobbly finance markets is lower than the benefits from an efficient credit formation process.

Summary and conclusion

Credit relations are at the very heart of the capitalist mode of production as they are based on formal devices and informal social relations to serve their purpose. On the one hand, credit relations are defined in contractual terms that stipulate mutual responsibilities between creditor and borrower, but on the other hand, they are based on the creditor's calculated estimate that the borrower will be able to fulfil his or her obligations. Credit relations are thus prima facie legal and technically determined contracts, but they rest on the socially fluid notion of trust. The creditor not only has to trust the borrower's capacity to honour the contract and his or her integrity and prudence, but also need to trust the general economic and social system wherein credit is being issued inasmuch as the borrower's stipulated projects (say, to run a small-scale business on the basis of the credit raised) are inevitably dependent on the overall functioning of the economic system. Already in this elementary, even rudimentary relationship between one creditor and one borrower—a typical textbook case in finance theory or legal theory—there are considerable implications that needs to be recognized. When economic transactions are conducted on the scale of billions of dollars per time units, and being co-dependent on one another either directly (as in the case of, e.g., commodities trade wherein positions made affect market prices), or indirectly (via, e.g., policy statements made by authorities and agencies), these elementary relations and their complexities are amplified on a logarithmic scale. It is frequently remarked that, for example, the US finance industry is one of the most regulated businesses in the world and certainly so from a historical perspective (Awrey, 2012; Ricks, 2011), and yet the industrial production of, for example, credit relations and contracts provides materials for thousands of academic scholars in finance theory and related disciplines. The mind-boggling complexity of the finance industry seems inexhaustible.

For scholars who do not only target more specific issues or relations, the sublime vastness of the financial economy may be daunting, and yet there is a need for scholarly texts that seek to include and combine scholarly literatures from different disciplines that actively map the underlying business practices. Such literatures include finance studies in economics, legal theory, management studies literature, and economic sociology, but also seemingly more peripheral disciplines such as anthropology and historiography. Hegel's adage that the owl of Minerva takes off at dusk, which commonly is understood as a warning that insight and wisdom can only be achieved, at best, after the fact, in medias res, in the middle of things, the fog of war precludes any meaningful analysis of the long-term consequences of conventional wisdom and decisions made, and only when the dust falls to the ground can the significance of such conditions and events be accounted for. The voluminous scholarly and popular literature that addresses the financial crisis of 2008 and the doctrines, legal reforms, and regulatory practices that resulted in the disastrous outcomes are recent evidence of the validity of Hegel's poetic declaration regarding the prescience of mankind. As always, it is easier to pass judgement and declare verdicts when assisted by the benefit of hindsight, and yet this is precisely what needs to be done when sociotechnical systems of great complexity are being developed and elaborated upon. To claim that individuals granted great authority failed despite their best intentions may appear to be ungrateful or a churlish thing to do, but unless responsibilities are accompanied by at least a justifiable critique in the case of failure, the governance system is unsustainable, as the new generation of policymakers and leaders may be less incentivized to learn from history. The new generation of policymakers and leaders may predictably fail to honour the ambition to learn from past failures, but being reminded of failures is arguably more helpful in that pursuit than to sweep historical debacles under the carpet.

Downer (2011), who examines aviation engineering failures ("plane crashes"), discriminates between *epistemic accidents* and what Charles Perrow (1984) refers to as *normal accidents*. Whereas a normal accident is caused by, for example, human failure and cannot be explained on the basis of insufficient know-how that resulted in the accident (say, a derailment), epistemic accidents are defined as "those accidents that occur because a scientific or technological assumption proves to be erroneous, even though there were reasonable and logical reasons to hold that assumption before (although not after) the event" (Downer, 2011: 748. Original emphasis omitted). In the case of an epistemic accident, the engineers' design of the airplane was based on the best and most reliable scientific data and evidence, and the inconsistencies or weaknesses of such scientific data only reveal themselves in the unfortunate event of an accident or an adverse event. Consequently, despite the best intentions of the community of aviation engineers, the oft-cited high reliability of airline travel (supported by robust evidence) is "necessarily built on highly specific insights gleaned from enlightening but unavoidable surprises" (Downer, 2011: 757). The technical and meteorological complexity of aircraft can be only partially simulated in the laboratory or in so-called in silico models, and therefore airplane accidents data and information are primary input material for ongoing aviation engineering projects. In analogy with aviation engineering, it may be that financial crises, at least on the "wholesale level," should be understood in terms of being epistemic accidents. For proponents of the finance industry, that would be a legitimate way to escape the culpability of finance industry actors themselves, whereas more critical commentators would regard the introduction of epistemic accidents as an explanatory factor as a way to shift blame from centrally located agents who act on the basis of their convictions and self-interest to some kind of unfortunate but basically unknown and unknowable condition that surfaced only after the damage was already done. Regardless of the position taken, whether finance crises, which, unlike in the aviation industry, are more frequent and growing in magnitude as finance markets deepen, are best characterized as normal or epistemic accidents is an open question. We may learn from history what explanations gain the upper hand when the books are closed.

Notes

1 In the finance industry, it is commonly discriminated between capital markets, which offers medium- to long-term contracts, with maturities "greater than one year," and money markets, which supply short-term credit contracts, with maturities "shorter than one year" (Hockett and Omarova, 2016: 1165, note 64).

2 Empirical studies exploring data sets from Italy and Germany, respectively, show that the liquidity crisis that followed from the collapse of the interbank lending market in 2008 resulted in lower investment in smaller firms more generally in the case of Italy (Cingano, Manaresi, and Sette (2016), and innovative firms more specifically in Germany (Giebel and Kraft (2019) during the period that followed. The average daily volume of interbank lending reached its peak at 20 billion euros in 2006 (which corresponded to 12.3 per cent of total assets of the average bank), but by the end of 2010, the comparable figure was 4.7 billion euros (Cingano, Manaresi, and Sette, 2016: 2742). Cingano, Manaresi, and Sette (2016: 2738) show that the "aggregate drop in investment" in smaller and younger firms, and firms dependent on banks for credit supply, is "traceable to the interbank market collapse." As smaller and innovative firms account for a considerable proportion of new job creation (Decker et al., 2014, 2016, 2017), the shortage of finance capital reduce job growth, and economic growth more generally, thus partially explain the secular stagnation being observed. Cingano, Manaresi, and Sette (2016: 2770) estimate that employment would have been 12 per cent higher in the absence of the financial crisis, and that the total investment expenditure in 2007–2010 would have been "almost 24% higher than that observed."

3 For instance, a widespread explanation of secular stagnation is that ageing populations save more and make less investment, but the current economic situation cannot be explained on the basis of demographic data, Acemoglu and Restrepo (2017) argue. Since the early 1990s or 2000s, periods commonly viewed as the beginning of "the adverse effects of aging" in much of the advanced world, there is no evidence of a "negative association between aging and lower GDP per capita" (Acemoglu and Restrepo, 2017: 174). On the contrary, the relationship between ageing and GDP per capita is "significantly positive in many specifications" (Acemoglu and Restrepo, 2017: 174). Furthermore, the conventional pro-business view and free market theory explanation for the decline in dynamism in the American economy—that the federal state or the state imposes costly or inefficient regulatory measures—is not supported by empirical evidence, Goldschlag and Tabarrok (2018: 32) argue: "Regulation does not appear to be a major explanation for the decline of dynamism seen in the United States and neither measurement error nor endogeneity bias appear to be large enough to reverse this conclusion." More generally, Goldschlag and Tabarrok (2018: 37) notice that "[m]any measures of declining dynamism are associated with greater GDP per capita." For example, on average there are "[f]ewer entrepreneurs and more large firms in more developed economies both cross-sectionally and over-time," Goldschlag and Tabarrok (2018: 37) write. Regardless of this observation, the alarming decline of entrepreneurial activities in the US economy is an issue that equally policymakers and scholars are concerned with.

4 In contrast to this sceptical view of offshoring, De Rassenfosse and Thomson (2019: 1498) argue that in the case of R&D offshoring, empirical evidence indicates that these business decisions "contribute positively to productivity in the home country, irrespective of the host country destination." Still, productivity growth per se does not of necessity translate into economic and social welfare in the home domicile, and the study examines the specific case of R&D offshoring wherein local expertise and know-how can be exploited to generate competitive advantages.

5 Lazonick and Mazzucato (2013: 1094) define innovation in formal terms as "[t]he generation of higher quality products at lower unit cost at prevailing factor prices." Prior to that, Damanpour (1992: 376) defined innovation in more open-ended terms, as "[t]he adoption of an idea or behaviour, whether a system, policy, program, device, process, product or service, that is new to the adopting organization." Either of these two definitions should be applicable when examining financial innovations.

6 The term *collateral* is of central importance for this volume, but it is relatively complicated to define in precise semantic terms. Furthermore, Spears (2019: 343) proposes, in traditional neoclassical descriptions of markets, the concept of collateral is absent, simply because the theoretical models assume that all economic agents "keep their promises." Nevertheless, in legal terms, Boy and Gabor (2019: 297) write, "collateralization means the creation of a real right to secure the performance of an obligation." Riles (2010: 797) points to the hybrid nature of collateral as being both a legal contract and a financial device:

> In legal terms, collateral is a hybrid of property and contract law. Legal rules concerning how collateral rights are created and enforced, who is responsible for maintaining collateral during the period of the swap, and

when parties must seek the authority of a judge to dispose of collateral or when they can act on their own differ considerably from one jurisdiction to the next. In the financial markets, however, one first encounters collateral as a mountain of specific preprinted forms that must be completed and filed before trading can begin and confirmation documents that must be exchanged after each trade.

As a consequence of this hybridity, collateral "[i]s not just a set of legal doctrines but also a set of practices of document production, filing, and exchange and associated modalities of sociality," Riles (2010: 797) writes. Collateral is produced by legal-technical experts in the back offices of financial institutions (Riles, 2011), a professional practice little attended to equally by news media and scholarly communities.

In practical terms, since the late twentieth century, liquidity has been upheld in finance markets on the basis of the trading of so-called repurchase agreements, commonly referred to as repos: "Collateralized promises to pay have taken a central role in the financial architecture since the late twentieth century in the form of repurchase agreements (repos)" (Boy and Gabor, 2019: 304). This means that the concept of collateral is more important today than, for example, neoclassical economic theory recognizes. Once discounted as a mere "'back office' technicality to secure financial transactions against credit risk," collateral has become "increasingly central to the way that financial instruments are valued and priced," Spears (2019: 364) proposes. For instance, prior to the financial crisis of 2008, financial traders used the LIBOR rate, an industry standard for estimating the cost of borrowing money in the (short-term) money market, in turn used to calculate the present value of OTC derivative cashflows. That is, the LIBOR rate was widely assumed to both represent the "risk-free rate of interest" and to denote the funding costs of large banks and financial institutions (Spears, 2019: 343–344). The downfall of LIBOR, which resulted in divergences in banks' funding costs, represented what Spears (2019: 344) refers to as "an intellectual crisis as some of the most fundamental assumptions of [financial traders'] models became invalidated." As a consequence, Spears (2019: 344) writes, "even the simplest uncollateralized derivatives sold by different banks became incommensurable goods." The absence of a market standard to calculate a (synthetic) risk-free rate of interest generated substantial liquidity and transparency problems that imposed considerable information costs on financial traders. In this situation, the elementary demand for shared rules and standards for calculative practices was undermined. "The existence of a market," Spears (2019: 346) writes, "requires that economic actors are able to cleanly 'disentangle' goods or instruments that are to be traded from their broader social context, thus rendering them calculable." In the face of what Spears (2019: 365) refers to as the break of an "institutional order," financial traders have sought— with only modest success, in Spears' (2019) verdict—"to make collateral itself the social basis of liquidity by standardizing its features." In the new institutional order that replaced the LIBOR standard, collateral plays a new role as a "valuation anchor" in addition to its more classic role as "risk mitigant," Spears (2019: 365) contends.

7   In fact, even credit rating agencies, which were supposed to serve as the watchdog that would alert finance market actors in the case of more lax mortgage lending

standards and its various consequences, failed to avoid this naive belief in almost endless housing prices. For instance, in March 2007, First Pacific Advisors discovered that Fitch, one of the "Big Three" credit rating agencies (the other two being Standard & Poor and Moody's) used a model that "assumed constantly appreciating home prices, ignoring the possibility that they could fall," Coval, Jurek, and Stafford (2009: 20) write. Such evidence has triggered an intense debate regarding the role of credit rating agencies in the self-regulation regime that dominated in the period (see, e.g., Naciri, 2015; Alp, 2013; Cornaggio and Cornaggia, 2013; White, 2013; Bolton, Freixas, and Shapiro, 2012; Hunt, 2009; Rom, 2009). Bubb and Prasad (2014: 1554) emphasize that "crucially, over-optimism about house prices in the recent housing bubble was not confined to homebuyers. The same 'bubble fever' infected lenders, securitizers, and MBS investors." Between 1985 and 2011, the outstanding amount of "non-mortgage-related ABS," simultaneously being a finance asset class associated with high risk and the capacity to innovate in terms of transforming illiquid assets into invest-able and tradeable finance assets, issued in the United States and Europe grew by over 1,800 per cent (Awrey, 2012: 270). This condition justifies what Bubb and Prasad (2014) refer to as *naive-investors theory*, wherein also professional investors and securities underwriters (and not only home mortgage borrowers, normally understood to be "naive" regarding projected house prices) are smitten by overoptimism.

8 Coffee (2012: 1060) summarizes the substance of the Dodd-Frank Act as a piece of legislation that "tied the hands of financial regulators in some respects," while "mandating relatively little." Ultimately, Coffee (2012: 1061) argues, the Dodd-Frank Act does not in any meaningful way address the "core problem" at hand, that "banks are inherently fragile." Banks and other finance institutions operate on the basis of a "fundamental mismatch" between "the short-term character of their liabilities and the longer-term character of their assets." That is, depositors expect and receive high liquidity, while borrowers "expect to repay their loans over a longer, multiyear period." In practice, this means that finance institutions balance their various asset and liabilities on the basis of their ability to access (longer-term) credit markets and (shorter-term) money markets, which makes them susceptible to market disturbances such as speculation on asset prices, imprudent business practices, bank runs, and so on. In Coffee's (2012, 2011) account, the Dodd-Frank Act does not accommodate these issues.

9 "Runs occur when holders of the short-term safe debt have (rational) doubts about the value of the backing collateral (which is also debt) and want cash instead," Gorton (2017: 549) writes. If a bank does not hold sufficient liquid resources to satisfy the demands for cash, it has to access liquidity through the sales of assets, but such sales may signal to market actors that the bank is in a state of imminent default, which creates uncertainty and consequently pushes down asset prices further and causes so-called "mark-to-market losses." In the end, herd behaviour generates enormous costs for society, which justifies a variety of insurances against bank losses from the sovereign state.

10 The quick expansion of high-frequency trading (HFT) in the finance industry is one such change in practices that further complicates regulatory oversight. Today, roughly two-thirds of all trading activity in the US financial market is based on HFT technologies (Johnson, 2017: 856). HFT is technically and legally complex (e.g. are the algorithms used in the trade to be treated as firm-specific assets, e.g.

protected from external reviews?), but it also enables the trade of what is called "dark pool assets," that is, securities that are "off-exchange" or "unlisted." This means that a specific class of securities are traded "without disclosure of trading information required on nationally regulated exchanges," Johnson (2017: 864) writes. The presence of dark pools raises several regulatory concerns as it reintroduces a series of issues pertaining to market fragmentation, the fairness of trade, access to market information, the risk of price manipulation, and how to ensure that what economists refer to as "price discovery" remains a transparent process. More specifically, Johnson (2017: 878–879) examines dark pool trade practices such as *spoofing* (described as "a bluffing tactic whereby traders submit and cancel a series of bids for the purpose of gaining an advantage in the market price") and *pinging* (which means placing small test orders in the market at a number of different price levels, and then the orders are quickly cancelled to extract market data that is used to generate a larger return on the trade of the specific asset), two practices that occur in a fraction of second and therefore cannot be reasonably assumed to diverge from the more analytical process to determine asset prices over a series of trade events. What Johnson (2017: 885) refers to as "alternative trading strategies and venues" has been widely criticized for being what generate risks that "threaten to disrupt the stability of financial markets." Other commentators have been more interested in the legal side of the trade, and have claimed that the use of HFT practices is either "deceptive" (and by implication an unlawful practice in finance trade) or that price manipulation techniques such as spoofing and pinging per se violate US federal law. Under all conditions, the quick and in many cases unchartered expansion of the use of HFT in the finance industry generates considerable regulatory challenges.

2 The institutional framework

The capital formation process in finance-led economies

Introduction

The previous chapter addressed the more formal features and mechanisms of the finance economy. In this chapter, the more practical work conducted in the credit formation process, which involve the production of high-quality collateral, will be examined in more detail. In order to outline how the credit formation is co-produced with the supply of collateral, the construction industry and its role in the financial economy is discussed. Even though local and regional variation is a factual condition, as housing markets and financing are fundamentally shaped by local conditions, customs, institutional conditions, legislation, regulatory practices, and so forth, a close-knit relation between the sovereign state, the finance industry, and the construction industry is stipulated in all advanced economies (see, e.g., Bohle, 2014, 2018).

Urban studies scholars have increasingly paid attention to what Guironnet, Attuyer, and Halbert (2016) call the "financialisation of property markets" (Beswick and Penny, 2018; Fields and Uffer, 2016; Weber, 2010). Also, political scientists such as Ansell (2014) have emphasized the new and emerging "political economy" of housing markets, and economists have committed considerable effort to examining the role of the home mortgage lending market in the finance crisis of 2008 that resulted in the resounding Great Recession that followed (e.g. Adelino, Schoar, and Severino, 2018). Empirical studies indicate that various forms of financial engineering and legal operations, including the use of legal corporate forms such as limited liability companies (LLCs) (Travis, 2019), novel ways to finance urban regeneration activities, including tax increment financing (TIF) (Searle, 2018; Pacewicz, 2012; Briffault, 2010; Lefcoe, 2010), and the incorporation of real estate developers in tax havens (Botzem and Dobusch, 2017), are now widely used business practices in real estate development and ownership, and urban regeneration programmes more widely. Critics argue that the influence of new finance industry investment models and practices have considerable social and economic consequences, including "social restratification" (Forrest and Hirayama, 2018) and may ultimately result in what Peck (2012) refers to as "austerity urbanism" (see, e.g., Desmond, 2012). Regardless of these important contributions to the understanding of the deepening relations between urban development, housing production, and finance industry operations, a more comprehensive theoretical model needs to be developed to connect the various mechanisms that render land, housing, and real estate attractive investment objects within current finance industry practices. The purpose of this chapter is to outline the connections between housing as collateral, home mortgage lending, and mortgage-backed securities issuances as capital formation activities, and the regulatory state.

The construction industry is frequently portrayed as an autonomous industry that produces housing, built environment, and related output on the basis of current and anticipated market conditions. At the same time, the construction industry is labour intensive and provides a broad variety of blue-collar work, which makes it the industry *per préférénce* to subsidize for political entities to stabilize economic growth over the economic cycle. "[H]ousing manufacturing, the production of the attendant infrastructure, housing sales and resales, and financing perhaps the most important engine of the US economy," Pattillo (2013: 512) writes. What is less commonly examined is the role that the construction industry plays in providing high-quality collateral, housing—preferably privately owned by households—and accompanying home mortgage lending within the capital formation in the finance industry (Levitin and Wachter, 2020). Being supportive of the production of affordable[1] and qualitative housing is a key political objective in most welfare states (Schwartz, 2012), and the conventional wisdom of policymakers over the last decades, is that private ownership of real estate serve to align household interest and preferences and macroeconomic objectives (Krippner, 2017). Housing policy is therefore a political domain wherein the construction industry plays a key role. Fligstein, Brundage, and Schultz (2017: 884) refer to this relation as "the housing-finance nexus." In addition, the supply of finance capital has many economic benefits as its lowers the cost for business promoters who raise capital to finance various ventures and entrepreneurial activities. As Krippner (2017: 2) remarks, the availability of credit in an economy is an "indispensable tool of statecraft" in the contemporary welfare state model, not the least in an economic regime wherein households' access to credit has "become a substitute for wage income and a prerequisite for full inclusion in the marketplace."

In order to expand the capital base, the finance industry demands assets be backed by the sovereign state. Such so-called *safe assets* are the foundation for capital formation activities, whereupon private-backed credit can be issued on the basis of the stock of safe assets (Gorton, 2017; Gorton, Lewellen, and Metrick, 2012). Over time, Gorton, Lewellen, and Metrick (2012) show, around one-third of all credit is safe assets, that is, credit insured by the sovereign state. This means that around two-thirds of all credit is backed by private finance institutions, but this expansion of the capital base, beneficial for the overall efficiency of the economy and conducive to economic growth as an abundant supply of capital which makes more ventures and entrepreneurial projects realizable, is dependent on a predictable supply of safe assets. Through these capital formation mechanisms, the construction industry is closely tied to the finance industry, insured and subsidized by the sovereign state, as the housing market provides prime collateral that supports both state-backed and private-backed credit.

The construction industry also benefits from contributing to the capital formation process as the industry has historically received much attention from policymakers during, for example, the downturn of the economic cycle, oftentimes resulting in various public investments, insurances, subsidies, and tax exemptions to restore economic growth (Levitin, 2014; Rosas, 2006). Furthermore, being dependent on a generous supply of low-cost finance capital, provided by efficient capital markets, to be able to realize its portfolio of projects and to be able to initiate future projects, the construction industry itself benefits from the expansion of the capital base as a second-order consequence. The activities and interests of the construction industry, the sovereign state, and the finance industry are therefore entangled through a number of mechanisms. When monitored closely by regulatory authorities, this tripartite model generates net economic welfare, but if imbalances are observed, including, for example, imprudent behaviour such as predatory lending to supply collateral (Agarwal et al., 2014; Bond, Musto, and Yilmaz, 2008; Engel and McCoy, 2007; Peterson, 2007; Eggert, 2002), but now with lower quality as the new pool of borrowers is less likely to be able to hold their contracts until maturation (Shin, 2009), various undesirable effects are generated, ultimately – in the worst case scenario – leading to a finance market crisis.

The remainder of this chapter is structured accordingly: first, the political goal to provide affordable housing as an integral component of the welfare state model is connected to the role of the construction industry as the primary and entrusted provider of high-quality housing. To finance home purchases, credit is issued as home mortgage loans, and this stock of loans is insured by the sovereign state, that is, treated as safe assets by finance institutions. Second, the chapter examines the role of safe assets within the broader capital formation process, serving to generate private-backed money claims. This process includes the securitization of home mortgage loans on an industrial basis, and securitization further expands the credit supply within the shadow banking sector of the finance industry (as discussed in Chapter 1). In the third section, the relationship between the construction and finance industries, recognized by the sovereign state and supported by the state's insurance of home mortgages loans, is discussed in terms of a trade-off between finance market *efficiency* versus *stability*, an issue that policymakers and regulatory agencies need to carefully consider.

Housing policy, home mortgage lending, and the role of the construction industry

Weiss (1989: 253) argues that the real estate business "revolves around money," and yet "surprisingly few" scholars engage in "tracing funds through the financial system." Weiss (1989: 253) lists a number of areas of research demanding scholarly attention, including "mortgage insurance, secondary mortgage markets, impacts of taxation policies, and public subsidies and programs." As Min (2018: 900) notices, "[h]ousing finance naturally produces liabilities that function as money." That is, the production of housing, which is the business of the construction industry, actively participates in capital formation. Schwartz (2012: 37) says that mortgage debt, securitized or not, constitutes the largest, or one of the largest, assets in most Organization for Economic Cooperation and Development (OECD) countries: "Housing and more particularly housing finance was an important systemic component of the postwar welfare state by virtue of the balance-sheet connection between long-duration liabilities and long-duration assets."

The role of mortgage lending in capital formation is based on a variety of premises. First of all, housing is a "social necessity" (Min, 2018: 921), and it is costly to develop and purchase, and has a very long depreciation period. Second, housing is part of the welfare state programme, so policy-making actively supports the production of housing. Consequently, home ownership campaigns and progressive housing initiatives have been part of equally centre-right and social democratic and left-leaning governments' economic policies over time. First, home ownership serves as what Ansell (2014: 384) refers to as a "self-insurance" inasmuch as "housing provide a stock of wealth independent from the dynamics of the labor market." Household wealth is estimated on the basis of housing prices, and a downturn in the economy can thus be mediated by private wealth stored in home ownership. Second, this sense of being insured against economic hardship tends to modify the preferences of voters who own property, which makes them less supportive of redistribution policies and "social insurance spending" (Ansell, 2014: 387). To some extent, for equally left- and right-leaning governments, this relieves the state from expectations that can be complicated and costly to fulfil (Levitin and Wachter, 2020). At the same time, low-income households, students, and labour market entrants (e.g. immigrants), who are less capable of affording home ownership, tend to suffer the consequences of this shift in policy. Conley and Gifford (2006: 56) found "an inverse relationship" between the levels of economic equality and "widespread home ownership," which indicates that home ownership policies have negative externalities as low-income households suffer from the loss in faith in, for example, redistribution policies. Consequently, Conley and Gifford (2006: 78) call for an extended scholarly research agenda wherein housing policy is treated as an "important part of the welfare state function." Such a research programme would shed light on what factors and conditions and active participation in, for example, lobbying activities that contribute to the production of housing and real estate, and the accompanying financial activities. For instance, as Ansell (2014: 387, footnote 2) proposes, "Congressional support for mortgage credit expansion is driven as much by mortgage-industry campaign contributions and district demographics as by partisan ideology." That is, rather than being propelled by a political commitment to welfare programmes or other reforms (e.g. market deregulation or market creation), finance industry interests largely determine housing production. Lawrence Lindsey, a chief economic adviser in the George W. Bush administration, admits that "no one wanted to stop the [housing] bubble" being observed during the first years of the new millennium as "[i]t would have conflicted with the president's own policies." In most OECD countries, housing policy is a key welfare state provision.

To finance home purchases, the state relies on finance industry institutions, or, as in the case of the United States, on so-called government-sponsored enterprises (GSEs) to issue home mortgage loans. In the United States, the two GSEs Fannie Mae and Freddie Mac serve this role (Richardson, Van Nieuwerburgh, and White, 2018). To finance mortgage lending activities, the two institutions have jointly issued approximately $5.3 trillion in mortgage-backed securities, collateralized mortgage obligations (CMOs), and corporate debt. GSE-backed securities "[m]ore than doubled their relative size between the 1970s and the mid-1990s," Caverzasi, Botta, and Capelli (2019: 1036) write. More specifically, to be able to serve as the principal providers of home mortgage loans to the American public, Fannie Mae and Freddie Mac issue three categories of liabilities: (1) corporate debt (known as "Agency debt"), (2) mortgage-backed securities (known as "Agency MBS"), and (3) collateralized mortgage obligations (known as "Agency CMOs") (Min, 2018: 912). These liabilities not only offer the possibility to finance housing purchases, which per se fulfils one political objective, but they also have a wider significance within the capital formation process. As these liabilities are understood to "carry an implicit federal guarantee against losses" (Min, 2018: 901), the three categories of liabilities are an important component in the supply of safe assets. GSE-backed assets make up no less than one-quarter of the stock of US safe assets, and one-tenth of the estimated global supply of safe assets (Min, 2018: 901). The safe asset mechanism is examined in greater detail in the following sections.

Capital formation, safe assets, and credit supply

Safe assets, including all financial assets being insured by the sovereign state, either in the case when they are issued by GSEs, or by private finance institutions such as banks, are thought to carry de minimis credit risk. Consequently, safe assets are strongly preferred as collateral in transactions (Min, 2018: 902). Banks are licensed by the sovereign state to create credit de novo when they estimate that the credit risk is limited. That is, the debtor is expected to repay the loan at the end of the contract period, and interest payment during the entire contact period. When the sovereign state provides insurances, the credit risk is minimal, but when it is a private institution that issues, for example, securities, the perceived risk increases as the private issuer—unlike the sovereign state—can become insolvent or default during the contract period. One implication is that the information about the issuer of credit become valuable, as such information can support the estimation of credit risk. As information is costly to acquire and to process (Merton, 1987), say, a loan can be collateralized to reduce risk. That is, there is a safe asset backing the loan. In that situation, the access to additional information about the borrower is no longer critical as the collateral per se serves to reduce the credit risk. To use a trivial example, a pawn broker who receives good collateral on a loan (say, an exclusive Swiss wristwatch) does not have to worry about the borrower's credit history or track record in repaying loans as the collateral itself covers the pawn broker's cost if the borrower fails to repay the loan. Expressed in theoretical terms, collateral helps "ameliorate the problem of information asymmetry in financial intermediation" (Min, 2018: 910). When safe assets, that is, low credit risk assets, serve as collateral in a transaction, economists say that the credit being issued is *information insensitive*. That is, new information issued, regardless if it pertains to the issuer of the credit or other macroeconomic or policy-relevant information, does not affect the liquidity of the asset as such (Gorton, Lewellen, and Metrick, 2012: 101). As in the case of the pawn broker, rumours that the borrower is in a dire financial situation do not affect the risk of the lender as the underlying collateral has a stable market value regardless of the financial fitness of its current owner. The collateral is information insensitive insofar as the introduction of new information does not affect the liquidity of the asset being held.

Information-insensitive assets such as the liabilities of private issuers of credit being insured by the sovereign state or GSEs, being the franchisees of the sovereign state (Hockett and Omarova, 2016: 147), are socially valuable if they constitute a stock of collateral that serves to assist the capital formation process. Gorton, Lewellen, and Metrick (2012: 101) point at the considerable growth of the total asset stock in the United States over the last six decades, wherein the total stock of assets was approximately four times GDP in 1952, and ten times GDP in 2010, a few years after the financial crisis. At the same time, the proportion of total assets that are considered safe have remained stable over time, accounting for roughly one-third of total assets. Such empirical data indicates that safe assets constitute a form of finance industry infrastructure that serves to leverage the credit supply in an economy. Gorton, Lewellen, and Metrick (2012: 102) define safe assets in performative terms, by pointing at what classes of assets that are considered safe in day-to-day finance market trading:

> The key components of "safe" debt include bank deposits, money market mutual fund shares, commercial paper, federal funds and repurchase agreements ("repo"), short-term interbank loans, Treasuries, agency debt, municipal bonds, securitized debt, and high-grade financial-sector corporate debt.

Consistent with a legal theory of finance, Gelpern and Gerding (2016) argue that safe assets is a legal concept at the same time as law is rarely mentioned in, for example, Federal Reserve speeches, except when it is introduced as "an occasional source of distortion" (Gelpern and Gerding, 2016: 366). Nevertheless, unlike, for example, physical entities, safe assets "are not to be found in nature" as they only exist in economic theory and in "market vernacular," Gelpern and Gerding (2016: 366) write. By implication, the term *safe* is a misnomer as this class of assets cannot be completely risk free, but on the contrary they should be understood as being "'safe enough' to ignore the risks for some purposes" (Gelpern and Gerding, 2016: 366). This means that safe assets is a form of "legal fiction,"[2] ultimately resting on the sovereign state's capacity and willingness to insure the finance industry against losses. That is, the degree of risk in holding assets such as mortgage-backed securities, bank deposits, or government bonds "ultimately rests on state capacity to regulate, collect taxes, and issue money, and state willingness to deploy these powers in specific ways for the sake of particular constituents and markets" (Gelpern and Gerding, 2016: 367). In other words, safe assets are not different in kind but only in degree regarding the parametric risks pertaining to asset holding, in turn being a combination of state-based insurances and regulatory practices and private business activities, a model that is "unavoidably distributive and fraught with distortions" (Gelpern and Gerding, 2016: 367).

Gelpern and Gerding (2016: 369) identify three mechanisms that are constitutive of safe assets. First, legal interventions such as the use of devices and mechanisms including "contracts, statutes, regulations, and administrative agency practices" promote the full and timely repayment of certain financial contracts, which reduce uncertainty and consequently affect the credit-formation process positively. Second, legal institutions can use the label "law" to certify that specific assets are "absolutely or relatively safe," which encourages market participants to buy such assets. Third and finally, legal institutions can issue guarantees that certain safe assets will maintain their value even in the face of severe shocks, such as system-wide financial crises or asset price drops in the market (Gelpern and Gerding, 2016: 369). This third mechanism is of great importance as safe assets serve to restabilize the finance market during episodes of turbulence. In the upward movement of the business cycle, public-backed and private-backed assets do not differ much in terms of risk assessment and price (in fact, the difference between state bonds and corporate bonds is treated as a qualitative measure of market stability), but at the peak of the economic cycle, what economists call the "flight to quality" (de facto meaning to shift high-return assets for less risky and more liquid assets, such as bonds rather than second-order derivatives such as CDOs), state-backed safe assets are preferred over private-backed assets as "private safe assets as a group have a poor track record of keeping their value in crisis" (Gelpern and Gerding, 2016: 376).

The process wherein the state issues safe assets is complicated by the participation in, for example, a monetary union, wherein the state "gives up control of its currency" to instead benefit from a regional bank and its regulatory practices (as in the case of the European Central Bank, ECB). In that case, the state submits to "external policy discipline" and must ensure that there are sufficient guarantees "to have its debt treated as a safe asset," Gelpern and Gerding (2016: 405–406, footnote 169) write. For instance, while, say, the state of the Netherlands previously issued safe assets (say, state bonds) outside of such agreements, it is now relying on the ECB to ensure that a strict fiscal policy and regulatory discipline are maintained in the whole of the eurozone, or else investors may downgrade Dutch bonds as the government of the Netherlands may be held responsible for, for example, costs derived from weak fiscal discipline in, for instance, Greece or Italy, two countries that historically have been subject to regulatory control. In other words, the issuance of safe assets is not only a legal matter but also a political process, wherein the degree of autonomy of the sovereign state becomes an issue to consider (see, e.g., Epstein, 2017; Lupo-Pasini, 2017; Brummer, 2015). Under all conditions, "safe assets" are on average not risk free but are safer than private-backed safe assets as the sovereign state is protected against default by the network of transnational agencies such as the IMF, the World Bank, the ECB (in the eurozone), and so forth. This means in practice that the sovereign state acts as one of the primary market makers in the credit formation process, as it issues credit itself and insures private credit issuers. This system is not risk free, devoid of externalities, moral hazard, and the possibilities for opportunistic behaviour, but it remains the most efficient way known to date to optimize the supply of credit in the economy.

Min (2018: 912) suggests that the global stock of safe assets includes both privately produced safe assets (such as AAA-rated asset-backed securities) and "government-backed debt issued or guaranteed by a select group of countries perceived as having low risk of non-payment of claims" (typically OECD nations). At the same time as safe assets have been in parity with the total stock of assets, it is noteworthy that the category of safe assets is more diverse today. In the 1950s and 1960s, bank deposits accounted for nearly 80 per cent of the stock of safe assets, and as late as 1978, the figure still stood at 70 per cent. Finance market deregulation and finance industry innovations (Funk and Hirschman, 2014; Frame and White, 2004), have reduced the role of bank deposits: By 2008, on the verge of the finance industry crisis, the share of bank deposits had fallen to 27 per cent, and by 2010, when the faith in global financial markets had been restored, the measure still stood at 32 per cent, less than half reported in 1978. This diminishing weight of bank deposits is indicative of the role of securitization and the global securities market in capital formation in the contemporary economic system. "The current US mortgage finance system is heavily based on capital market financing implemented through securitization," Richardson, Van Nieuwerburgh, and White (2018: 28) write.

Securitization and the credit formation process

Securitization was discussed in some detail in the previous chapter, but some of the specific conditions that pertain to credit formation on the basis of mortgage lending must be examined. The concept of securitization is disputed, and some commentators (e.g. Lipson, 2011) argue that the term is poorly defined, especially given the enormous importance of the asset class in the contemporary economy, being the mechanism through which credit is issued. Lipson (2011: 1233) defines what he calls "true securitization" accordingly:

> [A] purchase of primary payment rights by a special purpose entity that (1) legally isolates such payment rights from a bankruptcy (or similar insolvency) estate of the originator, and (2) results, directly or indirectly, in the issuance of securities whose value is determined by the payment rights so purchased.

There are several benefits of securitization. First, securities markets are claimed to increase the liquidity in finance markets as securitization is more efficient than traditional financing such as lending or issuing shares (Lipson, 2011: 1242). Second, securitization gives originators access to the capital markets, which they would perhaps not otherwise have been able to access (Lipson, 2011: 1244). This second benefit is disputed not by design but by implication, as for instance less prudent and poorly capitalized home mortgage lenders, targeting sub-prime borrowers, may access capital markets wherein traders carry considerable information costs to detect underlying low-quality collateral. The literature on predatory lending (e.g. Engel and McCoy, 2007) indicates that securitization enabled assets backed by both high quality and low quality collateral to be bundled in ways that increased information costs and thereby reduced market efficiency. Third and perhaps most controversial, securitization enables certain accounting practices that may result in the reported financial fitness being somewhat misleading.

The literature distinguishes between first- and second-order securities markets, wherein asset-backed securities (ABSs), which include all kinds of underlying contracts associated with a flow of payments, including home mortgage loans (translated into mortgage-backed securities, MBSs), car loans, student loans, and so on, are first-order assets. The second-order securities market includes a variety of derivative instruments that repackage and resell first-order securities. For instance, Lysandrou and Nesvetailova (2015: 273) refer to so-called CDOs as "second floor securities" that combine various assets and therefore constitute a heterogeneous asset class. In fact, Lipson (2011: 1234) suggests that CDOs are not securities at all as this asset category is not directly tied to a flow of payments. Lysandrou and Nesvetailova (2015: 273) explain the major differences between, for example, ABSs and CDOs:

> Asset-backed securities have a transparent conformity in that each type has a single asset class as collateral (residential mortgage loans, credit card loans, commercial property loans, and so on). By contrast, no two individual CDOs were alike because of the large variety of ways in which different asset classes (subprime backed securities, other nonconforming loan backed securities, prime ABS, and so on) could be mixed together as the backing collateral. CDOs could still be sold, but only as unique, customised products tailored to suit the specific needs of specific investors.

As the trade of CDOs is highly information sensitive, that is, the pricing process includes information costs and therefore demands expertise (Bluhm and Wagner, 2011: 217), this category of securities is not safe assets but is part of, in Ricks' (2011: 97) phrase, the "private-backed money-claims" asset category that constitutes the two-thirds of the finance capital stock. In terms of the sheer size of the two securities markets, in 2006, 11 trillion US dollars was issued as ABSs, whereof more than half, about 6.5 trillion US dollars, consisted of residential mortgage-backed securities. In addition, the second-order securities market was sizeable, including $3 trillion US dollars' worth of CDOs outstanding by the end of 2006 (Lysandrou, 2011: 325). In other words, securities markets are vital for issuance of private-backed money-claims, in turn being dependent on safe assets, whereof more than half are home mortgage loans, in turn dependent on the housing production activities of the construction industry.

State-backed safe assets and the question of financial stability

From the policymakers' and regulators' perspective, safe assets backed by the sovereign state are uncomplicated insofar as they are based on high-quality collateral, mortgage loans originated by prudent lenders who have strong incentives to ensure that their clients are capable of holding their contracts until maturation. In contrast, two-thirds of the stock of capital, backed by private issuers, may include money claims that create imbalances and risks that may be transferred and multiplied within the financial system. This in turn politically and financially justifies the thickly textured regulatory control of finance industry activities being in place today. "No other competitive industry is subject to remotely comparable regulatory constraints and oversight," Ricks (2011: 78) remarks.

Structural changes, legal reforms, and finance regulation developments have generated changes in capital formation activities. As for instance Murdock (2012: 525) remarks, prior to the year 2000, "real estate had been a relatively safe investment." In the new regime of securities issuances and the repackaging of complex derivative instruments to produce high-risk and illiquid financial assets, things changed dramatically. For instance, in the period 2003–2007, a relatively short period of five years, the number of sub-prime loans "jumped from 456,631 in 2000 to 2,284,420 in 2005" (Murdock, 2012: 525). As private-backed assets are subject to the same information sensitivity as any other assets traded on the market, the declining quality of the underlying collateral (the sub-prime home mortgage loan originated) generated considerable consequences once the US home mortgage market expansion had reached its peak by 2007. Several commentators point at the mechanisms of the securities market as a key factor explaining seemingly imprudent or illicit behaviour among thinly capitalized and late-coming home mortgage institutions:

> The anonymity of mortgage-backed securities may appeal to some investors, such as those engaging in tax evasion and money laundering. As previously noted, securitization allows investors to reduce their information costs by pooling the acquisition of information in the form of a single rating regarding the security of the pool.
>
> (Eggert, 2002: 547)

Speaking in more lenient terms, Rajan, Seru, and Vig (2015: 238) argue that "[s]ecuritization changes the incentives of lenders, and hence their behavior." To determine the quality of a specific home mortgage loan, the financial trader needs to access not only the "hard information," including, for example, the borrower's credit rating (estimated by a so-called FICO score; see, e.g., Karger, 2005: 46–47; Rona-Tas, and Hiss, 2010), but also the "soft information," which includes, for example, the borrower's future job prospects. The soft information is costly to acquire and to process, and as the loan originator has limited incentives to disclose such information within the securitization scheme, important information is left on the side, Rajan, Seru, Vig (2015: 238) argue:

> In the absence of securitization, a lender internalizes the benefits and costs of acquiring both kinds of information and adequately invests in both tasks. With securitization, hard information is reported to investors; soft information, which is difficult to verify and transmit, remains unreported. Investors, therefore, rely only on hard information

to judge the quality of loans. This eliminates the lender's incentives to produce soft information.

This means that, for example, MBSs, securitized home mortgage loans, are not information insensitive, especially not in the situation wherein the pool of securitized loans includes poor collateral. Furthermore, the possibility to securitize loans and to sell them off on the global securities market, the home mortgage lending industry became an even more lucrative business in the era of 2003–2007. As securitization is an exemplary case of a fee-based business, there were a variety of financial and legal firms that benefitted handsomely from participating in underwriting and trading securities. By the end of the period, the tail began to wag the dog as loan origination became a sort of sine qua non activity within securities trade. When the stock of prime borrowers run short (home mortgage lending is after all a local business, which makes the number of prime borrowers limited in comparison to the possibilities of global finance market trade), banks must lower their lending standards in order to maintain their securities issuance activities and to expand their balance sheets. When lending standards are compromised and other business objectives and concerns overrule prudent lending standards, systemic risk is likely to soar (Shin, 2009: 310). "In order to keep their pipelines going, integrated banks took on riskier mortgages and packaged them into bonds that turned out to be of lower and lower quality," Goldstein and Fligstein (2017: 505–506) summarize (see also Griffin and Maturana, 2016).

In hindsight, it is salient that imprudent lending practices, poor pricing of risk, and deteriorating credit rating jointly produced a situation that resulted in an excessive supply of unsafe private-backed money claims. This in turn raises the question whether the finance industry and the shadow banking sector should be entrusted with the authority to supply finance capital in advanced economies. For instance, Baumer et al. (2017: 588) report that nearly 25 per cent of residential mortgage loans that originated between 2003 and 2005 in the United States "contained one or more indications of suspected fraud" (see also Fligstein and Roehrkasse, 2016). In some areas, the figure was as high as 50 per cent. Based on a sample that included 132,401 securities (separated into the four asset classes of collateralized loan obligations, non-agency mortgage-backed securities, asset-backed securities, and collateralized debt obligations), grouped into 14,315 deals and issued between January 2000 and December 2010, Griffin, Lowery, and Saretto (2014: 2874) find "a negative relation between reputation and the quality of the securities produced." This robust evidence indicates that market actors failed to self-regulate on the basis of the credit rating mechanism, and that reputational loss is an insufficient penalty in highly liquid finance markets:

> The basic intuition is that it takes time to build a reputation, so a bank with a high reputation would never want to be so short-sighted as to

maximize current profits at the expense of jeopardizing streams of future revenues [...] We show that this intuition can break down with complex securities.

(Griffin, Lowery, and Saretto, 2014: 2873)

"The securitization of mortgages made mortgage lending less dependent on local savings, but weakened the incentives of the mortgage originator to lend prudently," Rona-Tas (2017: 54) writes.[3] Such evidence can rule out the "bad seed" argument that proposes that imprudent lending is a marginal phenomenon that, for example, regulators should not overstate. Instead, the combination of shadow banking expansion, securitization, and lowered home mortgage lending standards proved to be disastrous.

The purpose of this chapter is not to catalogue various actors bearing the responsibility for the sub-prime debacle (for the long-term consequences of the 2008 finance crisis, see, e.g., Redbird and Grusky, 2016) but to address the larger issue of how capital formation is dependent on the supply of safe assets, in turn to a considerable degree being backed by collateral produced by the construction industry. Gorton, Lewellen, and Metrick (2012: 102) argue that the constant demand for safe assets to multiply the finance capital base indicates that the role of the sovereign state, which generates safe assets, is critical for the vitality of the economic system: "[R]egulators and policymakers must adroitly balance the need to improve financial stability with the simultaneous need to maintain enough liquid, safe debt in the economy to meet the demand for such debt." Consequently, Gorton, Lewellen, and Metrick (2012: 101) argue that "regulators and policymakers should tread carefully when considering any new regulations or legislation that would potentially limit the production function of the financial sector." Given that financial stability is one of the key regulatory objectives, if the stock of state-backed assets, that is, informational-insensitive, safe assets, is reduced, the demand for safe assets would be substituted by private-backed assets. As private institutions, even in the contemporary oligopolistic finance industry that includes gargantuan banks (Murdock, 2012), have fewer opportunities than the sovereign state to finance their activities on the global finance markets, the supply of credit and the liquidity of the finance market would be impaired by a withdrawal of the state. A lower supply of finance capital would then affect the so-called real economy, which is undesirable for most governments in advanced economies.

The state debt mechanism

As Gorton and Pennacchi (1990: 66, footnote 8) remarked close to three decades ago, one of the unintended consequences of government budget deficits and state debt is that they supply a stock of safe assets whereupon private-backed money-claims can be issued, thus multiplying the capital base in ways that supply capital to a variety of investment opportunities. In this view, state debt and the "transactions system backed by money market instruments" (Gorton and Pennacchi, 1990: 66, footnote 8) jointly contribute to capital formation, vital for the functioning of late modern, finance-led economies. "Large *sovereign* debt markets are effectively prerequisites to the emergence and sustenance of large *private* debt and equity markets," Hockett and Omarova (2016: 1168. Emphasis in the original) suggest. Quinn (2017: 76) examines how the US federal budget, surrounded by detailed rules and standard procedures, is related to "financial expansion." In Quinn's (2017: 77) view, government officials may actively seek to circumvent budget rules to pursue policy goals, and this work includes a variety of policy forms including delegated programmes, public–private partnerships, public authorities, associational programmes, and "various other strategies that blur expected boundaries of the state." Such practices are part of the strategies of governance that closely connect fiscal policy and the finance industry, Quinn (2017: 78) argues:

> [B]udgetary constraints are not simply limiting or paralyzing but can generate creative strategies of governance. Contests over off-budget forms of borrowing and spending govern not only fiscal outcomes but can have particularly large spillover effects in the field of finance.

Government officials tend to discover that they access a variety of government capacities including guarantees, tax expenditures, incentives, regulations, authority over property rights, and the state's own position as a consumer of goods that actively support the credit formation process of the finance industry. Quinn (2017) shows that the Johnson administration successfully used GSEs such as Ginnie Mae and Fannie Mae in the 1960s to support home ownership policies. In the budget of 1968, despite the government maintaining close ties with Fannie Mae and absorbing much of the risk pertaining to its mortgage lending activities, the GSE was "officially no longer part of the U.S. government." In practice, this meant that $1.4 billion of planned expenditures were not included in the federal budget (Quinn, 2017: 72). In Quinn's account, the sovereign state always of necessity plays a key role in supporting finance industry expansion to promote the credit formation process. Consequently, state debt is a key mechanism to monitor as it provide a stock of safe assets that serve to leverage privately issued safe assets and to increase the supply of finance capital.

Expressed differently, the sovereign state, operating on the basis of democratic ideals, protects uninformed agents by insuring the deposits of the banking system (Gorton and Pennacchi, 1990: 51). The average citizen or voter should not, for instance, have to worry too much about their saving accounts as herd behaviour, which may result in bank runs (Gorton, 2017; Froot, Scharfstein, and Stein, 1992), inflicts excessive costs on the banking system, well above the parametric risk of bank default (Frieden, 2016). The sovereign state thus serves to insure certain bank activities to simultaneously ensure economic welfare and, when insuring also, for example, mortgage loans in the next stage, increase the supply of finance capital in the economy. In other words, "[t]he government's role is to create a risk-free asset" (Gorton and Pennacchi, 1990: 51). However, one of the most efficient ways to justify bank insurances and other subsidies and tax exemptions is to align the interest of home mortgage borrowers, the finance industry, and the state, and to insure mortgage loans that provide such benefits. By implication, politically justified motives serve the wider function to trigger a further expansion of the capital base, wherein two-thirds of total of assets in an economy include private-backed money claims, and whereof a significant proportion derives from the shadow banking system. In this view, state debt and budget deficits may be treated in a new light wherein the state's liabilities operate as a multiplier within capital formation activities. By the end of the day, the economic system is co-produced with political decision-making, which provides the state with a more productive role as the supplier of safe assets in addition to its legal and regulatory functions (Hockett and Omarova, 2016: 1149).

To subsidize the banking system is far from uncontroversial. Previous welfare state reforms, including, for example, public pension funds, unemployment insurance, and health insurance, have served to separate market risks from individuals and households. The welfare state carries some of the risk when supplying welfare provision in exchange for the taxation of declared income. In a similar manner, Schwartz (2012: 47) argues, the post-war government reconstruction of housing finance markets has helped "remove risk from the financial system." As the state finances and sponsors either banks or GSEs to issue home mortgage loans, safe assets are created, as examined above. This stock of mortgage loans is not only created de novo and ex nihilo on the account of borrowers, but is also connected to the cash flows in the form of premiums paid to, for example, pension funds and insurance firms, which amass liquid finance capital "that has to go somewhere" (Schwartz, 2012: 48). Managers of pension funds and insurance-based funds thus buy securities and other instruments to optimize their return. That is, liquid finance capital is exchanged for more illiquid commercial papers. By connecting these cash flows to housing finance, the welfare state can create stable connections between finance industry institutions and a labour-intensive and goods-producing sector of the economy—the construction industry—that is "macroeconomically significant" (Schwartz, 2012: 48). The benefits for the overall economic efficiency and welfare are numerous, but the downside is that the sovereign state creates moral hazard inasmuch as it insures a private industry against default, which may create incentives conducive to, for example, imprudent home mortgage lending. As home mortgage lenders have good incentives to offer generous loans—as these loans constitute the stock of safe assets, also the sovereign state shares this interest, at least initially—housing prices inflate not so much on the basis of an upward shift of the supply-demand nexus but on the basis of an oversupply of cheap finance capital. As the historical record indicates, ex post resolution activities such as bailouts benefit centrally located finance institutions, whereas the fringe, including individual households, are not prioritized (Pistor, 2013), for the most part being left to sort out their economic difficulties on their own (see, e.g., Andrews, 2009).[4] The housing-finance nexus is thus at risk to oversupply finance capital in the home mortgage lending industry, which results in net welfare losses in the case when households find themselves "below the waterline," that is, they hold mortgage loans that are larger than the current market price for their homes (Marshall and Concha, 2012: 559). The housing-finance nexus is therefore of key importance for household welfare:

> [A]s a consequence of financial liberalization, the links between the workings of the financial system and the health of the economy have become tighter. This connection is heightened by increased levels of business and household debt exposure in recent years and by the entry of pension funds and small investors to equity and property markets.
> (Bell and Quiggin, 2006: 631)

Despite home mortgage lending being a highly regulated industry, which includes both state legislation in the United States and federal laws including the Federal Trade Commission Act, the Real Estate Settlement Procedures Act, the Truth in Lending Act, along with its 1994 Amendments in the Home Ownership and Settlement Procedures Act, the Equal Credit Opportunity Act, and the Fair Housing Act (Peterson, 2007: 2225), the oversupply of finance capital easily results in households with mortgage loan contracts they can barely hold until the end of the contract period. The creation of welfare on the basis of insuring home mortgage lenders is a risky venture as the finance industry tends to outsmart its regulators and legislative entities, at least in a short-term perspective.

Credit supply shocks and the household debt channel

Mainstream economic theory has widely assumed that increased household debt is an indication of a well-functioning finance capital market, but following the 2008 finance industry collapse, a more refined and empirically oriented theory regarding relationships between mortgage lending, household debt, and financial and macroeconomic crises has emerged. Jordà, Schularick, and Taylor (2016) provide evidence that shows that home mortgage lending is today a major business activity for banks. In 1900, the share of mortgage loans in banks' total lending portfolios was about 30 per cent, but has today doubled to around 60 per cent. This has resulted in a sharp increase in credit-to-GDP ratios in advanced economies, and the core business model of banks is to act as a real estate fund: "banks are borrowing (short) from the public and capital markets to invest (long) into assets linked to real estate" (Jordà, Schularick, and Taylor, 2016: 110). Jordà, Schularick, and Taylor (2016: 137) define mortgage and non-mortgage lending accordingly: "Mortgage lending includes residential and commercial real estate lending. Non-mortgage lending is a less homogeneous category that includes business lending and other unsecured lending such as consumer finance." One of the consequences of sharply increased credit-to-GDP ratios is that the role of banks has changed as they no longer serve the intermediary role to channel household savings to productive investment in the business sector. The concern is that increased credit-to-GDP ratios, so-called credit booms, is the primus motor for financial crises (Jordà, Schularick, and Taylor, 2016: 111).

Jordà, Schularick, and Taylor's (2016: 114) highly detailed and differentiated data set demonstrates that the credit-to-GDP ratio in advanced economies plateaued at circa 40 per cent after 1900 and stayed at that level until the 1970s. Between 1980 and 2013, the average bank credit to GDP increased from 62 per cent to 114 per cent (Jordà, Schularick, and Taylor, 2016: 114). More specifically, the credit boom occurred during a relatively short time span, between the mid-1990s and 2008–2009. In Jordà, Schularick, and Taylor's (2016: 114) 17-country sample, the average bank credit to GDP ratio rose from 78 per cent of GDP in 1995 to 111 per cent of GDP in 2007—an unprecedented increase of more than 30 percentage points (p.p.) as a ratio to GDP in just 12 years. This translated into 2.5 percentage points per year during the period. Furthermore, the data reveals a remarkable growth of household debt in comparison to the non-mortgage lending-to-GDP ratio, which rose by a factor of three during the 140 years included in the sample, whereas the mortgage-lending-to-GDP ratio has grown by a factor of eight (Jordà, Schularick, and Taylor, 2016: 115). This is a concern for policymakers as empirical evidence reveals that mortgage lending booms predict financial crises, followed by a "post-crisis drag on growth" (Jordà, Schularick, and Taylor, 2016: 137). In contrast, non-mortgage credit booms "have virtually no effect on the path of the recession nowadays" (Jordà, Schularick, and Taylor, 2016: 139).

An important question for theory development and policymaking is, what are the primary drivers for the growth in mortgage debt-to-GDP in advanced economies since the mid-1990s? Mian and Sufi (2018: 31) suggest that the expansion of credit supply (rather than a shift in demand) is an "important driver of business cycles." Consequently, "a rise in household debt is a robust predictor of a decline in GDP growth across a large number of countries since the 1970s" (Mian and Sufi, 2018: 31–32). Mian, Sufi, and Verner (2017: 1757) examine the key question, "What is the fundamental source of the increase in credit supply?," based on the result that "models based on credit demand shocks alone are difficult to reconcile with our findings." To answer this question, Mian and Sufi (2018: 32–33) introduce the concept of "exogenous economic shocks" that affect the economic system:

> [A] shock that leads to a rapid influx of capital into the financial system often triggers an expansion in credit supply. Recent manifestations of such a shock are the rise in income inequality in the United States [...] and the rapid rise in savings by many emerging markets.

More specifically, a "credit supply shock" represents a "relaxation of lending constraints." That is, for the same potential borrower and same true risk profile, "lenders become willing to lend more or on cheaper terms" (Mian, Sufi, and Verner, 2017: 1782).

A credit supply shock needs to be explained, and the literature lists a few conditions, of which two are endogenous (growth in economic inequality and bank deregulation) and one exogenous (growth in overseas savings), yet interrelated in complex ways. Mian and Sufi (2018: 36) name "banking deregulation episodes" as being "perhaps the cleanest identification of credit supply shocks." Evidence shows that US states that deregulated their banking system earlier witnessed larger household debt ratios than non-deregulatory states, which eventually translated into a rise in the unemployment rate and a decline in house prices when the boom period ended in the deregulatory states (Mian and Sufi, 2018: 36). Mian and Sufi's (2018) findings are supported by Favara and Imbs' (2015: 960) work that explains soaring housing prices on the basis of "bank liquidity shocks," that is, credit supply rather than demand-side changes. Favara and Imbs (2015: 958) argue that the provision of credit is "not an exogenous variable," inasmuch as there is reason to believe that "credit supply depends on the price of assets, which may be used as collateral." This means that credit supply "responds endogenously to current and expected economic conditions." Favara and Imbs (2015: 960) examine the role of bank deregulation on state level in the United States, and they notice that only commercial banks with offices and business activities outside of the deregulated state expanded their credit: "independent mortgage companies, thrifts, and credit unions did not react" (Favara and Imbs, 2015: 984). Favara and Imbs (2015: 960) regard such evidence as what rules out demand-based explanations, that is, "deregulation must have triggered a credit supply shock for banks in deregulated states." Consequently, Favara and Imbs (2015: 984) propose that there is a "causal chain going from an expansion in credit to house prices." The expansion of credit was in turn caused by finance market deregulation, in many cases motivated by political objectives rather than on the basis of economic concerns (Favara and Imbs, 2015: 959). In the end, Favara and Imbs (2015: 984) propose that "deregulation can explain up to two-thirds of the observed increase in mortgage loans originated by commercial banks in the United States between 1994 and 2005."

The Swedish real estate boom in the latter half of the 1980s, following the deregulation of finance markets in the 1983–1985 period, is an illustrative case of a credit supply shock. In the first half of the 1980s, a local finance industry was developed in Sweden, stimulated by the budget deficits that were financed in the domestic market (Englund, 1989: 83–84). This new finance industry made banking regulation ineffective. When the banking sector was deregulated, banks entered the finance companies' markets and became their competitors, and given the banks' benefits of the banking licences granted by the state, finance companies "were pushed into higher-risk markets" (Englund, 1989: 85). The increased credit supply resulted in lending increasing by 136 per cent (73 per cent in real terms, after tax effects are considered) over the five-year period 1986–1990 (Englund, 1989: 84). The credit supply also resulted in the Stockholm stock exchange index rising by 118 per cent between 1985 and 1988. In this period, the household's financial assets grew from 82 to 102 per cent of GDP. Another effect was the growth of real estate asset market prices. In the latter half of the 1980s, the price increases for prime location commercial properties was considerably higher in Stockholm than anywhere else in Europe. At the same time, in the 1988–1990 period, investment in real estate (other than housing) nearly doubled in comparison to the 1983–1985 average, being 88 per cent above the benchmark. "[I]t is difficult to explain 1990 prices of real estate, and perhaps also of other assets, purely in terms of fundamentals," Englund (1989: 86) summarizes.

By the end of the Swedish credit supply boom in 1991–1992, real estate asset prices dropped by 35 per cent in 1991, and by an additional 15 per cent the year after (in total corresponding to a 55 per cent real estate asset price drop in two years). The real estate crisis generated a bank crisis that was calculated to cost around 2 per cent of the Swedish GDP. The bank rescue activities was based on the principle that the government should save the banks "but not the owners of the banks," which resulted in the state of Sweden assuming responsibility for the assets and liabilities of insolvent banks. The major bank Gotabanken was declared bankrupt, and its assets and liabilities were transferred to a state-controlled corporate entity. Englund (1989: 96) proposes that inflated real estate asset prices, an immediate effect of the credit supply shock, resulted in overbuilding, "which at some point led to vacancies and commercial rents falling short of expectations." This in turn initiated a downward spiral of asset prices, which rendered certain finance companies insolvent, and that created uncertainty regarding the creditworthiness and solvency of finance market actors. Englund lists three conditions that may explain this episode of "bad banking." First, bankers were not prepared or trained for the "new environment" (Englund, 1989: 96); being familiar with the rules and practices of the since long regulated banking sector, the mid-1980s brought a series of institutional changes whose significance and consequences were complicated to fully anticipate for all market actors. Second, a shortage of human resources and skills in the face of an overwhelming demand for credit resulted in a resource allocation problem for the banks. As Englund (1989: 96) remarks, in the end, it paid to be a prudent lender (as in the case of Handelsbanken, one of the two oldest and most prestigious banks in Sweden, being the only bank that was excluded from the bank rescue activities), but it demands a certain sangfroid to avoid being enticed to participate in a credit expansion boom when the opportunity emerges. Third and finally, Englund (1989: 96) recognizes the possibility of opportunistic behaviour in finance companies being on the verge of bankruptcy, now being weakly incentivized to act with prudence when insolvency looms: "it is conceivable that banks and finance companies close to insolvency realized that pay-offs were asymmetric and gave incentives for increased risk-taking." (Englund, 1989: 96).

Taken together, the Swedish deregulation of the finance industry (the "credit supply shock" in the episode) resulted in (1) sharply rising stock market prices, and (2) soaring real estate prices, especially for real estate in attractive locations in Stockholm. By the end of the credit boom, banks were found to have been overlending and now held what would be known as "toxic assets" during the 2008 finance industry collapse and bailout activities, which called for the government to commit considerable resources and skills to bank rescue activities. The consequences of the credit supply shock lingered until the mid-1990s, when the next boom-bust cycle was initiated, an episode that included the digital media industries hype and the idea of a "new economy" that generated a similar upsurge in investment activities and money-lending appetite, but that is another story.

The global savings glut

The question is still why the finance industry was deregulated in the first place, in United States, Sweden, and elsewhere. Kumhof, Rancière, and Winant (2015) compare the Great Depression of the 1930s and the Great Recession of 2008 and the following decade, and identify the growth in economic inequality as the principal driver for the expansion of credit supply. In both cases, a sharp growth in income inequality was mediated by a sharp increase in debt-to-income ratios among lower- and middle-income households (Kumhof, Rancière, and Winant, 2015: 1217). Between 1983 and 2007, the share of total income claimed by the top 5 per cent of the income distribution increased from 21.8 per cent in 1983 to 33.8 per cent. In the same period, the ratio of household debt-to-GDP doubled (Kumhof, Rancière, and Winant, 2015: 1220). Growing economic inequality increases the surplus finance capital in the top five per cent households, which propels the expansion of credit supply, especially if combined with deregulatory reforms:

> [H]igher debt leverage arises as a result of permanent positive shocks to the income share of high-income households who, due to preferences for wealth, lend part of their additional income back to poor and middle-income households. This increase in credit supply allows poor and middle-income households to sustain higher consumption levels.
>
> (Kumhof, Rancière, and Winant, 2015: 1243)

In addition to the restructuring of the American economy so that economic inequality grows and the finance industry is deregulated, the credit supply shock is also propelled by what has been called "the global savings glut," wherein export-oriented economies in, for example, South East Asia increasingly invest their financial surplus, which results in an expansion of financial services and investment activities. In what is called the "Flow of Funds data," the ratio of private domestic credit-to-GDP increased from 130.4 per cent to 292.3 per cent between 1983 and 2007. Furthermore, the ratio of foreign private credit assets to GDP increased from "2.8 percent to 34 percent" (Kumhof, Rancière, and Winant, 2015: 1226). Favilukis, Ludvigson, and Van Nieuwerburgh (2017: 151) provide more detailed information about foreign ownership in US Treasuries. Between 1984 and 2008, the foreign ownership of marketable Treasuries outstanding increased from 13.5 per cent to 61 per cent. In the 2008–2012 period, foreign holdings of long-term and short-term US Treasury and agency debt as a fraction of GDP increased from 31 per cent to 40.6 per cent. Foreign ownership strategies reveal a preference for safe assets: "As of June 2010, the bond market portfolio composition of FOI consists of US Treasuries (78 percent) and agency mortgage-backed securities (MBS) and US agency debt (19.5 percent)" (Favilukis, Ludvigson, and Van Nieuwerburgh, 2017: 152). Studies also show that the demand is inelastic, that is, unaffected by changes in other asset prices:

> [D]emand for US Treasury securities by governmental holders is completely inelastic, implying that when these holders receive funds to invest, they buy safe US securities such as Treasuries or agencies, regardless of their price relative to other US assets. Foreign governmental holders have very deep pockets and will pay whatever price necessary to push nongovernmental holders out of the safe US bond market when their demand is not met with an equal increase in supply.
> (Favilukis, Ludvigson, and Van Nieuwerburgh, 2017: 152)

It may be inadequate to refer to the global savings glut phenomenon as being entirely exogenous as it is essentially the consequence of policies enacted by the IMF, the World Bank, and the World Trade Organization (for an overview of these transnational governance organizations, see, for example, Conti, 2010; Chwieroth, 2010; Chorev and Babb, 2009; Girdwood, 2007; Neu et al., 2006; Arnold, 2005), operating under the aegis of the so-called Washington consensus, the free-market theory model that several commentators associate with the neoliberal politico-economic programme that dominated from the late 1970s until at least 2008 (Kentikelenis and Babb, 2019; Babb, 2013; Sheppard and Leitner, 2010):

> In response to financial crises in the late 1990s and early 2000s, governments in emerging markets began to accumulate foreign reserves, typically in the form of US-dollar denominated assets. In turn, this shift

led to declining global interest rates, the rise of dollar-denominated assets, and current account deficits in many advanced economies.

(Mian and Sufi, 2018: 50)

Bohle (2018: 200) uses the metaphor of a "wall of money" to underline the centrality of mortgage lending in the economy (see also Fernandez and Aalbers, 2016):

> The global wall of money results from the rise of accumulated corporate profits which are not being reinvested in the real economy or shared with workers, the recycling of trade surpluses of emerging and export-oriented economies, and the privatization of pension schemes and build-up of funded pensions. Housing and mortgage debt, which are considered high quality collateral, have absorbed an increasing amount of liquidity.
>
> (Bohle, 2018: 200)

Taken together, the shocks of economic inequality growth—itself an immediate effect of downsizing and outsourcing decisions in major American corporations (Ivanova, 2019; Jung, 2016; Bidwell, 2013; Bidwell, Briscoe, Fernandez-Mateo, and Sterling, 2013; Davis-Blake and Broschak, 2009; Milberg, 2008), which reduced job growth and served to push down real wage growth—finance industry deregulation, and increased overseas savings were the drivers, the "credit supply shocks," of the mortgage lending. At the same time, Mian and Sufi (2018: 50) add, the excess of savings relative to investment demand—a phenomenon Mian and Sufi (2018: 50) call "financial excess"—was amplified by behavioral biases, financial innovation, and even by "malfeasance within the financial sector" (Mian and Sufi, 2018: 50). Therefore, Mian and Sufi (2018: 32) contend, "[f]inancial crises and a sudden collapse in credit supply are not exogenous events hitting a stable economy." Mian and Sufi (2018: 53) summarize the mechanisms at work:

> [T]here is a global excess supply of savings coming from both the rise in income inequality in advanced economies and the tendency of some emerging economies to export capital to advanced economies. This excess savings leads to growth in the financial sector, a decline in interest rates, and a rise in household debt burdens of households in advanced economies outside the very top of the income distribution.

Such verdicts are further supported by the analysis of Levitin and Wachter (2020), who propose that there "was a glut of mortgage financing" during the 2003–2007 period: "the bubble was predominantly a supply-side phenomenon," Levitin and Wachter (2020: 147) summarize. What Mian, Sufi, and Verner (2017: 1812) refer to as "the household debt channel" is thus the principal mechanism that connects and explains a variety of financial and macroeconomic conditions. It is not the demand for credit that explains the expansion of mortgage lending, but credit supply shocks result in soaring housing prices and an increase in imports of consumption goods, at the same time as there is no change in the investment-to-GDP ratio (Mian and Sufi, 2018: 41). Once the credit boom reaches the end of the expansion cycle, a financial crisis is at the door: "[C]redit supply expansions are a precursor to crises," Mian and Sufi (2018: 36) contend.

The role of behavioural bias

One implication is that empirical evidence indicates that both finance market actors and policymakers fail to understand the negative effects of increases in private debt, Mian, Sufi, and Verner (2017: 1798) propose. For instance, lenders mistakenly extrapolate "previously low defaults when granting new loans," neglect tail risks (the heightened risk when lending to less creditworthy borrowers), and underestimate the "the true default risk of mortgages" (Mian and Sufi, 2018: 49). In policymaking quarters, forecasters such as the IMF and the OECD "systematically overforecast GDP growth at the end of household debt booms" (Mian, Sufi, and Verner, 2017: 1758), which is indicative of a limited understanding of the mechanisms connecting a variety of macroeconomic and financial conditions including household debt, housing prices, interest rates, domestic and overseas savings, and economic cycles. For instance, Kumhof, Rancière, and Winant (2015: 1218) remark that the literature on income and wealth distribution, and the literature on "financial fragility and financial crises" have largely been developed in isolation from one another. In the end, recent evidence demonstrates that Alan Greenspan's doctrine that "rational market can take care of themselves" (cited in Palma, 2009: 831), once a hegemonic belief, cherished in the Washington consensus-based policymaking as a free-market axiom (Turner, 2015: 169), was little more than wishful thinking clad in neoclassical theorizing in the absence of robust empirical evidence. In contrast, housing markets and mortgage lending have served as the de facto expansion mechanism inflating the finance industry. More specifically, soaring housing prices, which policymakers, economic advisers, and pundits regarded as evidence of a benevolent and well-functioning finance market, smoothed by qualified policymaking and governance practices, were in fact first-rate evidence of underlying growing economic inequalities and the consequences of the downsizing and outsourcing strategies of American corporations. Such tendencies were amplified by deregulatory reforms that generated additional finance industry activities and resulted in more lenient market regulation, which paved the way for, for example, the predatory lending practices in the sub-prime home mortgage lending segment.

The lesson learned from the recent literature is that mortgage lending and the housing market have served as the primary site for finance industry expansion since the early 1980s. In lieu of real wage growth and job growth, which hollow out and pressure not only working-class households but also the middle class (Temin, 2017; Davidson, 2014; Scott and Pressman, 2011; Pressman, 2007; Frank, 2007), policymakers opted for what Prasad (2012) refers to as "mortgage Keynesianism" to promote economic growth and short-term economic welfare on the basis of increased household debt (a phenomenon referred to as "debtfare"; Lavinas, 2018):

> In 1983, the top income group [the top 5 per cent] was more indebted than the bottom income group [the remaining 95 per cent], with a gap of around 20 percentage points. In 2007, the situation was reversed. The debt-to-income ratio of the bottom group, at 147.3 per cent compared to an initial value of 62.3 percent, was now more than twice as high as that of the top group, which remained fluctuating around 60.
>
> (Kumhof, Rancière, and Winant, 2015: 1221)

Policymakers interpreted soaring housing prices in sanguine terms, but in fact these conditions were the consequences of a series of interrelated conditions and mechanisms that they in hindsight seem to have only a limited understanding about.

Regulatory concerns: the question of how to balance credit supply and financial stability

Ricks (2011: 98) notices that the financial system suffers from a structural imbalance—what the economist John Hicks calls a "constitutional weakness" of the system—inasmuch as savers have a preference for holding primarily short-term and highly liquid assets, whereas borrowers want to issue long-term obligations, being considerably more illiquid assets than what the savers prefer (see also Calomiris and Haber, 2014; Coffee, 2012). Sissoko (2019) discusses the role of the repo (repurchase agreement) market that today serves to provide liquid holdings in the finance industry. Boy and Gabor (2019: 298) define a repo as "a contract to sell a marketable asset that is entered into simultaneously with a contract to repurchase it at a specified price and time." Elsewhere, the term *collateral* is included in the definition of a repo: "[R]epos involve the sale of an asset with the simultaneous agreement to repurchase it at a specified time at the original price plus interest, or in other words, an exchange of cash for collateral" (Boy and Gabor, 2019: 304). From an economic point of view, a repo is equivalent to a secured loan; from a monetary point of view, the repo entails a creation of shadow money. That is, the repo is a promise to pay "[w]hose par convertibility is constructed through complex legal and accounting processes centred on collateral" (Boy and Gabor, 2019: 298). The reliance on repo trade is the effect of the disintermediation of banks, derived from deregulatory policies intended to create what Sissoko (2019: 316) refers to as the "market-based" credit formation model. This new model gives regulatory agencies such as central banks a new role in the economy, Gabor (2016: 971) emphasizes:

> [T]he central banking community, with the Bank of England at its forefront, now increasingly accepts that financial stability in shadow banking, or market-based finance, means supporting liquidity in collateral *markets* in times of stress rather than supporting banking *institutions* as in the traditional lender of last resort (LOLR) model.

Unfortunately, the current model "gives lenders particularly strong contractual rights over borrower assets," Sissoko (2019: 316) proposes. Furthermore, the current model is susceptible to exogenous shocks that result in a flight to more liquid assets. That is, repo contracts are "inherently procyclical," Sissoko (2019: 325) proposes:

> The modern markets system is [...] characterized by repo-based leverage that generates an environment where liquidity events are accompanied by forced selling, the expectation of forced selling, and repo borrowers who realize losses. In short, as many have observed, repo contracts are inherently procyclical and can easily play a key role in transforming a simple price decline into a liquidity event, losses and bankruptcies.

"In short," Sissoko (2019: 330) writes, just as "liquidity begets liquidity," illiquidity also "feeds upon itself." Boy and Gabor (2019: 305) emphasize how this market-based model generates instability in the finance system:

> [T]emporary illiquidity cannot be hidden on banks' balance sheets but mark-to-market valuation forces actors to realize losses. The very relation which makes repo money—at par exchange between cash and collateral that finance has developed over the last 20 years—also makes finance more fragile and liquidity events 'endemic' as radical uncertainty bites harder and faster.

For the repo market to operate in a functional manner during the upward movement of the business cycle, so-called "long pools," which include pension funds, mutual funds, and hedge funds, that include holdings such as securities that finance governments, corporations, and that securitize "a variety of other loans such as mortgages" (Sissoko, 2019: 323), play a key role. However, to serve this role, fund managers exhibit a strong preference for the limited class of safe assets to be able to cope with liquidity events (Sissoko, 2019: 324). The paradox of the "market-based" model is that the repo market operates if, and only if, there is a supply of safe assets. That is, the sovereign state and the government are assigned a central role in maintaining the liquidity of the market. Wansleben (2020: 209) stresses this condition, and speaks about a "neo-patrimonial relationship" between repo market actors and central banks:

> [N]eo-patrimonial relationships have developed between public and private actors, which explain why public authorities remain duly committed to consolidating a "repo-based financial system," despite its apparent dysfunctionalities […] Extant market structures increasingly depend on subsidies and safeguards from state institutions, particularly central banks, even though they fail to accomplish the outcomes that are supposed to legitimize these public subsidies and safeguards.

For instance, the European repo market is "structurally intertwined with European government bond markets," Gabor and Ban (2016: 617) write. They go on to say, "around 75 per cent of repo transactions use government bonds as collateral." Over time, the role of collateralized lending has increased in proportion: in 2002, only 30 per cent of over-the-counter derivatives were collateralized, and by 2008, the proportion stood at 65 per cent; in 2013, 91 of "all OTC derivatives trades were collateralized" (Sissoko, 2019: 337, footnote 22). The failure of the repo market to self-regulate, and to be dependent on the sovereign state to step in to ensure the supply of safe assets has important theoretical implications, Sissoko (2019) argues. The elimination and disintermediation of banks, which served to stabilize financial markets, resulted in a financial system as prescribed by neoclassical economic theory, but such accomplishments waned as the financial system relied paradoxically so heavily on market liquidity that it caused liquidity to fail (Sissoko, 2019: 317):

> Neoclassical theory views markets as inherently liquid. Repo, by putting neoclassical theory into effect, exposes the contradictions in the theory. The final result is counterperformative. Repo, by taking neoclassical theory seriously, has played an important role in its ultimate rejection: now government is almost universally viewed as a far more important source of liquidity than markets.
>
> (Sissoko, 2019: 334)

In other words, the "repo-driven 2008 liquidity crisis" is an example of what Sissoko (2019: 318) calls "counterperformativity," because repos ultimately "undermined support for the neoclassical approach to market liquidity." In the more recent view, "governments, not markets, have begun to be viewed as the fundamental source of liquidity, displacing the neoclassical view," Sissoko (2019: 318) contends. Rather than being a truly market-based model for credit formation and credit supply, grounded in private ordering mechanisms, the current model paradoxically shuns the central role of the sovereign state, while it is intimately bound up with and dependent on it to remain operational. Ultimately, Sissoko (2019: 316) writes, the "modern 'market-based' financial system" fosters instability, which explains the excess demand for safe assets." Furthermore, the current market-based system "favour[s] lenders to the greatest degree possible" (Sissoko, 2019: 333).

The securities market provides a way out of the safe asset shortage predicament, but securitization as a fee-based business (Goldstein and Fligstein, 2017: 489) includes increasingly specialized actors (Jacobides, 2005) and therefore tolerates, for example, imprudent home mortgage lenders that operate on the basis of high-risk lending in the sub-prime sector. The solution to imprudent market behaviour and opportunistic behaviour has been to rely on the market-based credit rating as a form of a private ordering solution (see, e.g., Elkin-Koren, 2005; Schwarcz, 2002; Williamson, 2002; Katz, 1996; Eisenberg, 1975), but empirical evidence indicates that credit rating agencies and issuers of securities have joint interests when operating on the basis of the so-called "issuer pays" model (Besedovsky, 2018; Cornaggio and Cornaggia, 2013; Bolton, Freixas, and Shapiro, 2012; Mathis, McAndrews, and Rochet, 2009), and that such joint interests result in lower credit rating quality (Alp, 2013). That is, credit rating agencies have been overoptimistic regarding the quality of the securities being issued by the end of the upward movement in the business cycle. In lieu of strict market self-regulation, novel legislation and regulatory practices derived therefrom such as the Dodd-Frank Act of 2010 have been passed by the US Congress. A scholarly literature is sceptical regarding the possibilities of this legislation to push down systemic risks in an industry wherein assets based on poor collateral (e.g. sub-prime home mortgage loans) are combined with qualitative assets in the securitization process, and wherein second-level derivative instruments introduced to spread risks, such as CDOs, are ineffective in pricing risk properly (Krawiec, 2013; Wilmarth, 2013; Tillman, 2012; Coffee, 2011, 2012).

Finance industry regulators have to balance the preference for a generous supply of finance capital at low cost and a minimal operative stability in financial markets to maintain the faith in financial markets. In order to support the former goal, the production of safe assets, either issued by a GSE (as in the case of the United States), or private finance institutions fully insured by the sovereign state, serves as a key mechanism for the multiplication of finance capital—the capital formation process. As housing policy is part of the welfare state model, and home ownership is in many cases the largest investment made by individual households, oftentimes with home mortgage loan contracts with a duration of 25–30 years, home mortgage loans is the near-perfect collateral as they integrate and align at least three political objectives: (1) they ensure that a certain proportion of the population, that is, the voting public, own their homes, (2) they create a stock of safe assets that play a key role in the capital formation process (over time, around one-third of all safe assets are backed by the sovereign state), and (3) they create jobs in the blue-collar work-intensive construction industry, which serves as the provider of qualitative housing and is the largest sector of the economy after healthcare in most OECD economies. Through these mechanisms, the construction industry is closely entangled with the franchise model of finance capital in the contemporary advanced economic system; the sovereign state insures a certain stock of high-quality safe assets, and private-backed money-claims follow suit, in both cases relying on high-quality collateral, an underlying asset that has a reasonably stable and predictable market value.

Regulatory blind spots

Despite the central role of the housing-finance nexus in the economic system, studies show that even policymakers and regulatory agencies have a problem designing a robust and integrated regulatory model that includes all the mechanisms and connections between mechanisms and entities in the capital formation process. Ivanova (2017: 4) reports house price increases for specific years during the 2002–2005 period, with an 11 per cent increase in 2002 and 2003, and 15 per cent increase in 2004 and 2005. In the short period of four years, 2002–2005, US housing prices thus rose by no less than 63 per cent. By the early 2000s, White (2013: 104) writes, "there was a widespread belief that housing prices could only go up." Such beliefs translated into a self-fulfilling truth as home mortgage lenders and borrowers jointly participated in generating an upward spiral in housing prices (Mayer, 2011). Unfortunately, what at the time and not the least in hindsight seemed to be an unsustainable growth of housing prices, not possible to fully explain on the basis of a sudden upsurge in demand or an endemic shortage of objects (in fact, rising the S&P/Case-Shiller Index was accompanied by a construction industry boom in several regions, including Florida and Southern California), was not treated as a warning signal by regulatory agencies, Fligstein, Brundage, and Schultz (2017: 887) demonstrate. Based on studying the Federal Reserve's Federal Open Market Committee's (FOCM) meeting minutes, it can be seen that even the entrusted experts at the apex of the governance and regulatory system, recruited from the most prestigious quarters of the American society, failed to maintain an integrated and operational theoretical model wherein the finance industry was related to housing production and the home mortgage lending market. For instance, during one meeting, which discussed soaring housing prices, only seven of the 15 speakers expressed any concern regarding misaligned market prices, of whom four saw only low economic risks. The remaining three speakers, who did in fact recognize a potentially high economic risk, nevertheless all felt that the Federal Reserve did not need to take action (Fligstein, Brundage, and Schultz, 2017: 887). This sanguine view of the home mortgage market was endemic in FOMC. For instance, the New York Fed vice president Richard Peach gave a speech in 2005, which lambasted the news media and business press for reporting on the remarkable rise of the S&P/Case-Shiller Index: "Hardly a day goes by without another anecdote-laden article in the press claiming that the U.S. is experiencing a housing bubble that will soon burst, with disastrous consequences for the economy," Peach stated (cited in Fligstein, Brundage, and Schultz, 2017: 898).

According to Fligstein, Brundage, and Schultz's (2017: 900) analysis, the shared macroeconomic training of the entrusted FOMC experts served to blindfold them inasmuch as they "continued to view housing in isolation from the financial system." Operating on the basis of an analytical model that effectively placed macroeconomic fundamentals and concerns above finance industry operations, the FOMC experts entertained the belief that monitoring macroeconomic issues would be sufficient to uphold the stability of the entire economic system. Unfortunately, the housing-finance nexus included growing proportions of imprudent lending, securitization of home mortgage loans on an industrial scale, and deteriorating credit rating quality, a brew that resulted in the 2008 finance industry stalemate, an outcome that does not honour the credentials of the FOMC experts. The study by Fligstein, Brundage, and Schultz (2017) is indicative of how a one-sided or biased theoretical framework may mislead also purportedly highly qualified policymakers and advisers, susceptible to group think if they all share certain convictions regarding the mechanisms that regulate the economic system. Regulators and economic advisers do therefore not only need to have the capacity to cognitively process heterogeneous data accurately and to be experienced, but they also need to recognize and see the value of a diversity of know-how and views when monitoring integrated and dynamic economic systems. Some commentators such as Richardson, Van Nieuwerburgh, and White (2018) believe that these demands on regulators are unreasonable and therefore reduce net economic welfare in the housing finance sector. Richardson, Van Nieuwerburgh, and White (2018) instead advocate a market-based model wherein housing policy and home mortgage loans are separated, and market actors accommodate the risks of the home mortgage origination and securitization: "[T]he bulk of the mortgage finance system should not have national housing policy injected into it, as mortgage finance generally is an inefficient way of addressing the affordability and income-redistribution goals that are usually at the center of housing policies" (Richardson, Van Nieuwerburgh, and White, 2018: 28).

In the end, there exist intricate relations and interdependencies between the sovereign state, the finance industry, and the construction industry, jointly contributing to the process of capital formation. A scholarly objective is therefore to further explore how, for example, construction industry agents can negotiate new construction projects and other business-related benefits on the basis of this role as the entrusted provider of collateral, which serves the broader benefit to leverage the stock of finance capital in an economic system. Scholarly inquiries are arguably needed to shed light on these relations, carrying macroeconomic implications beyond the narrower political concern for affordable housing supply.

Summary and conclusion

The contemporary economic system of competitive capitalism is fuelled by the supply of low-cost finance capital that can, for example, fund various entrepreneurial initiatives, which eventually translates into new goods and services, new business models, and other business innovations (Adrian et al., 2017). Free market theorists regard this capital formation process as an exclusively self-regulating market-based activity, a form of private ordering, but empirical evidence shows the importance of the role of safe asset supply for capital formation activities, accounting for roughly one-third of the credit supply (Gorton, Lewellen, and Metrick, 2012). This indicates the active role played by the sovereign state in finance markets, which by implication makes what was formerly strictly regarded as liabilities, such as sovereign debt, in fact be treated as core mechanisms in the supply of finance capital in the economy (Gorton and Pennacchi, 1990; Hockett and Omarova, 2016). Risk-averse and prudent policymakers prefer not to let the defined agencies monitored by the sovereign state create safe asset ex nihilo, but instead insure, for example, home mortgage loans, which serves many purposes and political ends in the economy (student loans, representing an individual and social investment in human resources, is another example of a politically palatable policy that generates a larger quantity of collateral, also securitized by the finance industry). In this operational model, home ownership, associated with certain indisputable "user-value," the interests of the construction industry, the sovereign state, and the finance industry are aligned. Concerns that the finance industry is not monitored in sufficient detail, predictably surfacing after any episode of finance industry turbulence (Gerding, 2005), for example, the 2008 finance industry collapse, may be reduced on the basis of a detailed understanding of how safe assets are actively created and regulated by the sovereign state's agents. That is, the preference for finance market stability among policymakers and other constituencies must always be weighed against the macroeconomic benefits derived from an ample supply of finance capital at low cost. The one political objective cannot exclude the other, but macroeconomic growth and welfare and finance industry stability are closely aligned, yet distinctively different policy concerns, not to be confused, empirical studies indicate.

Notes

1 In many American federal programmes, affordable housing is defined in terms of the aggregated monetary costs of occupying a home. If this cost does not "exceed 30 percent of one's gross income," the housing is affordable (Glaeser and Gyourko, 2018: 4, footnote 1).

2 In lawyers' terms and in legal theory and scholarship, a "legal fiction" is a factual statement that a judge, a legal scholar, or a lawyer makes while "[s]imultaneously understanding full well—and also understanding that the

audience understands—that the statement is *not fact*" (Riles, 2010: 802; emphasis in the original). Legal fiction is thus an ambiguous term inasmuch as it is based on an "as if" logic wherein it is neither true nor not true, but is rather itself positioned as the very epistemological tension between what is true and what is not true. Riles (2010: 803) introduces the concept of "placeholder," a mathematical term that denotes an integer that forecloses a question for the moment, not by resolving it but by "papering over it," so that other issues can be addressed with greater precision. In this view, a legal fiction item (such as addressing the corporation as a "legal person") operates as a placeholder to enable a variety of legal issues to be discussed. In the example above, lawyers, legal scholars, and lay audiences know perfectly well that a corporation is not a person in the conventional semantic meaning of the term, and yet this legal fiction provides many benefits when addressing corporate activities of legal relevance.

3 It is important to notice that much research has emphasized the failure of mortgage lenders to uphold the quality in lending. There is research that stresses how the great mortgage expansion was propelled by the misrepresentations of factors such as borrower income, borrower assets, and "second liens and owner-occupancy status." (Ambrose, Conklin, and Yoshida, 2016: 2637–2638). Ambrose, Conklin, and Yoshida (2016: 2649) examine a data set acquired from the New Century Financial Corporation, "one of the largest subprime lenders in the run-up to the recent mortgage crisis," and with "a large portion of its business originated through independent mortgage brokers," and report that income falsification was "essentially a borrower-level phenomenon" (Ambrose, Conklin, and Yoshida, 2016: 2638). Furthermore, and unsurprisingly, mortgage borrowers who were the most likely to overstate income were concentrated in lower-income neighborhoods (Ambrose, Conklin, and Yoshida, 2016: 2643). As consumer protection law is premised on information asymmetry, it is mortgage lenders that carry the burden of proof in the case of mortgage contracts being terminated prior to the maturation date, but Ambrose, Conklin, and Yoshida (2016) reveal that the so-called low-doc mortgage market, intended to serve, for example, self-employed borrowers who have limited possibilities for or interest in disclosing their income, also provided an opportunity for low-income households to access credit in the credit expansion phase.

4 The differences between how the Icelandic and the Irish government handled the financial crisis is telling in terms of how there are in fact alternative approaches. In 1991, Sweden endured a major banking crisis, and the Swedish government opted for a resolution model wherein the banks were forced to recognize their losses, and no less than one-fifth of the banking system was nationalized (Murdock, 2012: 545). Based on this model, Sweden managed to turn around the banking system in two years. When Iceland, with a banking sector that had outgrown the GDP, was hit by the finance industry crisis, the country "essentially followed the Swedish model" (Murdock, 2012: 545). In contrast, Ireland, which experienced similar problems, rejected the Swedish model. Irish policymakers feared a capital flight, and "guaranteed the obligations of its banks, whose assets represented twice Ireland's GDP" (Murdock, 2012: 545). In the Icelandic model, policymakers "let its banks go bust," whereas the Irish model saved the banks "at enormous cost" (Bohle, 2018: 210). In the case of Iceland, the economy benefited from the substantial devaluation of the Icelandic krona, whereas Ireland "had to accept the straightjacket of EMU and pursue internal devaluation" (Bohle, 2018: 210).

The total cost for the bailout of the Irish banking system has been estimated to be €64bn, and the wider economic recession that followed resulted in a GNP decline by 8.5 per cent, soaring unemployment peaking at 15 per cent, and household incomes declining by 17.5 per cent between 2008 and 2012 (Waldron, 2016: 54). Icelandic policymakers protected their constituencies from carrying the costs incurred by overbanking and could push some of the costs of the crisis onto foreign actors; in Ireland, taxpayers had to foot the bill to protect the interests of primarily German and French bondholders (Bohle, 2018: 210): "The German banks and others who extended credit to the Irish banks were bailed out by the Irish taxpayers, while the Irish people bore the brunt of an austerity program that has kept the country in recession," Murdock (2012: 545–546) writes. The two ex post resolution models and crisis management approaches have their benefits and their disadvantages, and they also allocate the costs on the basis of different assessments regarding the culpability of various actors. The Icelandic policymakers protected their constituencies from the consequences of imprudent lending, whereas the Irish policymakers believed in protecting the credibility of the national banking system, also under the condition wherein Irish taxpayers were affected.

3 Thickly capitalized ventures

Housing production, illiquid assets, and social welfare

Introduction

As indicated in the second chapter of this volume, the supply of affordable housing is a key political objective in most welfare states, and for various reasons. First, housing has obvious user value inasmuch as it serves as residential homes for their owners or tenants. Second, housing and real estate serve as collateral in mortgage lending, and as it is widely assumed that the sovereign state insures this stock of loans against default, home ownership generates a stock of safe assets (Gorton, 2017). Safe assets in turn enable private-backed assets to be created in the form of credit, and are therefore an important mechanism in the credit formation process. Third and finally, housing and real estate projects in many cases serve to fuel the regional economy and promote job creation (Bryan et al., 2017). Taken together, the production of housing and real estate differs considerably from other categories of production, say retailing or commodities, inasmuch as the sovereign state, the construction industry, and finance institutions are closely aligned in the credit formation process, wherein the finance industry generates credit and the construction industry provides collateral within the realm of the sovereign state. "Housing is unique as an asset class in that property values are tied together and to their mortgage market. Housing is, in a sense, a communitarian asset," Levitin and Wachter (2020: xvii) say. In other words, the housing-finance nexus (Fligstein, Brundage, and Schultz, 2017: 884) operates within a jurisdiction wherein macroeconomic objectives (i.e. economic stability, long-term growth, enterprising activities) are part of the policymaking that regulates housing and real estate production. Says Weiss (1989: 267):

> One cannot study the history of real estate without fully appreciating the role of government in passing and enforcing laws, levying taxes, administering regulations, giving subsidies, building and maintaining infrastructures, providing services, settling disputes, making plans, buying and selling land, shaping agendas, and performing an exhaustive list of additional functions.

As discussed in Chapter 1, critical scholars introduce the term *financialization* to denote the process wherein the so-called real economy is managed, assessed, and regulated on the basis of a finance industry logic. In addition, there is evidence of both productive and dysfunctional financialization. That is, the credit generated within the financial system is to an insufficient degree reinvested in, for example, production capital, R&D, and human resources (Orhangazi, 2019), and instead surplus capital is invested in the secondary derivatives instrument market (say, in securities trade or in hedge funds; Cheffins and Armour, 2011). Expressed differently, a process of financialization needs to be understood as a gradual shift of authority from the political entities of the sovereign state and its defined agencies that implement legislation and policies, to the finance industry, which is granted a licence to issue credit as part of statecraft (Krippner, 2017). The tendency towards financialization is highly visible in the housing-finance nexus, the business of generating and financing new housing and real estate. Few other industries rely on as close and intimate relations between political entities, the deployment of productive resources in the construction industry process, and financial services including home mortgage lending and the securitization of such long-term assets into mortgage-backed securities and beyond.

The purpose of this chapter is to examine the literature that indicates that the political difficulties involved in providing "affordable housing" are not so much a matter of political controversies or indolence as they represent a mismatch between political objectives and assumed responsibilities vis-à-vis citizens, on the one hand, and the operational business model in the housing-finance nexus, on the other. The nature of housing and real estate, being costly to develop, as it is dependent on land resources owned by cities and municipalities, the magnitude of the investment and accompanying risks that households need to carry, and so on, is that housing production entails a situation wherein land needs to be translated into an investable asset. As Searle (2018: 525) remarks, to overcome the "fundamentally illiquid nature of land and real estate is complex; it takes work to make real estate into finance." That is, to be able to produce new housing and real estate, there has been an institutional transformation that is characterized by the predominance and authority of calculative practices derived from finance industry risk management models (Levitin and Wachter, 2020). The production of, say, affordable housing, is thus not simply a matter of providing land and contracting a construction company to complete the project, but involves a series of deliberations, agreements, and calculations that satisfy the interests of a variety of actors, and that render housing projects investable assets within current risk management practices. The outcome is commonly a stock of housing and real estate whose "affordability" can be disputed.

The remainder of this chapter is structured as follows: the first section examines how municipalities and city governments need to attract finance capital to fund their urban development projects. The second section discusses how the finance industry in its day-to-day operations actively translates illiquid asset holdings (e.g. home mortgage loan contracts associated with a defined interest and mortgage payment stream) into tradable assets, primarily first-level derivative instruments such as securities, but also second-level and more difficult-to-price instruments such as collateralized debt obligations. The third section turns to the source of new finance market assets, the municipalities and city administrations that own and control land that can be transformed into residential areas or be regenerated on the basis of urban renewal initiatives. As local government has few opportunities for raising taxes to finance projects, projected property tax revenues have served to construct investable assets within, for example, so-called Tax Increment Financing (TIF) programmes. The fourth section critically examines whether the alignment of housing policy, local government initiatives, and a finance industry-led housing and real estate market has produced affordable housing and to what extent externalities, leveraged systemic risk, democratic deficit,[1] and other unintended consequences of purposeful action have surfaced and been accommodated in the process. The final sections points at policy implications and theoretical contributions derived from the literature review.

Attracting finance capital to the housing sector

In practical terms, it is not primarily federal or state governments that matter when it comes to the production of, for example, affordable housing. A scholarly literature indicates that the finance-led economy is largely centred on cities and municipalities, because such administrative entities host the best possibilities for investment and offer collateral that benefits further capital accumulation. In 2016, it was reported that the estimated economic value of global real estate assets were \$217T, a figure which "represented 60% of all global assets, including equities, bonds and gold" (Gupta, 2019: 1131). City governments and municipality administrations, or more simply what Schragger (2009: 502) calls "the municipal corporation," operate in a milieu wherein the tension of "being open to global flows of capital and yet maintaining democratic accountability in the city" (Gupta, 2019: 1124) need to be reconciled and practically handled. Still, such policymaking and regulatory work are premised on the fact, Gupta (2019: 1125) writes, that "cities are not just where new forms of financial activities are taking place, but rather, cities themselves are being rebuilt and reconfigured—and even reimagined—at an astonishing pace by finance capitalism."

The municipal corporation thus needs to attract "mobile capital." That is, cities must appear to be "business-friendly," or offer other possibilities that finance capital investors appreciate, while at the same time robust economic regulation needs to be implemented to avoid the exploitation of the municipality's assets, including land and real estate stock (Schragger, 2009: 484). Schragger (2009: 313) is concerned that equally scholars and policymakers formulate numerous policy prescriptions based on these conditions, all being oriented towards making cities "ride the wave of urban popularity." Unfortunately, Schragger (2010: 313) argues, such policies "seem somewhat beside the point when considered in light of large-scale economic trends that affect city prosperity." That is, in Schragger's view (2010), most of the conditions that affect how successful cities are in term of attracting mobile financial capital are beyond the influence of individual local policymakers, economic advisers, and regulators. Consequently, Schragger (2010: 313) warns, "[a]ny claim that one policy or another will generate local economic growth should be made with a great deal of caution." In the free market system of the capitalist, finance-led economy, neither governments nor municipal corporations have the authority or capacity to command finance capital flows. On the contrary, in a free market system, Schragger (2009: 488) writes, finance capital "must be cajoled."

In practical terms, cities depend on revenues from fixed assets (e.g. real estate), immobile assets that cannot cross the city line at reasonable cost, if at all. Such revenues include property taxes from real estate ownership. To inflate the market value of real estate (i.e. the value of the real estate in the eyes of finance capital investors—not city governments, nor their defined agents), which also result in rising property taxes, cities unfortunately end up in the situation wherein they "extract as much as possible from less mobile capital while courting more mobile capital" (Schragger, 2009: 493). In this situation, city governments "give too much away" to attract mobile finance capital at the same time as they "extract too much from capital once it has become fixed in place" (Schragger, 2009: 485). In either case, these "two political pathologies," which Schragger (2009: 485) refers to as "giveaways" and "exploitation," respectively, are the consequences of the city's "particular economic and spatial predicament." From a political science perspective, based on public choice theory, wherein voters elect a city government and expect economic benefits and favours in return in a transactional relationship (i.e. political power and authority in the exchange for a variety of voter benefits), the current "giveaways" and "exploitation" model result in a situation wherein "local jurisdictions often foist benefits on nonvoting outsiders and impose costs on voting insiders" (Schragger, 2009: 497). What Schragger (2009: 497) refers to as an "over-attentiveness to mobile capital" generates counterintuitive outcomes. Behavioural theories (and more specifically what Simon, 1976 referred to as "administrative behaviour") partially explain such outcomes. Public officials often act within short-term horizons, and even if they do act honourably, they engage in giveaways because economically, "they have little choice," or because politically, "they need to be seen as doing something to enhance local competitiveness" (Schragger, 2009: 495). City management is therefore an intriguing practice in the finance-led economy as it is illustrative of a variety of qualities and conditions that are inextricably bound up with the global flow of finance capital.

Speaking in more practical terms, city governments deploy a variety of strategies and tactics to attract mobile finance capital. The more conventional approaches include instituting direct incentives such as tax breaks and subsidies that benefit investors, investing in local infrastructure improvements to indirectly benefit finance capital investor interests, and "the deployment of local amenities," that is, more generally making the city or town more attractive residential areas (Schragger, 2009: 507). More recently, and especially following the publication of Richard Florida's (2002) influential study of the "creative class" and its role in local economic growth, city governments have been incentivized to make investments that appeal to the purportedly creative class(es) or to wealthier households more generally. The concept of gentrification (see, e.g., Stein, 2019), a core term in urbanism discourses, effectively apprehends a variety of such investments made, oftentimes in "blighted" working-class neighbourhoods in metropolitan areas.

Despite city governments having the legal and political authority to act in ways that policymakers and officials believe benefit cities and the welfare of the population and voters, Schragger (2009: 495) is sceptical regarding the market analogy that is frequently used in accounts of city government: "[T]he market analogy is misleading. The city is not a preexistent entity that sells location services, but rather a result of cumulative location decisions." Schragger is critical of the market metaphor and the competition model that it implies, as cities were not introduced in a world wherein finance capital and markets for the investment of residual cash were already available. On the contrary, the cities are themselves the locale for the formation of finance capital and the creation of markets in the first place (most ancient and medieval towns emerged as marketplaces, but in some cases as military camps, for example, in the Roman Empire): "Cities do not arise after the establishment of cultural, legal, and political institutions. The city may in fact be a necessary precondition for them" (Schragger, 2010: 317). Furthermore, even if the struggle to attract mobile finance capital can be understood as a form of competition, the idiosyncratic history and specific location of cities cannot be ignored. Global "liveability" rankings of cities such as the Anholt city league table (Kornberger and Carter, 2010) may be inspiring and entertaining reading for policymakers, and may even provide some incentives to improve the economic and social welfare of the resident population, but to believe that, say, Stuttgart competes with Adelaide, or Dallas, in terms of attracting resources as if there were a global market for such city investment, is a misplaced and deceiving image:

> To say that the worldwide process of urbanization represents intercity competition for providing urban amenities seems absurd. Urbanization is occurring, but it is simply not plausible to describe it as the outcome of a market in local governments or to claim that some cities are winning in a kind of good governance race.
>
> (Schragger, 2010: 317)

In the end, the market metaphor is inadequate and vacuous inasmuch as it imposes a governance model, that of the market, which implies a set of mechanisms and legal devices (e.g. contracts and contract law) that only account for a subset of the practices involved in city governance and the work to attract finance capital investment. For instance, unlike incorporated businesses, which operate under the authority of bankruptcy law and its mandatory rules (expressed in various terms in different jurisdictions), cities and municipalities cannot declare bankruptcy in similar terms as corporations (in the United States, city bankruptcy is a legal device and a factual event, but the conditions diverge considerably from that of corporate bankruptcy cases; see, e.g., Webber, 2018: 128; Peck and Whiteside, 2016): "Financially speaking, US cities must operate in the short term, avoiding or evading current account deficits, but their responsibilities—for infrastructure, social and environmental sustainability, economic development—manifestly extend to the long term," Peck and Whiteside (2016: 247) write.

Regardless of all the legal, regulatory, political, and technical details pertaining to city governance and its capacity to attract and maintain mobile finance capital investment, cities are per se the principal location for financial accumulation and, writ large, the finance-led economy. For city governments and officials, this is equally a curse and a blessing, and even in cases such as New York City or London, the two global financial centres, which benefit greatly from finance industry taxation and tax income from the high net-worth individuals employed in the industry, the presence of the finance institutions creates specific governance problems, for example, a shortage of affordable housing for individuals employed in the various service industries and the welfare sector of the economy (being a major concern in, e.g., the San Francisco Bay Area, hosting the Silicon Valley computer industry cluster). As a factual condition, as illustrated by Gupta (2019: 1131), the finance-led economy is fundamentally urban in nature, not the least because real estate is the high-quality collateral of choice in the capital accumulation process.

Illiquid assets, asset prices, and the expansion of credit

To better underline the connections between the finance industry, construction project initiation (being a responsibility of local governments—here used as a shorthand term for municipality and city administrations and their defined decision makers), and the construction industry, some finance market terms need to be introduced. Illiquidity denotes the transaction costs involved when selling an asset (Adrian et al., 2017: 44). A highly liquid asset, say, shares in a Fortune 500 company, are easily sold off at the New York Stock Exchange. That is, there are only small costs involved in transforming a stock holding into currency on account. In contrast, a house is an asset that is illiquid inasmuch as it takes considerable time, effort, and cost to sell the house in return for cash. In many cases, there are property taxes and other legal and regulatory conditions that need to be considered which further increase the illiquidity of the asset. Furthermore, the degree of liquidity of different asset classes may vary over the business cycle, which affects the market price of an asset: "[T]he price that buyers are willing to pay for a high quality asset is depressed by the market's illiquidity," Guerrieri and Shimer (2014: 1876) write. They continue: "That is, even if a buyer somehow understood the quality of a particular asset, he would pay less for it because he would anticipate having trouble reselling it to future buyers who don't have his information." As several commentators have remarked (e.g. Greenwald and Stiglitz, 1986: 259), illiquidity is not to be understood as some market dysfunction but is better portrayed as a feature of various markets, a condition that needs to be managed by traders.

Second, asset prices, which per se are contingent on the overall liquidity of the market, affect how, for example, banks act in terms of, say, home mortgage lending. Banks manage their portfolios of assets and liabilities so that a favourable credit rating is maintained (Adrian and Shin, 2010: 436). A lower credit rating would increase the bank's cost of borrowing in the money market (i.e. the "short-term" credit market), and therefore banks actively manage the leverage of their portfolios when asset prices rise. When, for example, housing prices rise, asset holdings are worth more, and banks consequently can "expand their balance sheet" to make use of the "surplus capital," that is, identify new borrowers and issue more credit (Adrian and Shin, 2010: 420). Adrian and Shin (2010: 420) suggest that the banks' leverage is "procyclical." That is, "there is a strongly positive relationship between changes in total assets and changes in leverage." Adrian and Shin (2010: 436) can be cited at length here:

> When asset prices increase, financial intermediaries' balance sheets generally become stronger, and—without adjusting asset holdings—their leverage tends to be too low. The financial intermediaries then hold surplus capital, and they will attempt to find ways in which they can employ their surplus capital. In analogy with manufacturing firms, we may see the financial system as having "surplus capacity." For such surplus capacity to be utilized, the intermediaries must expand their balance sheets. On the liability side, they take on more short-term debt. On the asset side, they search for potential borrowers.

In the upward movement of the business cycle, housing market asset prices rise and banks leverage their portfolio through increased lending. This in turn increases the demand for home mortgage loan borrowers and collateral. That is, housing production needs to expand to better exploit the surplus capital situation. This mechanism easily results in inflated asset prices as generous home mortgage lending practices make naive market actors (i.e. households buying homes) believe in the accuracy of inflated market prices. The consequence is unsustainable asset prices and an increased leverage of banks, which result in market fragility and soaring systemic risk that can translate into asset price drops beyond the peak of the business cycle (Acharya and Viswanathanm, 2011).

The financial crisis of 2008 was triggered by this mechanism, Adelino, Schoar, and Severino (2018) argue. The extensive literature on the 2008 events tends to blame the expansion of the sub-prime home mortgage lending market, but Adelino, Schoar, and Severino (2018: 26) reject this explanation as the "increase in household debt was widespread among the US population and encompassed all income groups, especially middle-class borrowers." Empirical data indicate that debt-to-income (DTI) ratios "rose proportionally for all [US income] groups" (Adelino, Schoar, and Severino, 2018: 27), and consequently the 2008 crisis was not so much a sub-prime crisis as a middle-class crisis. Furthermore, finance institutions played an active role in supplying credit to expand their balance sheets to raise their return-on-equity performance, in order to better exploit the possibilities for leverage when asset prices rose sharply in the 2003–2006 period. "Between 1997 and 2006, the S&P/Case-Shiller Index of home prices rose by ~125% whereas the US Consumer Price Index rose by only 28%," White (2013: 104) writes. Such soaring housing prices were accompanied by growing mortgage lending. In the 1995–2003 period, residential loan origination grew by 600 per cent (Goldstein, 2018: 1109). "Banks seem to have taken house prices at face value and almost mechanically lent against these increased collateral values," Adelino, Schoar, and Severino (2018: 27) argue. They (2018: 27) continue: "The systematic mistake in the banking market appears to have been not taking into account the fact that collateral values were highly inflated, instead lending into the bubble while not guarding against a possible downturn in prices."

To return to the asset price/leverage mechanism that Adrian and Shin (2010) examine, the situation in 2003–2006, wherein housing prices soared, resulted in a situation wherein banks expanded their balance sheets and supplied credit to borrowers who could not reasonably be expected to dutifully fulfil their contract obligations as they did not have the means to repay the credit they were granted (Adrian and Shin, 2010: 436). In this view, banks were more concerned with their credit ratings and short-term bottom line results than to uphold prudent mortgage lending practices (see, e.g., Fligstein and Roehrkasse, 2016), and in the end the entire global finance industry was paralyzed when the demand for liquid assets widely exceeded the supply (Eichengreen, 2015). This demand brought an end to the vital interbank lending mechanism, the repo market, as it was now complicated to assess the degree of "toxic assets" (with the newly introduced term) on the balance sheets of various finance institutions (Frieden, 2016: 36; Gorton and Metrick, 2012: 447). In that situation, only finance capital infusion and other bailout activities orchestrated by the sovereign state could restore the faith in the finance market and render it operational anew (Levitin, 2011; Block, 2010). In the aftermath of these events, commentators have called for more robust macroprudential regulation to avoid "systemic buildup of debt across the economy" (Adelino, Schoar, and Severino, 2018: 28).

The key learning is that the liquidity/illiquidity continuum affects asset prices, and that rising asset prices generate a demand for more collateral and more mortgage loan borrowers. The "procyclical" mechanism of asset price increases and credit expansion unfortunately tends to create systemic risks that are complicated to measure and assess. Under all conditions, the finance industry is granted a licence to issue credit in the economy, a form of government franchise, Hocket and Omarova (2016: 1214) propose, but the credit issuance process still demands collateral, that is, housing and real estate assets. As it is local governments that have the authority to make decisions regarding the use of land and urban resources within their jurisdiction, the political nature of new housing and real estate project initiation is an unambiguous condition that needs to be considered. Nevertheless, despite local government discretion, the scholarly literature indicates that considerable efforts and interorganizational collaboration are demanded to render land or new housing projects investable. In the following, the political, legal, and financial operations activities preceding the actual construction project work will be examined.

Local government and the creation of housing project

Fernandez and Aalbers (2016: 72) remark that one of the key features of the "housing-centred process of financialization" is that it is "uneven in nature," a consequence of the fact that a global pool of capital and "national systems of housing and housing finance" need to be aligned through a variety of practices "on the ground" that are far from trivial, and not devoid of political controversy. In the following, some of these national and, more specifically, local practices to render the built environment as an asset class are examined.

The financing of urban renewal projects

In order to examine how local governments actively work to create construction projects in their communities, it is meaningful to distinguish between two types of finance industry-oriented activities. On the one hand, there is a credit supply that, for example, presumptive home mortgage borrowers benefit from, which includes conventional home mortgage loans that are securitized and sold on the global securities market to distribute risk (Gorton and Metrick, 2012: 430; McConnell and Buser, 2011). On the other hand, local governments participate in finance-related activities that serve the end to render housing, real estate, and urban regeneration projects investable for finance industry actors. In both cases, the construction industry serves as the intermediary that actively produces the physical buildings and the built environment that act as collateral in the credit formation process.

Fields and Uffer (2016) examine how the housing markets in Berlin and New York City have been subject to intense finance industry attention from the 1980s (in New York) and the 1990s (in Berlin, following the German reunification in 1989). In the mid-1990s, many German cities and municipalities started to privatize their housing stock, and thus opened up for finance industry investment (Fields and Uffer, 2016: 1488). Prior to that, housing was widely treated as a welfare state responsibility, and in West Berlin (arguably an idiosyncratic case for apparent historical reasons), in the period 1952–1970, 85 per cent of all new housing construction was subject to public subsidies (Fields and Uffer, 2016: 1491). However, in 2004, Goldman Sachs' real estate operation, Whitehall Funds, entered the Berlin housing market and created a "a herd-like movement of international investment firms following the money to Berlin's rental housing" (Fields and Uffer, 2016: 1493). This in turn resulted in a self-reinforcing speculation wave wherein investors were reselling their housing assets to other investors. In Germany more widely, Botzem and Dobusch (2017: 35) report, in the 2006–2007 period, roughly half of all apartment sales were "resales," wherein housing assets changed hands from "one investor to the other in a relatively short period." The speculation on housing assets, motivated by a lucrative return on equity investment, resulted in effects that "adversely affect tenants," Fields and Uffer (2016: 1489) write. The private equity funds that now owned housing facilities implemented "cost-cutting measures to maximise short-term value," which included "cutting back on services, repairs, and maintenance" (Fields and Uffer, 2016: 1489). The supply of affordable housing was consequently reduced as commercial interests rather than political objectives dictated the rules of the Berlin rental housing market. Regardless of such results, Fields and Uffer (2016: 1498) suggest that a financialization of a housing market does not operate in a deterministic manner. On the contrary, the increased influence of finance industry interest "continuously reshapes the urban landscape" (Fields and Uffer, 2016: 1498) as finance capital investors both discern existing investment opportunities and actively participate in the creation of investable housing assets.

Similarly, Searle (2018: 528), who examines the creation of Indian land resources into investable assets on the basis of a complex aggregates of actors, activities, and intermediaries, emphasizes that in order to transform physical land into investment objects, such resources need to be "reconfigured to be traded." In other words, they must be "disentangled" from existing social relations and be "standardized and abstracted." That is, to render a piece of land in India investable for finance institutions, the land must be transformed into an asset associated with "a plausible future asset stream," but this plausibility of predictable revenues is per se predicated on the various "valuations, forecasts, investment prospectuses, contracts and financial instruments" being introduced in the process (Searle, 2018: 528). As indicated by Searle's study of an investment fund traded on the London Stock Exchange—initially commercially successful, but eventually failing to generate a return for its investors—to transform physical resources into investable assets is by no means a trivial assignment.

Guironnet, Attuyer, and Halbert's (2016) study of an urban regeneration project in the Saint-Ouen municipality in Northern Paris also stresses the importance of taking a broader social and political view of the asset creation process, or else, local governments, for example, may assist a privatization of public assets that are inconsistent with stated political objects and are politically intolerable for voters and other stakeholders: "[R]isk-adjusted returns are not an abstract economic principle inherent to capitalistic accumulation but the output of a *social process* whereby financial investors in real estate translate categories of market finance into the built environment" (Guironnet, Attuyer, and Halbert, 2016: 1447).

Studies by Fields and Uffer (2016), Searle (2018), and Guironnet, Attuyer, and Halbert (2016) indicate that the creation of assets amenable for investment and that act as collateral in the credit formation process in the national economy, is a complicated professional practice that demands the active participation of a variety of actors, jointly capable of generating outcomes that are palatable to a number of constituencies. Beswick and Penny (2018) introduce the somewhat clunky concept of "financialized municipal entrepreneurialism" to denote how local government increasingly relies on finance industry calculations and vocabularies to be able to finance and realize defined urban regeneration projects and housing and real estate projects. In the United States, Beswick and Penny (2018: 616) argue, a "constitutive financialization of late-entrepreneurial metropolitan governance" is observable, yet is a complex socio-economic and political process "about which we currently know little." However, consistent with Fields and Uffer's (2016) and Searle's (2018) findings, Beswick and Penny (2018: 617) argue that the influence of finance industry motives is "neither a monolithic process" nor one that is "limited to owner occupation, or mortgage markets." In their very construction, housing facilities are simultaneously "an affordable, non-market tenure" and function as "the basis for a liquid financial product" (Beswick and Penny, 2018: 619). This dual nature of housing facilities inevitably implies finance industry engagement. The question for local government and other market participants, and not the least the finance industry itself, is how to blend various interests in new housing and real estate project initiation so that the outcome is beneficial and tolerable for a majority of stakeholders. As such processes are complicated to anticipate, the current literature on finance-oriented housing and real estate and urban regeneration projects needs to be examined, including not the least the literature that examine the financing model par preference, so-called tax increment financing.

Housing projects on the basis of tax increment financing

Weber (2010: 253) argues that local governments have the authority and capacity to actively participate in the construction of financial markets through the manufacturing of "new investment instruments and the under-lying assets that form their collateral." For instance, Weber (2010: 253) con-tinues, cities control "some of the most opaque and idiosyncratic assets," in particular private and publicly owned real estate. To render such illiquid assets eligible to "distant investors and rating agencies," active work is demanded to attract financial capital (Weber, 2010: 253). At the same time, despite the decision-making authority regarding the use of public assets, local governments are, Briffault (2010: 86) says, "largely dependent on their own resources to finance their activities."[2] Such "own resources" include revenues from tax payment, but the raising of taxes is surrounded by checks and balances and remains politically complicated, not the least because tax reforms may be inconsistent with voter preferences and/or campaign donors' expectations (Briffault, 2010: 86). Neither can local governments, as Molotch (1976: 320) remarks, enact policies that increase the economic growth and the taxable income in a local community to raise budgets. What can be done, though, under certain conditions, is to use the future tax revenues stream to create investable assets that attract finance capital owners. Briffault (2010: 89) refers to this tendency to transform tax income into investable assets as "fiscalization," itself being part of the "entrepre-neurial nature of most contemporary economic development efforts." As such operations provide local government with the opportunity to initiate urban regeneration projects, there is also evidence of externalities, unantici-pated consequences, and political deficits. Weber (2010: 253) suggests that there is evidence of recursivity in the creation of investable public assets and the collaboration with finance industry actors inasmuch as "the nature of these goods and services are often themselves transformed by the manner in which they are financed." That is, there is an evident risk that once various fiscalization initiatives are implemented, local governance is increasingly framed by a finance industry logic, which in turn undermines alternative or competing views (see, e.g., Marti and Scherer, 2015: 306), which potentially results in a democratic deficit.

TIF is an investment model widely employed in the United States. TIF allows local governments to designate a so-called "blighted area" for redevel-opment on the basis of the securitization of projected property tax revenues in the targeted area. The initial and ongoing redevelopment expenditure is thus covered by the future property tax revenues stream (Weber, 2010: 258). This means in practice that local governments sell off slices of their tax base (Weber, 2010: 258). As TIF provides local governments with the possibility to finance a variety of projects on the basis of finance market interactions, the model is remarkably widespread. Pacewicz (2012: 422) writes that "[s]everal major California cities have designated over 50% of their land area as TIF districts." At the same time, Briffault (2010: 66) writes, "TIF is highly controversial," and as Weber (2010: 258) remarks, "[t]he timing of TIF coincides with the dramatic expansion of capital markets and the global savings glut of the late 1990s and early 2000s." The development of

TIF-backed bonds—the financial instrument that local governments issue—mirrors the structured financial instruments being developed in other niches of financial markets, "which convert risky revenue streams into derivatives that rating agencies deem more secure than the underlying assets" (Pacewicz, 2012: 422–423). Legally speaking, TIF debt (corresponding to the stock of TIF bonds being issued) is not a "general obligation," which means that the securitized revenue stream is circumscribed to "projected tax revenues in city subsections, not the entire property tax base" (Pacewicz, 2012: 423). The local government thus isolates the designated area and its anticipated revenue stream from the wider city budget. This means in practice that a local government has no legal obligation to compensate investors if projected TIF revenues do not materialize (Pacewicz, 2012: 423). This in turn creates greater leeway for local governments as news media and the wider public are potentially less critical of failed projects if the cost of such projects is limited in terms of taxpayers' interests. Nevertheless, the repackaging of blighted areas into TIF bonds, being assessed by rating agencies and sold on the finance market place, the underlying asset was located "at the center of a fragile architecture of interlinked financial arrangements that is beset by a variety of risks" (Weber, 2010: 259). Expressed differently, "with TIF, municipalities are gambling on future appreciation in the value of the land and buildings within a small geographic area," Weber (2010: 259) summarizes.

In Chicago, a city that at an early stage used TIF as a standard device to finance urban regeneration project, TIF projects financed what Weber (2010: 254) refers to as the "Millennial property boom," roughly the 1996 through 2007 period. For instance, in 2007, the aggregated value of new property taxes generated within TIF districts represented one-tenth of the entire $5.5 billion budget of the city administration. The use of structural finance instruments such as TIF bonds thus played a key role in the debt-fuelled property boom in Chicago (and elsewhere) in the 1996–2007 period. Despite the successful use of TIF, sceptical commentators such as Briffault (2010) argue that TIF is overused inasmuch as it is no longer only "blighted" city districts that are regenerated on the basis of the use of structural finance instruments. "TIF is now increasingly used for greenfield projects on undeveloped land in the suburbs, at edge city highway interchanges, and in former cornfields," Briffault (2010: 72) writes. For instance, in an Illinois case "involving a proposal to convert farmland into a Wal-Mart," the blighting factors were "topographical issues" such as the need to have the land regraded and "the lack of utilities and a storm sewer system adequate to handle a large development" (Briffault, 2010: 79). In Briffault's (2010: 72) view, such land development activities have little to do with blight, being legally defined as "decayed or deteriorated structures, unsafe and unsanitary conditions, and economic and social distress." This more liberal use of the TIF instrument is unfortunate as the financial mindset that the use of the model inevitably nourishes may blindfold local government representatives and make them underrate the risks involved. For instance, in 2007, the City of Chicago suddenly instituted a new property tax rate to handle a $217 million budget deficit, an action widely understood as being implemented to cover unanticipated TIF expenses (Weber, 2010: 269).

In addition, the lack of a historical record regarding TIF projects, especially over the full business cycle, made this model essentially a speculative instrument. Over time, investors became overconfident about the future (a widespread phenomenon of especially the 2003–2006 period, *la belle époque* of finance, in Krippner's [2011] memorable phrasing), and the use of TIF thus contributed to "a dangerous oversupply of space" (Weber, 2010: 269). Until proven differently, the TIP project continued to be initiated based on what cognition scientists and behavioral economists call *positive asymmetry*, the tendency to ignore or underestimate discordant information, new information that is inconsistent with stated beliefs and the conventional wisdom (Cerulo, 2006). Finally, the professional identity of local government representatives and officials gradually changed as they increasingly regarded themselves as a class of finance industry entrepreneurs of sorts rather than as politically accountable professionals, Pacewicz (2012: 438) argues. The creation of new skills, professional communities, and departments contributed to a financing model that was unsustainable over time:

> Urban political leaders first turned to development professionals to leverage financial capital, but such efforts created a new set of development institutions within which development professionals create TIF-backed securities to live up to their own professional identities. In effect, a political and professional calculus is responsible for ever-higher rates of TIF spending, even though the actors involved recognize that the long-term consequences of this ratchet effect are fiscally unsustainable.
>
> (Pacewicz, 2012: 438)

Seen in this way, the use of the structural finance TIF model is "nicely congruent with the entrepreneurial nature of most contemporary economic development efforts," Briffault (2010: 89) argues. At the very heart of this entrepreneurial identity is the belief in the possibility of translating assets—not just specific assets, but *any* assets associated with a revenue stream (Peterson, 2007)—into financial assets amenable to finance industry investment, rating, and trade.[3] The transfer of blighted urban areas into TIF bonds on the basis projected property tax payment is a first-rate example of an entrepreneurial transformation of land into investable assets, predicated on a finance industry business logic.

The creation of affordable housing in finance-led markets

Ultimately, the question remains whether affordable housing is in fact produced within the current finance industry-backed development model.

Soaring housing prices speak against this scenario, and the supply of finance capital has arguably served to create an overconfidence among home mortgage borrowers, which has resulted in increasingly higher prices paid for built property. Although the capital formation process has inevitably contributed to what has been referred to as the "democratization of finance," there are apparent externalities in the current financing model. As Goldstein (2018: 1109) remarks, "by the height of the housing boom in 2005, there were more real estate agents than farmers in the United States," per se being an index of the attraction of the lucrative housing market. During an episode of swift home mortgage loan origination, more people jump the gravy train. Using data from 1,566 US municipalities over the 2000–2006 period, Goldstein (2018) demonstrates that the novel investment behaviour and risk-affirmative attitude that trickled down to even low-income households over time was not some rational response to economic fundamentals and economic policies, but was also triggered by social and cultural changes. In the period, virtually hundreds of thousands of Americans "became real estate entrepreneurs, buying millions of homes for short-term profit" (Goldstein, 2018: 1137). This new behaviour and accompanying identities and attitudes, Goldstein (2018: 1137) continues, were "predicated upon broad institutional changes that made investment an increasingly dominant idiom of economic action and reconceived houses as financial assets." As indicated by Fligstein, Brundage, and Schultz's (2017) study of the decision-making of the Federal Reserve's Federal Open Market Committee during the period, not even the highly qualified and seasoned economic experts at the apex of the governance system entertained a functional and plausible model that served to mediate systemic risks and to reduce expectations. Consequently, naive investors who actively participated in non-occupant investment (i.e. speculation in real estate) could not be rationally expected to know better than these formally appointed advisers and regulators.

At the same time, the idea that it was average American households that served to inflate the housing market prices on their own in this period is implausible. These tendencies are instead to be seen as a parable in line with the stories circulating around the time of the Wall Street crash of 1929, where also shoe-shine boys (i.e. non-experts), as the anecdote puts it, were prone to pass on their most recent stock purchase advice to their clients, a form of "democratization of speculation" that did not bode well, it may be learned from history (Deringer, 2015; Kindleberger, 2007; Abolafia and Kilduff, 1988). Instead, the active involvement of real estate companies is presumably the key driver of inflated housing prices and the loss of affordable housing as idea and political objective. Botzem and Dobusch's (2017) study of the German real estate market is arguably representative for the changes in the period preceding the 2008 finance industry crisis. In the period, primarily large Anglo-American investors were active in the German housing and real estate market. By 2007, the UK-based company Terra Firma owned 190,000 apartments, the company Fortress had more than 150,000 units in its portfolio, and Cerberus, Goldman Sachs' local agent, owned roughly 90,000 apartments (Botzem and Dobusch, 2017: 35). All these three major investors applied the same finance industry business model, which included acquiring relatively cheap real estate, the building of a considerable portfolio of assets relatively quickly on the basis of minimal equity investment and borrowed finance capital, and ending in a sale of the entire company or an initial public offering (IPO) (Botzem and Dobusch, 2017: 35). That is, investment in German real estate assets was from the outset a speculative venture with limited interest in long-term real estate ownership and facilities management.

Botzem and Dobusch (2017: 36) pay detailed attention to the German firm the IMMOFIRM Group (a pseudonym), which operated in accordance with this business model. Already from the outset, the company's goal was to "assemble a sufficiently large stock of real estate assets that was to be taken public" (Botzem and Dobusch, 2017: 36). Needless to say, this business model was premised on the condition that "renovation and modernization efforts of the property were kept to an absolute minimum" (Botzem and Dobusch, 2017: 36). To reduce operational and managerial costs, the IMMOFIRM Group outsourced the facility management for nearly all its properties and loan servicing firms were contracted to manage and monitor the rental payment revenue stream. Furthermore, to cut corners and to speed up the process towards an investor exit, IMMOFIRM Group's business model relied on auditing firms that recognized the certification of the value of the asset holdings, which relied mainly on two criteria: operative cash flow and market value. Botzem and Dobusch (2017: 40) remark that as accounting measures, each of these two criteria "depends heavily on assumptions" (as in the case of the estimation of rental vacancies) and reference values (e.g. market prices paid for "similar properties"). The use of such accounting and auditing methods is consistent with what Michel Power (2010: 205) has called a "de-legalisation of accounting," wherein "the 'shadow of law' is being replaced by 'the shadow of financial economics.'" This means that whereas traditional accounting standards rely on a historical record of actual transactions, verified by formal documents and records, a finance industry-oriented accounting model (e.g. Fair Value Accounting; see, e.g., Barker and Schulte, 2016; Bougen and Young, 2012) portray market-based valuation and the pricing of assets, in many cases on the basis "fictive prices," as a more "future-oriented" and finance industry-friendly way of describing a portfolio of holdings. One way to inflate the market value of a portfolio of asset holdings is thus to speculate about its future economic value rather than to strictly account for its current market pricing.

Finally, IMMOFIRM Group's financial engineering used the possibility to make a tax haven jurisdiction the domicile for the head office, a choice unsurprisingly made "primarily for tax reasons" (Botzem and Dobusch, 2017: 40). In addition, the whole business operation was enabled by a generous supply of finance capital. The investment of roughly 1 billion euros in real estate over a three-year period was accomplished on the basis of "virtually no net equity," Botzem and Dobusch (2017: 40) write. The case of the IMMOFIRM Group is a textbook case of entrepreneurial finance engineering, which includes low private equity investment, the acquisition of cheap (and preferably underpriced) real estate, the outsourcing of facilities management services and the minimization of services to tenants, the use of auditing firms to verify the value of assets holdings, the incorporation of the business in a low-tax jurisdiction, and a stipulated exit already from the beginning of the business operations. IMMOFIRM Group's participation in the German real estate and housing market is arguably inconsistent with political objectives pertaining to affordable housing. In contrast, Botzem and Dobusch (2017: 41) write, "financial services firms actively contribute to excessive price developments privileging financial over productive activities." The net economic welfare potentially generated can be expected to lie elsewhere, if to be found at all.

Everyday housing concerns and practices: the case of middle-class and destitute communities

The central role of the construction industry in the finance-led economy has several implications for households. Atkinson (2019) examines the American policy, in operation since the New Deal period, which actively promotes the access to credit as a social provision, and points at the inefficiencies of the policy doctrine. The Roosevelt presidency embraced what Prasad (2012) refers to as "mortgage Keynesianism," and provided government-subsidized consumer credit to promote home ownership (Atkinson, 2019: 1099). A generation of Americans (de facto primarily the white population) were thus able to take advantage of a government-sponsored private credit supply and real wage growth during more than two decades. The real wage growth resulted in the raising of property values, and the government-sponsored private credit therefore served as "a catalyst for building the white middle class" (Atkinson, 2019: 1100). Today, more than half a century after the post–World War II growth started to stagnate (by the latter half of the 1960s), the situation looks entirely different, but policymakers still advocate a private credit supply as a mechanism that promotes economic welfare. Unfortunately, this New Deal model worked only in a regime wherein economic growth and real wage growth are generated simultaneously, so that credit loans can be repaid at the same time as economic welfare increases. Atkinson (2019: 1101–1102) sketches a bleak image of the current situation and argues that the government-subsidized, private credit market targets vulnerable groups to extract rents:

> [P]olicymakers have left low-income Americans in a terrible position by decimating public-assistance forms of social provision […] yet failing to

solve the threshold problems of persistent wage stagnation and other entrenched social pathologies. Thus, high-risk, low-income borrowers must provide for their own welfare in the credit marketplace, where lenders build their business models on the expected transfer of wealth out of economically vulnerable communities. In this light, credit does not make sense as a form of social provision where economic growth is intractably arrested.

As private credit market actors value home ownership because it provides safe assets that further propel the credit formation process, the difficulties involved in financing housing for low-income groups generates considerable policymaking difficulties. Such difficulties are derived from the fact that real wages are stagnant or falling in the United States, which result in the expansion of the so-called payday loan market (see, e.g., Langley, Anderson, Ash, and Gordon, 2019), in turn being part of what Rona-Tas and Guseva (2018: 64) call fringe lending markets (see also Baradaran, 2015; Karger, 2005), wherein vulnerable groups access costly credit to bridge the days in between the end of cash and the day they receive their weekly or monthly pay cheque. The New Deal period, where government-subsidized private credit markets could expand on the basis of a growing economy, is long since over. In Atkinson's (2019) view, the policy idea that credit supply is a social provision that will help vulnerable groups become economically sustainable is mistaken, and policymakers "[e]ither fall prey to their own optimism or else indirectly endorse continued regressive redistribution," Atkinson (2019: 1105) proposes.

The loss of affordable housing is a consequence of misdirected policymaking that promotes the expansion of private credit markets, but without accompanying economic growth, and has considerable consequences for both middle-class and working-class communities. Manzo, Druta, and Ronald (2019) study how soaring housing prices in Milan, Italy, result in the need for what is referred to as "intergenerational exchanges related to housing," wherein the older generation of families have to step in to support the purchase of homes for the younger generation. In Manzo, Druta, and Ronald's (2019: 522) view, this phenomenon is explained on the basis of the relationship between the housing market and global finance:

> On the one hand, housing markets have become embedded in wider (often global) circuits of finance, influencing property values. On the other, access to credit as well as stable employment necessary for home purchase diminished, especially since the global financial crisis.

In addition, in many welfare states, since the early 1990s, welfare state retrenchment that includes "the progressive dismantling of affordable housing policies" in combination with increased labour market insecurity have added to the situation wherein fewer young individuals and households can realize their dream of homeownership (Manzo, Druta, and Ronald, 2019: 523). "For many," Manzo, Druta, and Ronald (2019: 523) write, "the tradition of buying a home before marriage has thereby become an unachievable aspiration, marking a shift from previous generations." In the end, to make ends meet and to accommodate all sorts of risks that intergenerational family households recognize, credit and assets (e.g. apartments or houses) are transferred between generations. Unfortunately, for younger family members who need to take advantage of the economic wealth of the elder generation, this arrangement was perceived as an anti-quated practice and a condition that reduces social welfare: "[T]he interfer-ence in everyday domestic life that proximity to, and dependence on, parents typically facilitated, was perceived as burdensome and frustrating," Manzo, Druta, and Ronald (2019: 532) write. Based on empirical evidence, Manzo, Druta, and Ronald (2019: 534) contend that homes are "essentially the point at which economic pressures associated with financialization and the progressive withdrawal of social safety nets interact with everyday family practices."

Houle and Berger (2015) demonstrate that there is a weak correlation between student loan debt and home ownership in the United States, which eliminate the explanation that the growing student loan debt stock in the United States (see Houle and Berger, 2015: 592, figure 1) results in a lower home ownership ratio among young adults. Still, if middle-class families suffer the consequences of the enfolding of local and regional housing markets and the global "circuits of finance," it is at a relatively lower degree of loss of economic and social welfare in comparison to low-income households. Desmond and Wilmers (2019) examine the low-end housing market in the United States, wherein families rent their homes and yet are subject to forms of exploitation inasmuch as they commit a sig-nificant proportion of their income to housing costs. "Most poor renting families today receive no housing assistance and reside in the private rental market, where over half spend at least 50% of their income on housing costs and a quarter spend over 70% on them," Desmond and Wilmers (2019: 1093) report. High rent is partially a consequence of the median landlord profit margins that are higher in neighbourhoods with consider-able poverty rates, "even after accounting for a wide array of expenses" (Desmond and Wilmers, 2019: 1113). Desmond and Wilmers (2019: 1100) provide data from Milwaukee, Wisconsin, that reveal that a 10 per cent increase in neighbourhood poverty predicts an increased landlord profit-ability by 13 percentage points. This translates into median landlord profit margins being twice those of median landlord profit margins in non-poor neighbourhoods (Desmond and Wilmers, 2019: 1115). In low-end housing markets, tenants make less money but pay higher rents in nominal and rela-tive terms than residents in non-poor neighbourhoods do, largely because of social dilemmas which result in tenants paying a premium for the risks that landlords are exposed to:

Because landlords operating in poor communities cannot know with certainty whether a new tenant will cost them money, they may attempt to mitigate that risk by raising the rents of all their tenants, carrying the weight of social structure into price.

(Desmond and Wilmers, 2019: 1116)

Desmond and Wilmers (2019) continue:

[C]ompared to their peers in affluent communities, landlords in high-poverty neighborhoods face more risks in the form of rent nonpayment and vacancies and are exposed to repair costs that are either higher (in the national data) or at least more concentrated (in the Milwaukee sample). Landlords anticipating potential risk may price up their housing units, just as landlords who have themselves incurred losses may recoup by asking future renters to pay for the misfortunes of past tenants, thereby generating widespread exploitation by socializing risk.

(Desmond and Wilmers, 2019: 1116)

According to elementary economic theory, the above-normal returns of real estate investment would attract new market entrants, which result in increased competition and a downward push on the rents paid by tenants. Unfortunately, there is little evidence of such dynamics, and Desmond and Wilmers (2019: 1118) speculate whether there is a premium on "dirty work," that is, to participate in a business activity that is "challenging and morally ambiguous" is associated with a higher return on investment. Poor neighbourhoods offer "strong profitmaking capacity" that investors may be aware of or detect, but as there is a stigma associated with owning real estate that serves poor communities (as derogative terms such as "slumlord" indicate), many potential investors may refrain from owning real estate in low-income neighbourhoods. In the end, due to the loss of competition in combination with social dilemmas that result in uncertainty regarding projected rent payment, housing costs are soaring in low-end housing markets.

This situation results in eviction and homelessness no longer being some abstract worst-case scenario, but becoming an actual outcome for many low-income households. As a matter of fact and as a consequence of housing market mechanisms and ineffective policymaking, "eviction is perhaps the most understudied process affecting the lives of the urban poor," Desmond (2012: 90) proposes. Drawing on the Milwaukee data set, a city of 600,000 inhabitants that includes several destitute neighbourhoods, Desmond (2012: 97) shows that 3.5 per cent of all tenants in occupied rental units are evicted annually. In comparison, 7.2 per cent of the tenants living in "high-poverty neighborhoods" (Desmond, 2012: 106) were evicted, a figure twice the city average. In particular, poor black tenants were subject to eviction. Furthermore, in the 2003–2007 period, around 60 per cent of the evicted tenants were female, a condition explained by the fact that women more often take care of families and children than men do, in many cases because men to a higher degree than women are sentenced to prison terms. "In poor black neighborhoods, what incarceration is to men, eviction is to women: a typical but severely consequential occurrence contributing to the reproduction of urban poverty," Desmond (2012: 120) writes. He adds, "These twinned processes, eviction and incarceration, work together—black men are *locked up* while black women are *locked out*—to propagate economic disadvantage and social suffering in America's urban centers" (emphasis in the original).

There are two principal explanations for the high level of evictions in poor neighbourhoods and low-end housing markets. First, welfare provision have been hollowed out over time as an effect of policymaking. As minimum wages have been stagnant or declining in the 1997–2008 period at the same time as "the cost of housing has increased by historic proportions" (Desmond, 2012: 106), the income of poor households has been outpaced by the climbing costs of housing. No matter how the long hours the "working poor" spend working, or how hard they try to find more lucrative positions, their real wage growth is outpaced by the growing housing costs. Second, Desmond (2012: 120) accounts for the "professionalization of the housing industry" and "property management" over the last four decades, which results in pressure to deliver a return on investment for shareholders. "Between 1970 and 2000, the number of people primarily employed as building managers or superintendents more than quadrupled," Desmond (2012: 120) writes. As indicated by Desmond and Wilmers (2019), real estate investment in poor neighbourhoods may not be an attractive investment for social reasons, but if real estate developers operate at a distance and hold a portfolio of diverse assets, the "shaming effect" may be diluted.

To further underline the vulnerable position of the tenants of Milwaukee's poorer neighbourhoods, Desmond (2012: 123) shows that more than 70 per cent of the American households that are evicted receive no legal representation. Furthermore, legal scholars have demonstrated that even in the case where tenants are represented by lawyers and get the proper legal assistance they are entitled to, courts are ineffective in enforcing the law. Summers (2020: 149) examines what she refers to as the "warranty of habitability operationalization gap" in US legislation, intended to protect tenants by imposing standards for what is the lower limit for tolerable housing quality in both absolute and relative terms (i.e. in relation to the rent paid in a specific case). Examining data from New York City, "the largest rental market in the country," Summers (2020: 193) found that "very few tenants with meritorious warranty of habitability claims actually benefited from the law." In fact, approximately 98 out of 100 tenants who took their cases to court were "being held to their full rental obligations regardless of defective conditions." This means that landlords are "rarely facing financial consequences for neglecting their properties." Landlords also overtly ignore the rule of the court of law as in no less than 72 per cent of the cases in which the landlord agreed to make repairs in a court-ordered settlement agreement, the tenants reported that those repairs were still outstanding in a subsequent court appearance (Summers, 2020: 151). For Summers (2020: 201), such ignorance is remarkable as courts have a broad legal authority to order the so-called Housing Code enforcement agency to "perform an inspection of the unit." The warranty of habitability operationalization gap that Summers (2020) accounts for in US legislation is thus directly caused by inadequate enforcement of the law, which deprives tenants of their legal rights and provides opportunities for landlords to act with impunity, even after courts have made decisions that prescribe what actions they need to take.

In the end, this means that primarily black women who work hard to support their families under the most difficult conditions suffer the consequences of policymaking that results in a reduced minimum wage compensation purchasing power, are disfavoured by the effects of a global finance industry expansion that mandates a return on real estate investment (and which benefits indirectly from soaring real estate prices as it fuels the credit formation process), and are disadvantaged by a legal system that offers few opportunities to have disputes regarding contractual agreements determined in a court of law. In comparison to the intergenerational transfer of economic resources and assets in middle-class families, the black urban communities in America's poor neighbourhoods are considerably worse off, with homelessness always looming unless the rent is duly paid, no matter how much of the household budget it consumes. For these communities, more generous access to private credit markets is by no means the answer to their predicament. Real wage growth and economic growth more widely, resolute housing market policies, and an emphasis on court-based decisions in the unfortunate case of prolonged disputes over rental contracts or remuneration would be a viable approach to the current situation. That is, a series of institutional changes and novel practices and policies are needed to amend the situation and to increase net economic and social welfare in the domain of housing.

Thickly financed industries and the quest for affordable housing: is the subsidizing of housing production supportive of economic welfare?

The housing-finance nexus is a central pillar of the advanced differentiated economic system of competitive capitalism. It provides housing as part of statecraft and a welfare provision; creates jobs, including a considerable share of blue-collar jobs, not the least for male breadwinners; acts as a countercyclical public sector investment opportunity as premised by Keynesian economic theory; and actively contributes to the capital formation process through the production of safe assets on the basis of robust collateral (e.g. home ownership and home mortgage borrowing, insured against loss by the sovereign state). Deregulatory campaigns, financial innovations (e.g. second-level derivative instruments such as CDOs), and the creation of a global and heavily integrated finance market, based on self-regulation through credit rating, are institutional changes that have fundamentally transformed the housing market from being primarily a political concern, subsidized by the state, to an ongoing market creation activity (see, e.g., Vogel, 2018) within the realm of the state that provides insurances to equally finance institutions and construction companies and building societies.

The most significant and visible consequence of this institutional pressure towards transforming land and real estate into investable assets is an unprecedented rise in housing prices, a process that for the most part has been unmonitored, unregulated, and, ultimately, only poorly understood since influential free market theorists such as two Federal Reserve chairmen, Alan Greenspan and Ben Bernanke, were fully convinced soaring housing prices were indicative of successful deregulatory reforms, in turn justified by ideological beliefs regarding the accuracy of market pricing as the outcome of superior but distributed information-processing capacities. "[T]hese price increases largely reflect strong economic fundamentals," Bernanke, by then chairman of the Council of Economic Advisers, stated in a speech before Congress in October 2005 (cited Mian and Sufi, 2014: 78). Furthermore, these office holders stipulated, the deepening of securities and derivative instruments markets would *reduce* rather than *inflate* systemic risks (see, e.g., Turner, 2015: 169), a proposition that poorly stood the test of empirical data (Fligstein and Roehrkasse, 2016; Gorton and Metrick, 2012; Piskorski, Seru, and Vig, 2010; Shin, 2009; Keys et al., 2009). Greenspan, for instance, Mallaby (2016: 594) writes, was "programmed to believe in progress," and though he "understood the fragility in finance," he still "underestimated the cost in doing little about it" (Mallaby, 2016: 579). Lehman Brothers was "a poster child for the financial practices that Greenspan had defended," Mallaby (2016: 660) says. Unfortunately, Lehman's spectacular bankruptcy in September 2008, which remains the largest US bankruptcy to date (McDonald and Robinson, 2009; Swedberg, 2010), was an event that made the levees break and resulted in the most severe crisis of competitive capitalism in the post-war period (for a detailed account of the Lehman bankruptcy, see Ball, 2018).

One of the major risks with a finance industry-led development of markets is that the reproduction and expansion of the finance capital stock are no longer treated as a means to provide economic and social welfare, but become a primary concern in their own right, as in the case of Group's business activities (Botzem and Dobusch, 2017). Wansleben (2018: 775) argues that the inflation-targeting policy of central banks serves to "actively foster market-based versions of banking." That is, the uncompromising focus on low inflation (consistent with finance industry preferences as it enables an efficient use of calculative practices, including vital risk management models) results in an "institutional convergence," wherein all market participants share a commitment to finance capital revenues at the expense of other social and economic objectives (e.g. low levels of unemployment). In the end, and in the worst-case scenario, finance capital either contributes to the inflation of housing prices, which undermine the political objective of affordable housing (as in the case of Botzem and Dobusch's, 2017, study), or housing and real estate become unattractive, even non-investable assets (Hockett and Omarova, 2016: 1215). It may be, as Forrest and Hirayama (2018) speculate, that the post–World War II period is a unique episode of economic development wherein middle- to low-income households were incentivized and subsidized by economic welfare policies to pursue home ownership. In this view, Forrest and Hirayama (2018: 259) write, it may be "more appropriate to regard the postwar 'generation own' as the exception—a historical moment in which a propitious combination of demographic, social, political and economic factors enabled an idiosyncratic growth in mass home ownership." As the housing market is determined by a variety of complex macroeconomic conditions and political decisions, and not least the finance industry operations and interests, it may be that "financially literate, real estate accumulators" are best placed to negotiate "the shift from a 'consumer' to a 'market' society and the changed household strategies which this entails," Forrest and Hirayama (2018: 273) conclude. This scenario is, practically speaking, already a factual condition as soaring housing prices, considerably diverging upward from both consumer prices indices and real wage growth, has resulted in a considerable growth of household debt (Zinman, 2015; Turner, 2015).

Bubb and Prasad (2014: 1621–1622) explicitly advise against the current US policy wherein the finance industry is subsidized and insured en bloc with the intention to benefit presumptive home mortgage borrowers as the primary political objective. In this model, too many possibilities for an extraction of economic returns in between stipulated policy and material outcomes are introduced, which generate additional costs in every step of the fragmented home-mortgage lending industry (Jacobides, 2005; Peterson, 2007):

> [I]f there is a public policy goal of expanding homeownership through subsidizing mortgage loans to low income households, then the subsidy should be explicit and transparent. The current practice of allowing extremely high leverage mortgages to proliferate in a housing boom is an opaque and costly form of public subsidy. As recent events demonstrate, the costs of such high leverage loans are ultimately borne by society more generally through the severe economic fluctuations that they can produce. Perversely, these costs fall disproportionately on low income households.
>
> (Bubb and Prasad, 2014: 1621–1622)

An alternative model would be to introduce legislation that defines a leverage limit on "any mortgage loan taken on a home," for instance, a maximum "combined loan to value" ratio of 90 per cent (Bubb and Prasad, 2014: 1610). In that situation, the presumptive mortgage borrower needs to save 10 per cent of the market price of the house to be able to pay the down payment, which would incentivize them to be more risk averse when entering mortgage loan contracts. A similar model is already in place in, for example, Sweden, which is suffering the same inflated housing prices as in many other advanced economies. It is beyond the scope of this volume to assess the efficacy of this legislation, but it appears as if this policy in combination with other, stricter market rules has resulted in more moderate growth of housing prices.

Scholarly research and economic policy should better reflect this new market situation and the market society being actively promoted through, for example, a central bank's inflation target policies. Rather than speaking more narrowly about the "supply and demand" on the housing market, the entire underlying economic, financial, legal, and regulatory apparatus should not only be explained to the wider public, but also needs to be subject to more detailed scholarly research. Not the least, antiquated euphemisms such as "affordable housing" should be removed from political campaign vocabularies, political speeches, and declarations as such political objectives are now abandoned because the housing-finance nexus is granted the franchise to develop such services. In this business, "affordable" is not defined in principal terms but denotes any price market participants are able and willing to pay, and little else. In the business model, it is low or no income households that suffer the adverse effects the most. Whether such consequences are politically tolerable remains to be determined.

Summary and conclusion

The housing and real estate market demonstrates a curious combination of state-led market making, including insurances and subsidies, and market pricing mechanisms. It is virtually impossible to examine the housing and real estate market without recognizing the state as the primary market maker (Weiss, 1989: 267). At the same time, housing policy is a key component in the welfare state model (Conley and Gifford (2006: 78). Furthermore, various market participants benefit from the state as active market makers. For households, home ownership serves as a "self-insurance" (Ansell, 2014: 384) as home ownership stores wealth and gives a sense of economic stability during episodes of labour market turbulence or economic hardship. The construction industry provides housing, jobs, and collateral, which is part of the capital formation process. That is, assets insured against loss enable private-backed asset creation. This in turn generates a credit supply that benefits non-financial firms, economic theory predicts. Home ownership is made possible through home mortgage loan lending, a finance industry service and a finance market niche that is dependent on secondary securities markets to render illiquid holdings tradable assets. Furthermore, asset prices in the housing market affect finance institutions' lending practices as soaring asset prices lead to possibilities for an expansion of the balance sheet, which results in a search for new borrowers so that credit ratings can be maintained at a favourable level (Adrian and Shin, 2010). This means that rising house prices have historically resulted in increased credit supply, which leverages systemic risk and attracts less prudent and oftentimes thinly capitalized mortgage lenders to the industry. A sizeable scholarly literature indicates that the finance industry-led housing market is based on advanced financial engineering and the use of legal and auditing opportunities enabled by deregulatory reform. Empirical cases raise doubts regarding whether this business practice has in fact supplied affordable housing, but additional scholarly research may provide more detailed data that substantiate or question such results.

Notes

1 The term *democratic deficit* denotes the situation wherein the political policy-making process is determined by the interest of specific groups so that majoritarian interests and/or preferences are marginalized or ignored. A substantial literature indicates that democratic deficit is a systemic feature of, for example, the US Congress (Gilens and Page, 2014; Carnes, 2013; Gilens, 2005). "[E]conomic elites and organized groups representing business interests have substantial independent impacts on US government policy, while mass-based interest groups and average citizens have little or no independent influence," Gilens and Page (2014: 565) conclude in their study of policymaking in Washington, DC. They continue: "Interest group alignments are almost totally unrelated to the preferences of average citizens [...] The composition of the U.S. interest-group universe is heavily tilted toward corporations and business and professional associations" (Gilens and Page, 2014: 574). The primary implication is, Gilens and Page (2014: 576) contend, that "[a]verage citizens' influence on policy making [...] is near zero." This does not mean that ordinary citizens do not get what they want, or do not see the policies they favour being enacted; in fact they do, but only insofar as such preferences are aligned with the interests of the economic elites "who wield the actual influence" (Gilens and Page, 2014: 576).

   Based on these research results, Gilens and Page (2014: 577) are concerned that the current regime, wherein policymaking is "dominated by powerful business organizations and a small number of affluent Americans," poses a serious threat to America's claim of being a democratic society. In a study published in 2005, Gilens drew a similar conclusion and pointed at the implications:

   > Most middle-income Americans think that public officials do not care much about the preferences of "people like me." Sadly, the results presented [...] suggest they may be right [...] [I]nfluence over actual policy outcomes appears to be reserved almost exclusively for those at the top at the income distribution.
   >
   > (Gilens, 2005: 794)

Empirical evidence indicates a secular decline in the faith in the American political system in the United States. By the end of the Eisenhower presidency (1953–1961), over 70 per cent of Americans said they trusted the federal government, but by the early 1980s, after the 1970s political crises and an economic recession accompanied by the neoconservative and libertarian campaign to discredit the federal government, only 25 per cent of Americans testified to having trust in their elected government (Hacker and Pierson, 2016: 197). This erosion of trust in democratically elected institutions has continued unabatedly, and in 2017, only 12 per cent of Americans said they have either "quite a lot" or a "great deal" of trust in Congress (McCrain, 2018: 1369, footnote 1). Gilens and Page (2014: 576) say that wealthy Americans and corporate executives "[t]end to know a lot about tax and regulatory policies that directly affect them," but ordinary citizens are in many cases dependent on "Social Security, Medicare, food stamps, or unemployment insurance," that is, social provisions that this community of influential political actors know little about, and may not even care for as part of their political convictions or ideologies. This democratic deficit makes even mainstream commentators such as economists concerned with the state of the American political system: "Let me be clear: the corrupting power of money in politics in the United States is perhaps the gravest threat facing democracy in America," Carl Shapiro (2018: 716) writes. Shapiro (2018: 746) remarks that this ability to influence policymaking is now also visible in the legal system, which is constitutionally separated from the political system: "I am deeply concerned about the current state of the American political system, and specifically about the political power of large corporations and the cramped definition of corruption that has been adopted by the Supreme Court."

When questions regarding the role of lobbyism and campaign donations are added to the policymaking process, the democratic deficit is even more pronounced. Zingales (2017: 122–123) says that large US corporations in fact spend a surprisingly low proportion of their revenues on lobbying, presumably because they face only limited and dispersed opposition to their agendas. Such propositions are supported by empirical evidence. Kang (2016: 270) calculates that investment in lobbying activities in the energy sector in the 2007–2008 period, wherein 559 firms and associations spent a total of $607.9 million on lobbying activities, had average returns in the range of 137–152 per cent. Such calculations reveal that lobbying is highly lucrative for industry. In 2016, the lobbying industry reported a turnover of $3 billion (McCrain, 2018: 1369), and empirical research indicates that if, for example, a lobbying firm organizes a senatorial fundraising activity, the chances of the senator accepting the lobbyist's policy proposal or amendment is 3.5 times higher than in the case where no such fundraising activity is taking place (McKay, 2018: 876). The quid pro quo relations generated by the lobbying industry further amplify the democratic deficit, many commentators argue (e.g. Drutman, 2015).

2 Studies of, for example, the municipality bond market reveal that municipalities are disfavoured vis-à-vis other market actors, which impose costs in terms of higher interest to be paid for taxpayers. Despite the municipal bond market being "the largest and most important US capital market for state and municipal finance," with about "$4 trillion in market capitalization, 55,000 issuers, 1.5 million bond issues, and 100,000–200,000 new bonds issued each year" (Cestau, Hollifield, Li, and Schürhoff, 2019: 66), and growing from "less than $1.4 trillion in par

value outstanding in 1996 to almost $4 trillion outstanding by 2017" (Cestau, Hollifield, Li, and Schürhoff, 2019: 67), Schwert (2017: 1684) suggests that generally speaking, only limited scholarly work has examined "the pricing of default risk in the municipal bond market." The default risk (the risk of the municipality declaring bankruptcy during the contract period) accounts for "74% to 84% of the average municipal bond spread" (i.e. the lower price paid by the investor in comparison to safe assets such as US Treasury bonds to compensate for higher risks) in the 1998 to 2015 period. Schwert (2017: 1717) remarks that the typical municipal bond investor is a "buy-and-hold retail investor," and this class of investors pays attention to default risk rather than to liquidity risks. Research also indicates that the trading costs "are substantial," with median markups "between 1.3% and 2% of transaction value" (Cestau, Hollifield, Li, and Schürhoff, 2019: 74). Such research findings indicate that if policy intends to lower state and local government borrowing costs, then alternative approaches to merely improve the liquidity in the municipal bond market should be considered. Second, Cornaggia, Cornaggia, and Israelsen (2017: 2076) examine how credit rating, and more specifically the credit rater Moody's recently established "more stringent municipal rating scale," affect the pricing of municipality bonds. Results indicates that Moody's "dual class rating system" disadvantages municipalities inasmuch as it costs taxpayers "an aggregate $960 million annually in excess interest" (Cornaggia, Cornaggia, and Israelsen, 2017: 2076). Cornaggia, Cornaggia, and Israelsen (2017: 2076) regard this estimate as "conservative." Also, court cases substantiate the claim that municipality bonds markets are disfavoured. The State of Connecticut settled a lawsuit against rating agencies, and legal representatives of the state declared that "the credit rating agencies and bond insurers have enjoyed enormous profits, at the expense of taxpayers, as a result of this deceptive dual rating system. The harm to taxpayers across the country is real and substantial" (cited in Cornaggia, Cornaggia, and Israelsen, 2017: 2077).

Third and finally, Cestau, Green, and Schürhoff (2013: 593) examine the pricing of so-called Build America Bonds (BABs), a new class of financial asset introduced from April 2009 to December 2010 to give municipal issuers "access to a 'deeper' or 'broader' market." Policymakers' intention was to let municipalities issue a specific class of taxable bonds associated with a tax exemption to attract new types of investors. The bonds issued in the period were worth $145 billion in face value. Unfortunately, BABs were "notoriously illiquid," which resulted in the underpricing of the bonds, and ultimately resulted in "unintended subsidies" that benefited finance industry actors rather than taxpayers (Cestau, Green, and Schürhoff, 2013: 594). Any underpricing of a bond represents a cost of "financial intermediation to the issuers," Cestau, Green, and Schürhoff (2013: 604) write. There may be "money left on the table" due to "inattention by the issuer," or it may represent the market power of so-called underwriters with whom the issuer (i.e. the municipality) collaborates. Finally, underpricing may be understood as a form of compensation to the underwriter and other intermediaries for the "costs of identifying and distributing bonds to the final investors with the highest valuations" (Cestau, Green, and Schürhoff, 2013: 604). Under all conditions, a key policy question is why the issuers, the municipalities acting on behalf of taxpayers, tolerate underpricing and why they "do not bargain more effectively" (Cestau, Green, and Schürhoff, 2013: 595). These issues seem to be in need of theoretical explication as Cestau, Green, and Schürhoff (2013) provide no conclusive answer. In the end, the BAB programme, initiated as a response to the global finance industry crisis and intended to reduce the borrowing cost for municipalities and states, failed to increase the liquidity in the finance market, Cestau, Green, and Schürhoff (2013: 594) conclude.

Under all conditions, the studies of the municipality bond market presented by Schwert (2017); Cornaggia, Cornaggia, and Israelsen (2017); and Cestau, Green, and Schürhoff (2013) demonstrate that municipalities and city governments encounter higher costs than comparable market actors when lending finance capital to fund, for example, housing or infrastructure projects. Financial markets pass on costs derived from estimated default risks, biased credit ratings, or the underpricing of bonds being issued to taxpayers, which increase the costs to finance a renewal of the built environment on the basis of finance market lending. Whether this situation is tolerable for policymakers remains a question to be further explored.

3 "Expanding far beyond home mortgages, Wall Street now securitizes credit card debt, automobile loans, commercial loans, equipment leases, and loans to developing countries," Peterson (2007: 2206) writes. He continues: "Indeed receivables from virtually any income-producing asset can be securitized, including physician and hospital accounts, oil exploration, lawsuit settlement proceeds, entire business ventures, or even baseball stadiums." With this new financial innovation, any asset associated with a projected revenue stream can be translated into a tradable security.

4 Thinly capitalized ventures
Financing science-based innovation in entrepreneurial firms

Introduction

William Baumol's *The Free-Market Innovation Machine* (2002) celebrates competitive capitalism as a superior economic system in terms of its capacity to optimize the use of economic resources and to maximize economic welfare for billions of people. In this account, it is competitive capitalism per se that should be credited for what is a human accomplishment that includes a variety of technical, social, legal, and cultural conditions and institutional changes over the course of the last century. Vogel (2018) provides an alternative account of these accomplishments and changes, and argues that market making and the economic growth that derives therefrom is a matter of statecraft in the advanced and highly differentiated society, and that the sovereign state and its defined agencies and accompanying transnational agencies have played an unambiguous role in creating the advanced contemporary economic system of competitive capitalism. Furthermore, the Baumolian innovation machine would not have been made possible without the cultural and attitudinal changes brought about in the post World War II period, which today penetrate and define a variety of institutional settings. Vallas and Christin (2018: 11) talk about an "entrepreneurial turn" in economic policy, and suggest that an "entrepreneurial discourse has indeed become a ubiquitous feature of the economic landscape for many workers" (Vallas and Christin, 2018: 27). Unfortunately, recent research indicates that entrepreneurship is in decline across the board (e.g. Decker et al., 2014, 2016, 2017), with fewer new businesses being created, and with new businesses now providing fewer new jobs than during previous economic cycles.

This literature sketches a somewhat dissonant image of the economic system of competitive capitalism, which on the one hand maximizes the output on the basis of committed resources, while on the other hand distributes the wealth generated in such economic activities unevenly among participants and other economic agents (Tsui, Enderle, and Jiang, 2018; Scheidel, 2017; Killewald, Pfeffer, and Schachner, 2017; Gilens, 2012; Lysandrou, 2011). Rather than being coincidental or unrelated occurrences, enterprising and entrepreneurial ideologies, economic growth, and economic inequality are likely to be interrelated and co-produced, or at least that proposition is worthy of scholarly inquiries. "[O]n balance, there are more forces in our economic system pushing towards excessive, unjust, or ineffi-cient inequality than there are forces pushing towards excessive equality," Philippon (2019: ix) suggests. The last three decades' almost univocal cele-bration of entrepreneurship and enterprising may for instance have veiled the fact that the expansion of the supply of finance capital in advanced economies (an effect of the liberalization of derivative instruments trade, including the securitization of illiquid holdings, in the period) has not been accompanied by a supply of venture capital in parity with the expanded capital base.

According to elementary mainstream economic theory, mature industries are cash-rich but offer by definition limited high-growth investment oppor-tunities. In that situation, mature industries should return the residual cash to their shareholders (whereof roughly three-fourths are institutional investors, holding stock and other financial assets in their portfolios). Shareholders (and finance capital owners more widely) are motivated by the opportunity to make an above-average return on the money invested, and consequently they are incentivized to reinvest their residual cash in high-growth potential industries, such as knowledge-intensive and innovation-oriented ventures and companies, say, in the life science, biotech, or digital media industries. This is not necessarily the case in the current regime:

> To the extent that we live in a world of rising household income inequality […] it could be argued that the lower marginal propensity to consume at the top of the income pyramid could generate additional savings that then flows into some sort of investment. Yet investment growth is both unusually weak and at historically low levels as a share of GDP.
>
> (Schwartz, 2016: 227)

"Why does the extra saving by higher income households not translate into growth promoting investment?" Schwartz (2016: 227) asks. As, for example, fund managers are compensated on the basis of their ability to maximize the return for fund investors (given a stipulated level of risk), the investment in high-growth potential industries is complicated by the presence of risk man-agement models that discriminate and for large parts exclude investment objects that include non-parametric risk, that is, uncertainty. As most devel-opment work, and in life science ventures which include clinical trials whose outcomes are complicated or even impossible to predict, includes degrees of uncertainty, many of the high-growth potential companies are excluded from investment. That is, they are rated non-investable.

This factual condition leaves economic policymakers with a sizeable problem: if private finance capital owners only insufficiently supply finance capital to support entrepreneurial activities such as start-ups and new business creation, who should then supply additional capital? An alternative perspective on the perceived shortage of venture capital (accounted for in the scholarly literature) is to claim that the supply of enterprising activities seeking venture financing is too large, but such claims are inconsistent with the widespread acclaim of entrepreneurialism in the contemporary economy (see, e.g., Audretch, 2007; Colyvas and Powell, 2007). If the supply of enterprising activities that seek venture financing is deemed justifiable, even being at a desirable level, then the corollary concern is to determine whether it is private capital or tax-funded capital investors (e.g. state-controlled investment funds) that should supply the capital needed. If private capital is targeted, the uncertainty of investment must be complemented by subsidies and tax exemptions to incentivize owners of finance capital to make uncertain investments (in comparison to a reinvestment of the residual cash in, e.g., hedge funds, or some other high-risk/high-return finance asset). If the state and its defined agencies (say, state-controlled investment funds, incubators) that supply finance capital are deemed most suitable for making investments in high-risk ventures (which, e.g., Gilson, 2003, and Lerner, 2009, strongly dispute), then investment vehicles need to be established and carefully monitored. In either case, it is the sovereign state that supplies finance capital to innovative ventures in the absence of risk appetite among private finance capital owners. As opposed to Baumol's (2002) affirmative view of competitive capitalism, in this situation, it is not so much the economic system per se but politically determined decisions that uphold and maintain innovative activities. This casts a shadow of doubt on the nature of the "innovation machine" as a non-governmental franchise.

Given the concerns stipulated above, this chapter examines how the growth and financing of ventures and start-ups, including not the least so-called venture labour, salaried work in thinly capitalized companies that is not fully compensated for increased market risks (Styhre, 2019; Neff, 2013), is dependent on complex collaborative activities between finance capital owners, the finance industry, and the sovereign state. As opposed to the inherited and affirmative view of finance capital owners as the investors of "smart money"—finance capital that generates a return in excess of comparable state-funded investment (Sørensen, 2007; Gompers, Gornall, Kaplan, and Strebulaev, 2019)—the analysis indicates that the presence of uncertainty deters private finance capital investors. Consequently, a market failure situation that can only be handled by the sovereign state, which accommodates a considerable proportion of market risks, is generated. In this view, as indicated by Vogel (2018), "marketcraft" is essentially a responsibility of the sovereign state and transnational agencies that institute, regulate, and monitor markets in advanced competitive capitalism.

The remainder of this chapters unfolds as follows: the first section addresses how there is a perceived endemic shortage of venture capital that can support entrepreneurs and new business, itself being indicative of the inherited expectations on finance capital owners to commit their financial resources to risky and uncertain development work. The second section shifts the focus to the scholarly literature that portrays entrepreneurs as the primus motor of the dynamic capitalist economy, while at the same time turns a blind eye to the venture labour conduced in thinly capitalized new businesses. The third section turns to the question of the role in venture capital for this stock of new businesses, and the literature indicates that qualified and experienced venture capital investors make a material difference when they select the firms wherein they invest. The final sections of the paper discuss theoretical contributions and policy implications.

The endemic shortage of venture capital and the taming of uncertainty

Life science ventures constitute a class of high-growth/high-risk investment objects, which includes the deployment of advanced scientific and technological know-how to create new drugs, therapies, medical technologies, diagnostic tools, and so on. Such innovations all contribute to net welfare as they enable new medical practices, prolong human lives, reduce suffering, or cut healthcare costs in various proportions. Despite being textbook cases of innovation-driven ventures that should attract cash-rich investors, life science ventures remain thinly capitalized on average. Fleming (2015: 273) deplores the decline of venture capital investment in the life sciences, and shows that the finance capital invested in life science companies recently "shrank as a percentage of total investments, from 35.7 percent to 19.9 percent." What is particularly worrisome is that the share of the investment committed to "early-stage investments" such as so-called pre-seed and seed money has been subject to a "dramatic reduction from 62 percent to 45 percent," Fleming (2015: 273) continues. Life science venture capital investment is essentially a "winner-takes-all" business.

A more detailed analysis of the stock of capital that is defined as venture capital reveals that roughly three-fourths of the funds represent buyout capital investments. Harris, Jenkinson, and Kaplan (2014: 1852) demonstrate that "the asset class" that includes buyout funds and venture capital funds have persistently generated higher returns than "public markets" since 1984. Still, of the 70 million euros invested as venture capital, 74 per cent of the finance capital was in buyouts, Deeg (2009: 568) reports. Furthermore, every single investment in buyout activities was relatively sizeable in comparison to the funds committed to, for example, life science ventures, with an average buyout investment in the range of 27 million euros (Deeg, 2009: 568). In other words, in Europe, circa three-fourths of committed "venture capital" fund resources are used to finance buyout activities. This venture capital investment is not primarily committed to the development of new business enterprises, innovations, and other business contributions, but instead targets *existing businesses* with the intention to run them more effectively than the current owners or management team do for the time being. Harris,

Jenkinson, and Kaplan (2014: 1862) demonstrate that the average perform-ance of buyout funds peaked in the mid-1990s, but remained relatively high in the early 2000s. More recently, the situation has changed, and the average venture capital fund has "underperformed public markets by about 5% over the life of the fund" (Harris, Jenkinson, and Kaplan, 2014: 1880–1881). Apparently, investments made in the 1980s and 1990s provided a generous supply of businesses that justified buyout bids, and venture capital investors could harvest what previous generations of less risk-averse business owners and managers had developed over time. More recently, such opportunities are more complicated to detect and buyout investment appears to be less lucrative, potentially caused by previous underinvestment in R&D and human resources (see, e.g., Hall, 1993)

The key issue when it comes to venture capital investment is how to cope with the uncertainty that all investment in start-ups entails. "Investors, analysts, and finance professors can employ a number of comfortably familiar mathematical techniques to value economic ventures that are merely risky. But they have not yet figured out how to deal with uncer-tainty," Belinfanti and Stout (2018: 597) remark. Uncertainty denotes non-parametric risk that cannot be accommodated by risk management models and algorithms, and consequently the assessment of uncertainty is a matter of professional judgment, that is, non-calculative deliberations (Huang, 2018: 1824). Regardless of the supply of venture capital in an economy, and how much effort is invested in turning, for example, academic researchers into entrepreneurs, the supply of capital remains predicated on the capacity of investors to accommodate risks.

The entrepreneurship ideology and venture capital supply

Much of the scholarly literature emphasizes the entrepreneur as a key economic figure that upholds the dynamics of the capitalist mode of production. Baron (2008: 328) defines entrepreneurs as "individuals who recognize and exploit new business opportunities by founding new ventures." Ventures, in turn, denote "privately held entrepreneurial firms with significant external equity investment from professional investors" (Garg, 2013: 90). In Schumpeter's (1928) view, an entrepreneur is by def-inition indebted, running a business that will generate future revenues but only after the ongoing development work has been funded and carried out. To invest in entrepreneurial activities is therefore a bet on a future beset by combinations of risk and uncertainty to a varying degree. Like perhaps no other domain of economic affairs, entrepreneurial activities are subject to fierce competition and a high rate of failure. Furthermore, as Kalecki (1971) notices, it is above all the access to finance capital that sifts out successful entrepreneurs from failed projects:

> Many economists assure, at least in their abstract theories, a state of
> business democracy where anybody endowed with entrepreneurial

ability can obtain capital for starting a business venture. This picture of the activities of the "pure" entrepreneur is, to put it mildly, unrealistic. The most prerequisite for becoming an entrepreneur is the *ownership* of capital.

(Kalecki, 1971: 109; emphasis in the original)

In other words, no matter how promising a business idea may be, and how hard the entrepreneur works to develop a business, unless the entrepreneur is successful in convincing investors about the future revenues derived from the business development activities, the enterprise will not subsist. Furthermore, the entrepreneurship literature (and the popular business literature and press) at times portrays entrepreneurship as a business practice grounded in affective faculties, being essentially a matter of passionate commitment to venturing and business creation, but such romantic images are at best secondary to actual market potential and the quality of firm-specific assets. In fact, as Gielnik et al. (2015: 1017) indicate, "entrepreneurial passion did not predict entrepreneurial effort"; entrepreneurial passion is the mere afterthought of entrepreneurial skills and committed resources. In addition, most of the entrepreneurship literature tends to consider venturing from an entrepreneur-investor relationship perspective, wherein the entrepreneur is a protagonist who seeks the attention and support of presumptive investors (Huang and Knight, 2017: 81). This model also recognizes the investor as a protagonist, even as a patron of entrepreneurship, as, for example, venture capital investors have a track record in examining the commercial potential of new ventures, and thus serve what may be referred to as a curatorial function in selecting businesses to commercially support, and to actively engage with through the firm's governance function, that is, the board of directors (Gompers, Gornall, Kaplan, and Strebulaev, 2020). This bilateral model arguably explains in hindsight why certain businesses become successful, and stages the entrepreneurial function of competitive capitalism as a form of nexus wherein enterprising skills and novel business ideas on the one hand, and finance capital supply on the other, meet and cross-fertilize.

The success of start-ups is measured in terms of job creation (by policymakers and labour market analysts) and the creation of economic value that generate a return on investment for entrepreneurs and investors who hold stocks. Therefore, venture labour (Neff, 2013), salaried work in thinly capitalized ventures, is an important component of the "entrepreneurial culture" that Gilson (2003) calls for. Neff (2013) quotes a series of statements from business promoters and venture capital investors who praise the risk tolerance of individuals who start businesses and conduct salaried work in such firms. "It is to a certain extent in the best interest of venture capitalists to encourage people to keep trying, to not be afraid of failure. We need people to take a chance," Tom Perkins, a partner in a Silicon Valley venture capital firm, Kleiner Perkins Caufield & Byers, says (cited in Neff, 2013: 5). Furthermore, venture workers not only accept or tolerate, even embrace risk, but actively construct entrepreneurial identities for themselves, and make decisions individually for the benefit of the business venture: "I don't want someone who's going to ask, 'What's my job?' I need someone who's going to figure out that on their own," a co-founder of a news website says (cited in Neff, 2013: 18). Venture labour is thus a line of work that on the one hand is expected to be carried out *as if* the venture worker is entitled to future returns from a successful venture capital investor exit, while in fact being undercompensated in terms of the absent risk premium that can be reasonably expected when working in a thinly capitalized firm. The question is still to what extent such firms are in fact thinly capitalized. The extant literature suggests that is in fact the case, which consequently is an important component in the predominant venture capital investment model.

The significance of venture capital investment

Only a very small proportion of all new firms created receive venture capital investment. In a sample that included the 25-year period of 1981–2005, Puri and Zarutskie (2012: 2248) found that on average, 0.11 per cent of all new firms (i.e. a one-in-a-thousand ratio) received venture capital from professional venture capital investors. During the period of swift capital formation and finance market deregulation efforts, in the 1996–2000 period, the ratio doubled to 0.22 per cent (i.e. a two-in-a-thousand ratio), which is arguably still an insignificant proportion of all new firms. Also, Shane (2017: 68. figure 4.1), who otherwise is at pains to convince his readers that American entrepreneurship is in healthy shape, reports that merely 0.83 per cent of all new jobs were created by venture capital-backed companies. That is, one job out of 120 new jobs were created in venture capital-backed firms. Consistent analysis regarding enterprising and entrepreneurial activities provided by Decker and colleagues (2016, 2017, 2018) indicates a similar tendency, that new firm growth is in decline and that fewer new jobs are created by such ventures. At the same time, empirical research indicates that companies that do receive venture capital investment, regardless of their small proportion of the entire pool of new businesses, do perform better on several parameters than non-venture capital-backed companies.

Puri and Zarutskie (2012: 2248) found that the employment generated by venture capital-financed firms accounted for between 5.3 per cent and 7.3 per cent of the employment in the United States during the 2001–2005 period, a considerably higher figure than the 2.7–2.8 per cent of employment in the 1981–1985 period. Regarding economic performance, Kerr, Nanda, and Rhodes-Kropf (2014: 30) examine data from the Thompson Venture Economics database for the 1985–2009 period. The analysis reveals that the chance of return-on-investment in ventures is relatively small as about 55 per cent of the start-ups that received venture capital over this period were terminated at a loss (Kerr, Nanda, and Rhodes-Kropf, 2014: 30). At the same time, 6 per cent of the start-ups were capable of returning more than five times the original investment, and jointly accounted for circa 50 per cent of the gross returns generated over the period (Kerr, Nanda, and Rhodes-Kropf, 2014: 30). Furthermore, Kerr, Nanda, and Rhodes-Kropf (2014: 34) use Census Bureau data for the 1986–1997 period to demonstrate that venture capital-backed companies account for a significantly higher growth of employment vis-à-vis firms with no venture capital backing, a difference of 364 per cent versus 67 per cent of employment growth. Such figures indicate that venture capital investors do a difficult but important job in selecting businesses that generate a return for equity investors, but also generate jobs and, by implication, tax revenues that benefit the state.

Whether venture capital investors are successful in selecting the right firms from the pool of investment objects remains complicated to determine, but the high failure rate in the portfolio of selected companies indicates that the risk tolerance is quite substantial in the investor community, which suggests a relatively liberal selection of investment objects despite small the numbers of selected companies. Under all conditions, the research findings of, for example, Puri and Zarutskie (2012) and Shane (2017) indicate imbalances in the venture capital market, wherein the supply of finance capital is considerably lower than the demand (as suggested by, for example, Fleming, 2015). This results in a situation wherein ventures lead a hand-to-mouth existence wherein venture capital infusions follow capital-raising campaigns that take place whenever the venture is on the verge of becoming insolvent.

Junior stock market financing

The alternative model is that new ventures at an early stage choose to trade their stocks on one of the junior stock markets that are created in North-America (e.g., NASDAQ in the United States and TSXV in Canada) and Europe (e.g. AIM in the United Kingdom, Neuer Markt in Germany, and Le Nouveau Marché in France; Revest and Sapio, 2012). The concern is that, for example, life science companies that need to spend considerable periods of time and resources on development work, now operate within a legal framework wherein they have to commit considerable resources to corporate governance activities and market communication. Furthermore, many investors on junior stock exchanges are so-called naive investors, that is, actors who invest their private surplus equity such as savings, and therefore are easily disappointed whenever the stock market value of their holdings does not grow as fast as they anticipate. Disgruntled naive investors may thus spread negative market information that prevents other investors from committing their finance capital to the venture's development work, and the focal firm therefore needs to communicate extensively with investors to avoid negative market assessment.

As indicated by Birch (2017), many biotech companies delist from junior stock exchanges as this model for raising finance capital is inconsistent with their long-term needs, and because this financing model induces costs in excess of the benefits. One venture capital investor recognized this concern: "Well, a lot [of companies] will delist because they're not raising the money, it might be finding the corporate governance and the reporting requirements too onerous, too restrictive, too difficult, and too threatening" (cited in Birch, 2017: 478). Another indication of thinly capitalized life science ventures is that comparably fewer firms conduct clinical trials today in comparison to the past, simply because this is too costly and associated with sizeable high market risks as the outcome from clinical trials are complicated to predict on the basis of either in vivo or in vitro studies (Birch, 2017: 481). When the private equity market recedes, arguably a matter of the difficulties involved in calculating risk when investing in ventures that include uncertainties of various kinds, the state remains the investor of last resort, a model that qualified commentators believe is inefficient and sub-optimal as state officials, first, lack incentives to generate economic returns, and, second, tend to combine political and economic objectives in ways that are detrimental to firm growth:

> [I]t is a poor idea for government to seek to pick and promote individual firms. After all, even the most-experienced venture capital firms have substantial success in only one of every ten investments they pick, so we shouldn't expect inexperienced and possibly not-very-objective politicians to do better.
>
> (Kerr, Nanda, and Rhodes-Kropf, 2014: 43)

In this situation, there are macroeconomic implications from the unwillingness among finance capital owners to commit resources to new ventures, especially in uncertain life science start-ups.

The state as the venture capital market maker: some concerns

As a matter of fact, there is considerable evidence of the state acting as a de facto venture capital investor and with favourable outcomes in terms of economic growth. For instance, Conti (2018), Howell (2017), and Keller and Block (2013) account for how various state initiatives to support early-stage development work in new ventures are conducive to economic growth. More specifically, these studies indicate that state initiatives are complementary to private equity investment inasmuch as, for example, R&D grants may serve to verify certain innovation concepts so that the threshold is lowered for venture capital investors. In this view, the state productively contributes to innovation-led growth and a dynamic economic system.

An alternative view of state-financed initiatives is to consider the scenario wherein such funds are no longer supplied, and markets are exclusively assigned the role to supply finance capital to enterprising activities. In this scenario, it is important to recognize alternative investment opportunities that private equity holders examine. The foremost investment opportunity is to reinvest the residual cash generated on the basis of stock ownership in mature industries in the finance industry itself. The deregulatory policy of the last three decades in the United States and in Europe was intended to promote capital formation, which would result in a lower cost to acquire capital and therefore be supportive of increased entrepreneurial activity. One of the key mechanisms intended to serve this end is considerably more liberal legislation pertaining to securitization, wherein the cost for transforming illiquid asset holdings into tradeable assets is lowered (Shin, 2009). Given these stated policy objectives, the current situation wherein ventures suffer from an endemic shortage of venture capital supply, and this despite the sharp growth in the monetary base on various levels of analysis, is disappointing. Whereas, for instance, thinly capitalized banks can borrow money on easy terms during the upward turn of the business cycle (Adrian, Kiff, and Shin, 2018: 7), which increase the inflow of finance market actors and thickens finance markets, it remains complicated for equally thinly capitalized ventures to acquire even considerably lower amounts of finance capital to continue their development work.

Investment opportunities that attract residual capital

The legislative reforms and new deregulatory policy thus created a situation wherein the expansion of the finance industry and the monetary base fail to substantially increase the stock of operational venture capital. A critical commentator may then inquire where the surplus capital generated is channelled? The first immediate response to the collapse of the sub-prime mortgage market in 2007–2008 was investment in commodities trade, which resulted in a spike in the price of certain commodities (Williams and Cook, 2016; Sockin and Xiong, 2015; Tang and Xiong, 2012; Mayer, 2012; Nissanke, 2012). For instance, between 2007 and 2012, the volatility in oil prices was "exponentially greater" than during previous episodes of oil shocks, for example, the 1973 Organization of Petroleum Exporting Countries (OPEC) oil embargo, the 1979 Iranian revolution, and the 1990–1991 Persian Gulf war, Greenberger (2013: 709) writes. During this period, economist Mike Norman asserts (cited in Greenberger, 2013: 722), "oil prices are high because of speculation, pure and simple. That's not an assertion, that's a fact." More recently, there is evidence that hedge funds, providing first-rate high-risk/high-return investment, have grown considerably in size and number. Hedge funds are notorious for their "confrontational approach" as fund managers seek to extract residual cash from companies that have "sound operating cash flows and returns on assets, typically have a low share price relative to book value and low dividend payout ratios" (Cheffins and Armour, 2011: 57). The demand for hedge fund investment indicates that the appetite for high risk (as opposed to uncertainty of any kind) may be considerable among investors. By the early 1990s, there were around 300 hedge funds, managing assets worth US$40 billion. By 1998, less than a decade later, these figures had grown almost tenfold. In 2006, there were more than 8,000 hedge funds, holding more than US$1 trillion in assets (Cheffins and Armour, 2011: 79, 88). Lysandrou (2018: 55) reports that the aggregated hedge fund assets being managed "more than tripled between 2002 and 2007," rising from US$600 billion to about US$2.2 trillion, while "the number of firms operating within the industry" doubled from circa 5,000 to 10,000 in the same period.

Furthermore, finance capital has been invested in tax havens. "The global rich," Palan, Murphy, and Chavagneux (2010: 5) write, "held in 2007 approximately $12 trillion of their wealth in tax havens. It is as if the entire U.S. annual GNP were parked in tax havens." The transfer of capital funds to these jurisdictions is also a direct consequence of changes in the global financial system. For instance, when the American sub-prime mortgage market became moribund in the 2007–2008 period, funds were transferred to, for example, Switzerland: between 2009 and early 2015, the total amount of foreign wealth managed in Switzerland "has increased by 18%" (Zucman, 2015: 60).[1] Alstadsæter, Johannesen, and Zucman (2019: 2074) examine data from the "Swiss Leaks" and "Panama Papers" in combination with tax amnesties conducted in the aftermath of the financial crisis of 2008–2009 for the three Scandinavian countries of Denmark, Norway, and Sweden. Without tax evasion activities, the top 0.01 per cent richest Scandinavians would have on average a marginal tax of 49 per cent in 2006, and on average the top 0.1 per cent would pay about 45 per cent of their income in taxes. In practice, when considering tax evasion efforts, the top 0.01 per cent of households effectively paid taxes at the level of 35 per cent. "[T]ax evasion erodes the progressivity of the tax system, and, accordingly to our estimates, makes it regressive at the top," Alstadsæter, Johannesen, and Zucman (2019: 2099) say, in summarizing their results. Furthermore, while the Scandinavian countries are commonly portrayed as ranking high regarding respect for the rule of law and with the highest "tax morale" (Alstadsæter, Johannesen, and Zucman, 2019: 2075), it is likely that tax evasion is even higher in other countries and regions. It is noteworthy that regressive tax systems are today implementing fiscal policies in, for example, the United States, wherein in 2018, for the first time in a hundred years, the "top 400 richest Americans have paid lower taxes than the working class" (Saez and Zucman, 2019: 22). Such empirical evidence regarding the magnitude of tax evasion in especially the top 0.01 per cent income groups is indicative of finance capital owners reinvesting their residual cash in various finance asset classes, but preferably not in new ventures. Expressed differently, the traditional role of capital owners as investors in production capital is abandoned and left for others to handle.

Rentier interests exclude uncertain investments

"[M]ore than 60 percent of the labor force in the United States is engaged in activities in the 'information sector' in the economy [...] This sector includes the processing, recording, analysis, and dissemination of information," Baumol (2002: 2) remarks, to indicate that the contemporary economy is primarily based on know-how and other intangible assets that are complicated to price, and whose outcome may be difficult to anticipate or to value ex ante. Such celebrative accounts of the new innovation-led economic regime and the role of the entrepreneurial turn in economic policy (Vallas and Christin, 2018: 11) are well-known themes in the business press and in the scholarly literature. Yet studies of actual activities in these sectors of the economy reveal a situation wherein rentier interests are in many cases prioritized over entrepreneurial activities. As Garg (2013: 90) points out, a venture is a closely held entrepreneurial firm with "significant external equity investment from professional investors." According to Schumpeter (1928), entrepreneurship means debt, that is, to operate in collaboration with finance capital owners to develop a business activity. Unfortunately, empirical evidence demonstrates that entrepreneurial activities are in decline in the United States: "Startup rates and other measures of young firm activity have declined since the 1980s, with accelerated slowdowns in high-growth young firm activity since 2000" (Decker, Haltiwanger, Jarmin, and Miranda, 2017: 322). Based on such data, Decker, Haltiwanger, Jarmin, and Miranda (2014: 18) deduce that "[i]ncentives to start new businesses appear to be declining in all sectors." The last three decades' strong emphasis on enterprising and entrepreneurship in economic policy, in scholarly research, and in popular culture thus coincides with a discordant trend, an entrepreneurial culture in decline. The question is, what mechanisms that triggered this situation?

Several commentators indicate that institutional, legal, and regulatory changes in the global economic system have resulted in what Larry Summers (2014: 67) refers to as "a significant shift in the natural balance between savings and investment." The 1970s advocacy of an inflation-targeting ("price stability") economic policy, preferably orchestrated on the basis of independent central banks that act outside of the political system, has resulted in a low-inflation situation in advanced economies (see, e.g., Wansleben, 2018). This in turn has led to a downward shift in what Summers (2014) calls "the normal real rate of interest." The inflation-targeting economic policy in combination with finance market reforms fuelled an expansion of finance industry trading, especially after 2000, which ultimately has made investment in entrepreneurial firms unattractive as it includes unruly uncertainties that cannot be accommodated by existing risk management models. Decker, Haltiwanger, Jarmin, and Miranda (2016: 21) summarize the argument in favour of finance capital investment in entrepreneurial activities:

> Aggregate productivity growth depends not only on innovations and technology investments within firms but also on the economy's ability to reallocate resources from businesses with lower productivity to businesses with higher productivity. Evidence suggests that young firms

devote disproportionately more resources to innovation, so the high growth of young firms is particularly important for aggregate productivity growth.

A finance industry that primarily expands its trading activities on the basis of innovations such as first- and second-level derivative instruments, for example, CDOs and other complicated-to-price assets, acts through hedge funds to extract additional residual cash from competently managed and sound companies, and that no longer serves to transfer surplus capital to new and expanding businesses, is at risk to undermine the incentives to start new businesses. As previously shown, Hockett and Omarova (2016: 1214) use the term *financialization* to denote the situation wherein the finance industry fails to allocate finance capital so that the economy's full production capacity is utilized. In this view, the "logic of financialization" reflects a situation wherein financial institutions

> find it more profitable to channel credit toward markets in financial instruments, in which they have significant informational and institutional advantages, than toward real-economy projects with long-term payoffs that depend on a variety of macroeconomic factors these financial institutions cannot control.
>
> (Hockett and Omarova, 2016: 1215)

This "flight from uncertainty" is indicative of a rentier-led economy wherein the finance industry starves the non-financial economy (and its entrepreneurial activities in particular) of cash, which over time reduces the rate of renewal and growth of the economy.

The current situation demands attention from policymakers and scholarly communities alike, and indicates a need for new economic policies that incentivize finance capital owners to channel their surplus capital to new ventures. Alternatively, the sovereign state can expand and deepen its venture capital investment activities on the basis of tax-money income (which several commentators advise against, arguably for good reasons). In either situation, there is a need for reforms and new economic models and policies that incentivize finance capital owners to commit their resources to business venturing.

Summary and conclusion

To actively maintain competitive capitalism as the "free-market innovation machine" that Baumol (2002) envisages, new economic policies, new economic models, and new economic doctrines need to be developed and implemented, and preferably soon enough. The deregulatory advocacy that dominated until the finance industry crisis of 2008, embodied by the Federal Reserve chairman Alan Greenspan, was justified by the scenario wherein the lower cost and abundant supply of finance capital would benefit all constituencies. Unfortunately, the unintended consequence of such campaigns was to promote a rentier economy that pushed down "the normal real rate of interest" and largely abandoned investment in entrepreneurial activities as a finance capital owner's virtue and responsibility.

Note

1 Recent shifts in international policy have pressured traditional tax havens to disclose information so taxes can be collected in the domicile of overseas tax-haven account holders. This has resulted in changes in how taxes are evaded. For instance, South Dakota, a prairie state with fewer than 900,000 inhabitants, has become the site *par préférence* for so-called *perpetual trusts* or *dynasty trusts*. South Dakota has no income tax, no inheritance tax, and no capital gains tax, and state law protects the interests of nonresident and, increasingly, overseas clients. In 2014, South Dakota hosted trusts that managed funds worth $226 billion (up from $32.8 billion in 2006) (Scannell and Houlder, 2016), and by 2019, the value of the trusts stood at $335.2 billion (Bullough, 2019). Dukeminier and Krier (2002: 1304) argue that what is called "the Rule against Perpetuities" in common law prescribes that funds created by an individual to protect his or her financial interests must be dissolved within 21 years after the demise of the individual. However, US states such as South Dakota, Delaware, Alaska, and Nevada have passed state laws that encircle the Rule against Perpetuities to promote a thriving local financial services industry. This state legislation, protected by federal law, runs counter to the claim once made by Alexander Hamilton (cited in Dukeminier and Krier, 2002: 1324–1325) that "We do not want a large leisure class in this country; we want to give people an incentive to work." Dukeminier and Krier (2002: 1316) explain how the South Dakota financial services industry, seated in the state capital of Sioux Falls, now provides full protection against tax authorities in various countries and US states:

> One South Dakota trust company now offers dynasty trusts fashioned to provide maximum flexibility to nonresident clients. They are welcome to have their trusts drafted elsewhere, overseen by their own out-of-state investment managers, and so on, but the trusts have their situs in South Dakota. Books and records are kept in South Dakota, trades are executed there, trust administration is provided by the local trust company. These are sufficient contacts to qualify the trusts for the benefits of South Dakota law.
>
> (Dukeminier and Krier, 2002: 1316)

States like New York have complained about both the loss of billions of dollars to "trust-friendly states" and the leakage of income tax, estimated to be in the range of $150 million in 2013 alone (Scannell and Houlder, 2016). More generally, it has been estimated that $7.6 trillion is kept in tax havens globally, which translates into at least a global loss of annual tax income of $200 billion (Scannell and Houlder, 2016). "The protection offered by states such as South Dakota are undermining global attempts to control tax dodging, kleptocracy, and money-laundering," Bullough (2019) argues. Needless to say, South Dakota financial services representatives think otherwise and regard their work as what protects clients' interests on the basis of state law and what enables economic security for future generations of trust beneficiaries. Regardless of the more perfidious consequences of, for example, South Dakota legislation that Bullough (2019) points out, legal scholars and experts argue that perpetual trusts or dynasty trusts will eventually become very difficult to manage as there will be "tens of thousands of beneficiaries" in the future, which would even make it difficult to arrange the annual meetings being prescribed by law. In this view, what Dukeminier and Krier (2002: 1316) refer to as "the fall of the Rule against Perpetuities," and the "rise of the perpetual trust" may be beneficial for a handful of local financial service industry actors in states such as South Dakota, Nevada, and Alaska, but impose costs on everyone else as the Cayman Islands, Panama, and the English Channel islands are no longer the primary tax havens when they are subject to legal and regulatory reform, and when the jurisdictions in the American heartland take their place. At the same time, local financial service providers may eventually have difficulties protecting themselves against international competitors. For instance, in 2014, a Swiss trust company opened an office in Sioux Falls to take advantage of the liberal legislation, very much to the discontent of local agents (Scannell and Houlder, 2016).

5 The institutional logic of the finance-led economy

Introduction

> L'espirit de moderation doit être celui du legislateur; le bien politique, comme le bien moral, se trouve toujours entre deux limites.
>
> Montesquieu (1788b: 1)

A popular story from the Hellenic period, arguably a piece of consolation for scholars who believe their work is underappreciated, King Dionysos once asked Diogenes, a renowned philosopher of the Cynic school, why philosophers come to knock on rich men's doors, while the rich do not come to those of philosophers? "Because philosophers know what they have need of, while the rich do not," Diogenes (2012: 136) responded. Part of wisdom is being able to value the access to money and other material resources, but a bountiful supply of monetary means does not of necessity translate into an understanding of the value of other, non-pecuniary resources. Regardless of such ancient exchanges, the relation between wisdom and knowledge, on the one hand, and economic wealth and welfare on the other, does not need to be disjointed, as Diogenes suggested. Know-how and expertise, albeit of a specific kind, are integral to economic affairs and business ventures. This final chapter will address some of the issues pertaining to this foundational relationship, especially accentuated in the contemporary economy wherein roughly 80 per cent of the economic value of public corporations consists of intangible assets (Haskel and Westlake, 2017; Brynjolfsson and Saunders, 2010; Pagano and Rossi, 2009: 670. figure 2.). However, when paying attention to the details of the finance-led economic system, it is possible to observe that what from afar may appear to belong to a similar class of objects (say risk, liquid assets, collateral) may display marked differences upon closer inspection, which indicates that what may appear to be unworthy of closer scholarly or regulatory inquiries during, for instance, the upward movement of the business cycle may in fact play a major difference in the succeeding downward phase. This means that species of, for example, finance market trade do in fact reveal considerably differences during, for instance, episodes of finance market liquidity contractions.

Such evidence indicates that the regulatory control of finance markets, characterized by a high degree of innovation such as new asset classes that are essentially illiquid, that is, are costly and/or complicated to price, especially in the absence of long-term price series, is a non-trivial assignment. To better address such regulatory challenges, a broader historical and institutional perspective on finance industry trade will be taken, so that for, instance, the question regarding rentier returns versus entrepreneurial and innovation-led growth is examined as a question pertaining to the finance-led economy. The end of the chapter summarizes the key contributions of the volume and points at further scholarly projects to be pursued and some of the regulatory and legislative implications.

The institutional logic of the finance industry

Institutional theory is a widespread and cross-disciplinary analytical framework that includes the concept of *institutional logic*. Friedlander and Alford's (1991: 248) much-cited paper defines "logic" (the description "institutional" is already implied in the term) as a "set of material practices and symbolic constructions." A rich literature has applied this term to shed light on practical work in a variety of settings. The various definitions that are provided in the literature include a number of concepts and constructs, and there is both consistency and variation in the use of the term. Thornton (2002: 82) says that institutional logic defines "the norms, values, and beliefs that structure the cognition of actors in organizations and provide a collective understanding of how strategic interests and decisions are formulated." This definition underlines the cognitive dimension, both individual and collective, of the dominant institutional logic; the institutional logic shapes the cognition, and hence the perception and other sense impressions, of actors. Reay and Hinings (2009) and Dunn and Jones (2010) in turn underline the cultural element of institutional logic, and speak about how taken-for-granted rules (Reay and Hinings, 2009: 629) and cultural beliefs (Dunn and Jones, 2010: 114) shape the cognition of actors. Such "belief systems and associated practices"—the institutional logic rendered manifest—"define the content and meaning of institutions," Reay and Hinings (2009: 631) say. The concept of institutional logic has been used to study science and research policy (Berman, 2012) and policymaking more broadly (Nigam and Ocasio, 2010), in studies of health practices and organizations (Goodrick and Reay, 2011; Dunn and Jones, 2010), and in studies of changes in professionalism (Lander, Koene, and Linssen, 2013; Meyer and Hammerschmid, 2006) or unionism (Martin, 2008). Furthermore, the concept of institutional logic has been applied in more analytical examinations of, for example, commensuration practices such as ranking and rating practices (Zhou, 2005) or identity work (Pache and Santos, 2013; Lok, 2011). Finally, and of relevance for this context, institutional theory has informed studies of finance industry and finance institutions, such as in the case of Yan, Ferraro, and Almandoz's (2019) study of socially responsible investment, the study of the risk exposure of banks (Almandoz, 2014), or the increased emphasis on financial objectives in the construction and real estate industries (Bryan, Rafferty, Toner, and Wright, 2017). These studies reveal that agents tend to consider a "financial logic" as being a set of guiding principles, norms, and beliefs that structure day-to-day work and decision-making.

Almandoz (2014: 458) reports that members of the board of banks who were more prone to act in accordance with a "financial logic" rather than the alternative, "community logic," were more risk tolerant and accepted "risky deposits" to a higher degree. Yan, Ferraro, and Almandoz's (2019: 473) study of socially responsible investment (SRI) professionals demonstrates a "a great deal of resistance toward SRI coming from actors deeply embedded in the financial logic." This unwillingness to accept the SRI framework was partially explained by the epistemic difficulties these professionals encountered when they could no longer use an unambiguous measure—that of return-on-investment ratios, unmediated by measures of the degree of "social responsibility" taken in their portfolios and holdings—for how well they performed in comparison to other investors. Third and finally, Bryan, Rafferty, Toner, and Wright (2017: 502) argue that the construction and real estate industries now display "a financial logic of risk and risk shifting," wherein the possibilities for high returns on investment objects are recognized in more favourable terms than they used to be. Seen in this view, the finance industry and "financialized" non-financial industries adhere to and reproduce a certain set of "norms, values, and beliefs" (Thornton, 2002: 82) that are consistent with finance theory descriptions of ideal finance markets and their calculative practices. The institutional logic of the finance-led economy therefore represents a departure from, perhaps even a rupture with, previous institutional logics. In the following sections, three consequences of the institutional logic of the finance-led economy are examined: (1) how rentier interests tend to overshadow those of entrepreneurs and enterprising activities in need of finance capital; (2) how the difficulty of regulating the finance industry and global finance markets increases; and (3) how policy-making that renders credit supply as social provision is no longer possible to maintain as a larger proportion of, for example, the US population and households is excluded from the credit supply circuit.

Rentier interests and the entrepreneurial function

Joseph Schumpeter ([1928] 1991: 201) identifies "the rentier class" as one among six social classes in the differentiated society. As opposed to the two classes of workers and the "professional" and the "clerical class," the rentier is not equally dependent on salaried work as the rentier holds assets that generate a projected return. Several commentators have associated the rentier with "passivity" as the income the rentier lives off of is not directly dependent on the rentier's active engagement (even though rentier returns may be dependent on selling off and acquiring new assets, which demands active decision-making and money management). This activity–passivity continuum does in many cases play a role in defining the rentier more formally. Robinson (1966: 247) uses the term *rentier* in an "extended sense," that is, "to represent capitalists in their aspects as owners of wealth, as opposed to their aspect as entrepreneurs." The rentier make an income on the basis of "dividends as well as payments of interest," whereas the entrepreneur runs his or her own business (Robinson, 1966: 247). The concern for Robinson is that the entrepreneur as a specific species in the economic system generates new businesses, but such business creation activities demand finance capital. That is, the entrepreneur is by definition indebted. Rentiers, who acquire a surplus on the basis of their asset holdings, thus need to transfer their surplus finance capital to entrepreneurs so that the next generation of profit-generating companies can emerge. "To maintain a steady state of accumulation over the long run it is necessary that the ratio of rentier saving to profits should not be rising," Robinson (1966: 276) says. To be willing to commit surplus finance capital to business ventures in an expansive stage, the rentier surveys the entire economic field and examines the current situation, and increased uncertainty results in higher interests, which reduce the willingness to invest in entrepreneurial ventures as rentiers have a stipulated preference for holding wealth "in a liquid form" (Robinson, 1966: 277). The entrepreneurial function of the capitalist economy is therefore dependent on both macroeconomic stability that reduces the impact of the liquidity preference, and that rentiers have positive expectations regarding projected returns of the pool of available entrepreneurial business ventures that seek financing.

The impact of rentier interests in the economy has been debated over the decades. John Maynard Keynes (1953: 376) took a sanguine view of the rentier's role in the economic system, and stated that "[t]he rentier aspect of capitalism [is] a transitional phase which will disappear when it has done its work." More recent commentators are more concerned that the rentier has been revised and reintroduced under the label of shareholder primacy governance, the predominant idea advocated since the mid-1970s that shareholders are the "residual claimants" of the corporation, and that they consequently are entitled to the residual cash that the corporation they hold shares in generates on an annual basis (that is, if the firm is run at a profit). For commentators who are critical of this idea, the shareholder primacy governance model is a form of an upgraded version of rentier claims. Roberts and Kwon (2017: 517) propose that financialization denotes a situation wherein "the social pact between capital and labor" is transformed in ways that redistribute income to "elite financial actors," such as mutual funds or hedge funds, These "elite" actors have as their main purpose to "to increase the rentier income of affluent households," but at the expense of "production-based workers and less-affluent households." In a similar vein, Tomaskovic-Devey, Lin, and Meyers (2015: 542) portray the "shareholder value movement" as a campaign that actively encourages corporate decision makers to "replace equity with debt and to reduce employment." By replacing equity with debt, corporations boost the return-on-equity ratio, which finance market analysts may regard as an indication of a commitment to serve shareholder interests. Combined with increased repurchase announcements and actual stock repurchases, more frequent in the 1990s (Chan, Ikenberry, Lee, and Wang, 2010; Baker, Powell, and Veit, 2003; Kahle, 2002; Westphal and Zajac, 2001; Grullon and Ikenberry, 2000), shareholders were further compensated as stock prices inflated.[1] Reduction in employment, referred to as "downsizing" in the new managerial vocabulary, serves to push down labour costs directly and indirectly as fewer blue-collar jobs are available. Studies show that the announcement of downsizing activities is associated with higher executive compensation (Jung, 2016: 362), which indicates that executives are incentivized, through their compensation packages, to attend carefully to market evaluations of the company's stock. The welfare of shareholders has been primarily produced on the basis of the loss of income and benefits of labour, not on the basis of some realization of some previously unexploited resources or synergies, a sizeable literature suggests. "Income inequality has resulted primarily from the shift in the balance of power toward rentiers and away from workers," Van Arnum and Naples (2013: 1177) say. Taken together, for the critics of the shareholder primacy governance model, the corporate system's willingness to commit to rentier interests generates considerable externalities:

> [T]he shareholder value movement produced a perverse set of incentives to reduce total production and perhaps in the long-run total profit, while boosting stock prices and dividend payments on the remaining equity. Our results suggest that financial investment strategies, in concert with the shareholder value movement and CEO compensation strategies reduced the long-term value of the non-finance corporate sector and transferred income to financial service firms and rentier capital in general.
>
> (Tomaskovic-Devey, Lin, and Meyers, 2015: 542)

It is important to notice that the critique of shareholder value does not only centre on the redistribution of wealth from labour to shareholders and rentiers as additional externalities are addressed. From a regulatory perspective, the key concern is that a rentier-oriented finance industry, propelled by the shareholder primacy governance model that transfers economic wealth from non-financial corporations to finance institutions, tends to display a tendency towards volatility and increased systemic risk: "[T]he more 'shareholder friendly' the firm's corporate governance system, the less attention is likely to be paid to externalities, and the greater the exposure to volatility and systemic risk," Coffee (2011: 807) writes. Ireland (2010: 852) explicitly states that the rentier-oriented finance industry is characterized by a series of undesirable behaviours and conditions, which includes "a massive increase in speculative financial exchanges, regular financial crises, numerous corporate scandals, falling growth rates, a reduction in the rates of productivity growth and soaring executive remuneration." Deutschmann (2011: 383) argues that the liquidity preference of rentier investors, in combination with a sharply raised supply of new financial asset classes to invest in, makes it unattractive for the rentier to commit finance capital to entrepreneurial businesses, which are deemed to be too uncertain, and that yield a return only after a considerable period of time. Consequently, rentiers reinvest surplus finance capital in the finance industry itself, which has grown considerably in volume over the last decades: "Confronted with the lack of primary investment opportunities in the real economy, the financial industry invented secondary (and tertiary etc.) investment opportunities in the financial sphere itself" (Deutschmann, 2011: 383).

In hindsight, Keynes's assertion that the rentier would soon become a marginal figure in the economic system appears to be mistaken, several commentators write. Deutschmann (2011: 382) speaks explicitly about a mismatch between rentier and entrepreneur interests:

> There is considerable evidence that the mature economies of Western capitalism are faced with a growing general mismatch between rent seeking financial assets on the one hand, and declining real investment opportunities on the other. What lies behind the phenomenon of financialization is the actual transformation of advanced capitalism into a rentier society, where the private asset holder has become dominant over the entrepreneur.

In addition to an endemic shortage of finance capital supply for entrepreneurial companies—the advancement of the shareholder primacy governance model coincided with the massive campaign to promote entrepreneurship as the primus motor of the economy in the 1990s —and increased systemic risk in the finance industry (two conditions that should be a concern for intellectual rentiers, being concerned about the resilience of the capitalist economic system), the current system has resulted in increased economic inequality (an issue that rentiers cannot be assumed to be immediately concerned with, but still being an issue for political entities and various interest groups). Flaherty (2015: 434) names the combination of "banking liberalization" (including two major pieces of legislation in the United States in 1999 and 2000, which resulted in the repeal of the Glass-Steagall Act, a primary piece of New Deal legislation) and "weak governance" as the primary causes of the current situation wherein "the scope of rentier income streams" has been enhanced. If the socio-economic consequences of the rentier-oriented and finance-led economy can be left to the side for the time being (which does not indicate that it is not relevant), the lingering question is how to determine the resilience of the current economic system. That is, issues such as increased systemic risk and the consequences of long-term underinvestment in entrepreneurial projects need to be examined. The tendency to reinvest surplus finance capital in increasingly complex finance assets cannot expand infinitely, as systemic risk grows and as return on finance assets demand high-quality collateral at some point, these issues are a rentier concern regardless of the evidence of soaring economic inequality, which per se may undermine the legitimacy of the current economic system and result in the radicalization of groups who believe they are disadvantaged by the current distribution of economic resources.

Given the difficulty to monitor rentier activities and the influence of rentier interest in day-to-day finance industry trade, it is possible to sketch two future scenarios in the finance-led economy. The first scenario is market oriented and further extends the possibility to introduce new finance asset classes in new domains of the economy. The second scenario increases the regulatory control of the finance industry insofar as central banks are assigned the role to not only optimize the efficiency of the credit formation process, but also consider finance market stability (measured, inter alia, in terms of the degree of systemic risk) as a regulatory objective. Political entities may of course chose a combination of these scenarios, but for the sake of didactic purposes, the two scenarios are presented below as if they were mutually exclusive. In either way, political entities and their representatives may pay increased attention to the question of growing economic inequality and instability in the finance industry in the future, which calls for new thinking in terms of how the finance-led economy should be regulated.

The difficulty to regulate the finance industry towards welfare ends: the case of social impact bonds (SIBs)

In addition to the concern regarding how to balance rentier interests and the interests of entrepreneurs and business promoters, and the question of how to monitor and keep systemic risk at the level where a system-wide finance industry collapse is avoided, there are questions related to how the political system and its legislative and regulatory branches can possibly use the finance industry to achieve welfare goals enacted by democratically elected assemblies. This concern includes two basic issues: (1) how to determine preferences of subjects (citizens), and (2) how to maintain de facto regulatory control over the finance industry. Awrey (2012) discusses the former issue, and proposes that outside of paternalist or neo-paternalist regimes, which would simply stipulate desirable outcomes on the basis of authoritative beliefs, it is complicated to determine both the interests and the preferences of subjects. In addition, even if such information were possible to acquire at a reasonable cost, predictions about the future are complicated to make, which further obscures the possibility for formulating a "social welfare function" that regulatory agencies could use as a guideline for their operation:

Regulators cannot directly observe the preferences of their constituents, nor do they have any practical means of aggregating these preferences into a social welfare function. Simultaneously, they possess imperfect knowledge of (exogenous) future events and the (endogenous) welfare consequences of their policy choices.

(Awrey, 2012: 276)

Furthermore, Blair (2013) points out another complication, which is that even if such social welfare functions were possible to formulate on the basis of available data, regulatory agencies have fewer opportunities these days to actively shape business decisions in the finance industry as many of the transactions are located to the shadow banking system, formally outside of the sovereign state's bank regulation system:

The Federal Reserve, which is the governmental body that is supposed to control the flow of money and credit in the economy in order to promote economic activity while keeping inflation under control, actually has much less influence over the supply of money and credit than it has had historically, except through its influence on interest rates. A substantial part of money creation is now in the hands of the private sector.

(Blair, 2013: 434)

In many cases, it is not so much political entities and regulatory agencies that drive the development of the finance industry towards social and economic welfare goals, as it is the finance industry itself on the basis of its capacity to continuously introduce new financial assets that maintain the upper hand. One such case that is illustrative of finance industry inventiveness is the use of so-called social impact bonds (SIBs), a finance instrument that is designed to supply finance capital to social services and to assist welfare objectives. Whether the use of SIBs is an efficient and potentially game-changing use of the finance industry's ability to employ calculative practice to benefit welfare objectives, or a cynical use of the powers of the finance industry to colonialize also the sovereign state's welfare sector, is currently debated. For instance, Block and Somers (2014: 156) argue that attempts to "privatize and voucherize" social security have been unpopular, simply because the long-term consequences of such alliances between the sovereign state's welfare sector and the rent-seeking finance industry are complicated to overview. Before such judgements can be passed, the mechanisms of the financing model need to be described in some detail.

Empirical studies of SIB financing

Warner (2013: 303) says that SIBs represent a new form of finance device, being "a form of outcomes-based contract between public or nonprofit service providers and private investors." The contract stipulates that a "private financier" provides "upfront funding for interventions to improve specific targeted social outcomes" (Warner, 2013: 303). The SIB contract operates over a fixed period of time, but does not guarantee a fixed rate of return. In theory, the SIB device enables government to reduce the cost for social welfare carried by taxpayers as the financial risk is formally transferred to the private sector (Warner, 2013: 303). Whether this is de facto the case when all costs are included is less clear and consequently subject to discussion. SIBs have been used to handle social issues such as "homelessness, juvenile delinquency, prisoner re-entry, and early childhood education" (Warner, 2013: 304),[2] areas wherein the sovereign state assumes a responsibility but nonetheless tends to "underinvest in prevention," and instead pay for "remediation once the social problem becomes clear" (Warner, 2013: 304). Rather than investing in social welfare activities *after the fact*, when social problems have been observed and documented, the SIB device is intended to serve as a precautionary measure, which also, its proponents claim, may have a positive pay-off for the investor. For critics, this use of a finance industry device to handle social welfare responsibilities involves a long series of concerns, which includes, for example, a "serious under-pricing of public assets" (Warner, 2013: 308). That is, in order to make SIBs generate a return on investment, considerable costs related to, for example, prisoner re-entry programmes must be left outside of the calculative practices. That is, the issuer of SIBs can generate a return but externalize the additional costs so that taxpayers still have to fund the welfare activities, while it still involves an actor with access to the money and capital markets, and who can extract rent also on social welfare initiatives. In such a situation, the sovereign state creates a new market for finance industry investors, whereas the net economic welfare may not necessarily be positively affected. In fact, critics worry that the finance industry can use new classes of financial assets to extract finance capital from the sovereign state, which thus transfers resources from welfare activities to private businesses, notably already subsidized and insured by the state.

Cooper, Graham, and Himick (2016: 67) examine the use of SIBs in the UK welfare system, and review a handful of initiatives wherein SIB investment has been applied. In 2010, 3,000 short-term prisoners released from the Peterborough prison were supported by SIBs. The return for investors was calculated on the basis of the cost to avoid recidivism, that is, a form of "negative return" derived from a stipulated cost that would never be incurred in the case wherein the former inmate acquired a regular job and avoided future prison sentences. The SIB model was thus based on a "pay-for-performance contract" wherein the former inmates' self-discipline and capacity to digress from a criminal career was the primary mechanism for determining the "success" of the investment model. By its design, the SIB included a number of actors and contracts, that is, "a commissioner or government department," the "delivery agency or agencies," which could be charities, and "investor(s)" (Cooper, Graham, and Himick, 2016: 67).

Cooper, Graham, and Himick (2016: 67) remark that the UK government expressed great enthusiasm over the prospect of using SIB on a regular basis, and the minister for civil society issued a press release wherein the SIB device was portrayed as a "radical approach to solving complex and costly social problems." Unsurprisingly, this enthusiasm was shared by finance industry actors, always pushing for the creation of new market segments within the realm of the responsibilities of the welfare state. Cooper, Graham, and Himick (2016: 78) write that the management consultant firm McKinsey & Company has prepared "videos, booklets, and toolkits for organizations contemplating SIBs," and investment banks such as Goldman Sachs have already been "particularly active in the United States." Furthermore, the so-called Big Four global accounting firms are prominent promoters of SIBs, including Deloitte, which has been active in Canada wherein it has circulated the booklet *Paying for Outcomes* as part of their SIB advocacy campaign (Cooper, Graham, and Himick, 2016: 78). According to the standard account, the Peterborough prison SIB project was sufficiently successful to continue to experiment with new financing models, and new projects have been initiated in the United Kingdom.

Cooper, Graham, and Himick (2016: 69) report empirical data from an SIB initiative at St Mungo Hospital in London. The study included interviews with St Mungo employees, the Greater London Authority (GLA) solicitor, representatives of the Triodos Bank who prepared the SIB, and employees of other charitable organizations offering services similar to those of St Mungo's Hospital. Cooper, Graham, and Himick (2016) are not so much concerned with the immediate outcomes of the SIB funding initiative but emphasize the underlying operative model upon which the SIB model rests. Cooper, Graham, and Himick (2016: 79) argue that the SIB model and the metrics it uses to determine the outcomes of the rehabilitation activities stipulate "profound assumptions about the capacity and responsibility of the individual to act as an entrepreneur of the self." That is, a normative model of how individuals should preferably act in society is stipulated. In this model, self-interested behaviour is directed towards fulfilling contractual objectives, and the capacity to act in accordance with this linear model is construed as individuals' capacity to "function as moral citizens" (Cooper, Graham, and Himick, 2016: 79). In this contractual model, intended to generate social welfare at lower cost (so that equally taxpayers and SIB investors can share the benefits), society is more or less written out of the equation. Cooper, Graham, and Himick (2016: 80) describe this idea that society (i.e. the state and its various agencies) can be simply eliminated as an influential actor that fruitfully contributes to the solution of the problem at hand as being neoliberal:

> As an ostensibly market-based solution to a social problem, it carries with it the plethora of neoliberal rationalities. It "cures" homelessness not by "curing" society but by removing society from the equation. In

society's stead, it introduces contracts, profit incentives, risk taking, and outcome measurement; or alternately put, it eliminates from the notion of "society" everything except these calculative aspects of self-interest that suit a market ideology, even if no market exists.

Expressed differently, by its very design, the SIB model reduces the question of citizenship, a legal and political construct defined and protected by law, regulations, and international agreements, to a matter of the individual capacity to fulfil contract obligations, ultimately to the benefit of investors. Cooper, Graham, and Himick (2016) question this assumption on various grounds, regardless of the efficacy of the SIB model as such. "[E]ach of our interviewees appeared to express a genuine desire to help homeless people. However, their approaches and rationalities were strikingly neoliberal," Cooper, Graham, and Himick (2016: 69) summarize their findings.

Pauly and Swanson (2017: 721) provide additional evidence in a study on the use of SIBs, and they conclude that the SIB model may be used efficiently only under certain conditions: "[I]f investors in SIBs are not only socially motivated but also have special skills or effort to contribute to the production side of the public good or externality mitigation in question, then (and only then) might SIBs play a useful role." This means that SIB financing is not a "wholesale model" solution to the financing of the welfare sector, as SIB financing may attract investors who do not share this commitment to social welfare issues, nor have the "special skills" needed to make such investment decisions. SIB investors thus need to demonstrate both "performance incentives" and "sufficient expertise or involvement in implementation to contribute productively to program success." In the end, SIB financing may be relatively limited in the scope wherein it productively applies.

Policy implications

Taken together, learnings from the scholarly literature indicate that SIB financing is "very complex" (Warner, 2013: 315) inasmuch as a variety of actors and interests need to be aligned and tightly integrated in a contract that stipulates the rights and obligations of the various participants. In the end, SIB financing is promoted on the basis of two principal ideas: (1) that SIBs will "bring rigor to social service interventions," and (2) that SIBs attract private finance to areas where "public investment is lacking" (Warner, 2013: 315). Regarding the former issue, it is not clear whether the contractual features of the SIB model have a lasting benefit, or are more effective than conventional professional social service activities and interventions. A few individuals subject to direct contracting may regard this arrangement as a motivator, and as something that would help them act in ways that are consistent with stipulated policies (e.g. to avoid recidivism among former inmates), but that may not be the case for all, or even the majority of the subjects. Furthermore, Warner (2013: 316) suggests that it is complicated to acquire quality data regarding the outcomes from SIB projects. In addition, participants may be biased towards overoptimistic or positive evaluations as their payout is at risk unless the outcome converges towards anticipated outcomes (Warner, 2013: 316). In the end, SIB-funded projects need to be carefully monitored by regulatory agencies to avoid decision-making based on biased data that portray the SIB model in overtly positive terms which overstate its practical value.

Regarding the latter question, whether SIBs are attractive assets to invest in or not is equally complicated to determine. Warner (2013: 315) is sceptical regarding the attractiveness of SIBs unless most of the risks and additional costs are neutralized and absorbed by the sovereign state, being the principal of welfare programme activities: "Experience to date shows private investors do not appear willing to invest in proven programs, even with high returns, unless their risk is guaranteed by a subordinated investor. Thus, the core rationales behind the SIB movement may not hold up," Warner (2013: 315) writes. Warner (2013: 315) here cites a previous study which is considerably more sceptical than Warner herself, saying that it is doubtful whether the SIB model is "better than nothing," as social services officials may claim to justify the creation of a new class of financial assets:

> If you are perpetuating a model, that is dysfunctional at its core, I don't believe it is better than nothing, although it's a great way for a new industry to make money. These SIBs will create an industry of intermediaries and deal makers and brokers and accountants and lawyers and they'll be making a lot of money, I am sure taking this money off the top before it ever makes it to underpaid nonprofit workers or the beneficiaries of the program.

Seen in this sceptical view, the SIB asset is highly illiquid as it demands considerable expertise regarding how to formulate goals and performance metrics within the underlying social programme. This illiquidity makes an asset class less attractive vis-à-vis other asset classes, and this calls for concern regarding the sovereign state or its agencies carrying larger costs than they practically should if SIBs did not externalize certain risks and costs derived therefrom. In the end, SIBs may be successfully employed in certain cases and under specific conditions, but what these conditions demand is considerable information, especially over the economic cycle, to determine this.

The broader political and ideological issue is to what extent social welfare should be subject to private investment at all. Some commentators are concerned that the finance industry, which continuously introduces new financial asset classes and other innovations, is given the opportunity to extract finance capital from the welfare state organization, but without bearing all the costs and the uncertainty, which from a long-term perspective may undermine the legitimacy of the fiscal system and fiscal discipline, which ultimately impair the sovereign state's capacity to provide welfare services. Furthermore, the larger democratic issue is to what extent it should be possible to extract profits from the welfare sector in the first place, being an act that speculates on vulnerable groups' predicaments. Some commentators would regard that as unethical business practices, both in a short-term perspective (because it is deemed inadequate) and in the medium- to long-term perspective (because it undermines the social contract that stipulates all citizens as full legal subjects, not merely as contract-holders granted specific services). Given the historical track record of the finance industry regarding the capacity to advance new financial innovations, and to successfully encourage policymakers to create new markets for financial services, the use of SIBs and similar instruments is likely to be a model experimented on, debated, and subject to scholarly research in the coming period.

Household level implications: questioning credit as social provision on the basis of diminishing returns on finance industry subsidies and insurances

One of the consequences of the expanding finance industry is that credit supply is governed as a social provision by the sovereign state and transnational governance organization (Krippner, 2017; Mcfall, 2014; Peñaloza and Barnhart, 2011). Despite all the best intentions to lift poorer households out of their current situation, this policy has not served its purpose, Atkinson (2019: 1157) argues: "The reality [is] that credit is not for everyone." As credit is ultimately a matter of being a social relation (Crowston, 2013; Polillo, 2011; Calder, 2009; Carruthers, 2005; Hoffman, Postel-Vinay, and Rosenthal, 2000; Muldrew, 1998), an increased supply of credit does not necessarily solve underlying economic conditions, Atkinson (2019) writes. Robinson (2020: 982) addresses this concern:

> [M]arket-friendly policies—despite their mainstream appeal—do not necessarily or inevitably make real markets on the ground […] [O]fficials' effectiveness in selling credit expansion as a market-friendly policy option should be understood as an accomplishment, not a given: it hinges on the work of credit agencies and other intermediaries in cultivating beliefs and perceptions among various audiences that such policies genuinely stimulate market forces.

Decades of empirical data suggest that "low-income Americans can consistently expect to be in worse economic shape as time passes" (Atkinson, 2019: 1099), and more recently, there is also a "persistently grim economic prognosis" for the middle class in the United States (Atkinson, 2019: 1104). This structural economic inequality cannot be resolved on the basis of increased credit supply.

> Because the benefit of credit is contingent on the underlying circumstances of its user, credit is not suited to animate policies of social provision for the working poor who, for structural reasons, can scarcely hope for a brighter economic future. If anything, they are likely to pass on their problems to their children.
>
> (Atkinson, 2019: 1104)

As an elementary fact of credit supply, a person or household in a situation wherein cash is short in supply can borrow money from the anticipated future person or household that is purportedly better off, but only *because* this original loan was granted in the first place. This is the logic of, for example, student loans, wherein poor students increase their debt to be able to compete for future job positions that are more generously compensated, and that provide both a premium for study diligence and cover the costs (amortization and interests) for the student loan. Unfortunately, such optimistic prospects are not supported by empirical evidence in all cases: "Credit is built on expectation of economic progress, something that many low-income (and middle-income) borrowers have not seen in their lifetimes" (Atkinson, 2019: 1162). For instance, "while approximately 95% of children born in 1940 earned more than their parents earned, just 41% of children born in 1984 realized the same absolute mobility," Atkinson (2019: 1150) writes. In the case of low-income households, the chances of social mobility are negligible, which means that an increased credit supply has not resulted in the leverage of social and economic welfare that policymakers declared they actively promoted.

If Atkinson's proposition is substantiated, the question is then, how credit supply "come[s] to enjoy such seemingly universal support as a source of meaningful social provision for the working poor?" (Atkinson, 2019: 1099). Atkinson (2019: 1141) traces the change in policy to the Reagan presidency, an era wherein the Republicans reduced direct subsidies to the poor to "incentivize poor people to become economically self-sufficient" (Atkinson, 2019: 1141). "The cure for economic woes had to lie in the private sector," Ronald Reagan stated in a speech (cited in Pargendler, 2016: 365). The "pro-business" policy that the administration initiated included the largest tax reform in the post–World War II era, and top-level taxes were lowered from the maximum of 70 per cent to 50 per cent and later, in 1986, to 28 per cent (Jones, 2012: 265). An immediate effect of this policy was a rise in the proportion of people "living below the poverty line" (Atkinson, 2019: 1141): "In the 12 years before Reagan's presidency, from 1970 to 1981, inequality grew by 4.53 percent, but it expanded by 11.2 percent in 12 Reagan-Bush years from 1982 to 1993, or by 2.5 times as much" (Jacobs and Myers, 2014: 767). The response to rising poverty levels in American society, itself generated by shifts in policymaking, was to encourage lending to households, "especially but not exclusively low-income ones," the economist Raghuram Rajan says (cited in Atkinson, 2019: 1120, footnote 147). As Rajan notices, this support of credit-supplying institutions, the finance industry, and government-sponsored enterprises (GSEs) such as Freddie Mac and Fannie Mae in particular, is "politically expedient" because more generous access to credit may in fact "[o]bscure deeper economic problems such as income stagnation" (Atkinson, 2019: 1120, footnote 147).

For critics such as Atkinson, four decades of policymaking that increasingly insures and subsidizes the finance industry has accomplished relatively little in terms of curbing soaring levels of poverty or inequality. On the contrary, it generates the unintended consequence—whether the outcome was in fact intended or not is of course a question of political and scholarly debates—of amplifying economic inequality as revenues from financial asset holdings to a higher extent benefit households in the top income strata. Consequently, Atkinson (2019: 1158) calls for a critical discussion about the role of credit supply in the American welfare model: "[t]he balance in the public-private American welfare regime has shifted too far toward individualism and private provision." Needless to say, given the polarization of American society and its history and traditions, to reclaim the initiative to promote economic welfare within the realm of the state is a formidable challenge. The market liberalism preference and "limited government" credo of policymakers is complicated to circumvent, and the inertia of the American polity and its close connections to lobbyists, think tanks, and campaign donors are conducive to stalemate and status quo and elite interest fulfilment, rather than being a reform-oriented milieu that would benefit low-income households (Gilens and Page, 2014, Gilens, 2005). In this perspective, the prospects for economic equality and increased social welfare should not be overstated.

Alternative routes: a new view of finance industry regulation

In addition to structural and institutional changes in the finance industry, also new theories and doctrines regarding the nature of markets and their capacity to accommodate information have been advanced. Allen, Vayanos, and Vives (2014: 2) argue that prior to 2007, the study of finance industry crises was "a niche subject primarily studied by those interested in economic history or international economics." Finance industry crises were in short treated as a curiosity at the fringe of the economic discipline and policymaking activities, but merited little more than that as finance markets were assumed to be self-regulating and vaccinated against the adverse effects of opportunistic behaviour on the basis of the informational efficiency of the price-setting process (Brine and Poovey, 2017). Policymakers therefore, the conventional wisdom stipulated, only needed to monitor the whole of the economy from the top down, by checking a handful of macroeconomic fundamentals, such as interest rates (Fligstein, Brundage and Schultz, 2017).

A leading figure of the economics discipline and a long- serving official of the US finance industry, Harvard professor Larry Summers (2014: 65) admits that this regulatory model is no longer widely endorsed:

> Macroeconomics, just six or seven years ago, was a very different subject than it is today. Leaving aside the set of concerns associated with long-run growth, I think it is fair to say that six years ago, macroeconomics was primarily about the use of monetary policy to reduce the already small amplitude of fluctuations about a given trend, while maintaining price stability.

The conventional wisdom prior to circa 2008 was that short-term debt, that is, the supply of liquid assets in the economy, was the primary cause of a crisis, but the newly earned insight is that there are "many other factors that can contribute to the severity of a crisis" (Allen, Vayanos, and Vives, 2014: 6). In other words, crises in the finance industry, occurring at increasingly higher frequency (Calomiris and Haber, 2014), are not simply caused by monetary conditions or inadequate regulatory control, as the conventional wisdom proposed, but also mechanisms and practices internal to the finance industry and global financial markets play a key role.

This revision of the macroeconomic doctrines that dominated regulatory oversight prior to 2008 has served to question a variety of central ideas and assumptions that have been treated as indubitable axiomatic principles of an almost Euclidean standing. One such issue is the doctrine that central banks (1) should be independent from the political system so that the board of directors and officers who serve in central banks cannot be corrupted by the swings in political opinion, and calls for political and regulatory changes derived therefrom, and (2) that inflation (and, by default, interest rates) should be kept at a low (in the span of 1.5–2 percentage points per annum) and predictable rate (Polillo and Guillén, 2005). This essentially monetarist doctrine has been implemented on a broad scale across the majority of advanced economies (Blancheton, 2016; Kus, 2012), but the long-term consequences of this model have been questioned on the basis of theoretical concerns and empirical evidence (for an overview, see Tucker, 2018). In the following, some of the key arguments of this critique will be examined, and thereafter the empirical evidence regarding the efficacy of the independent central bank model will be examined.

Theoretical view of the central bank independence legislation

Hartwell (2019) claims that the very idea that politics and economic affairs can be neatly separated into a policymaking and legislative branch, and an executive branch in time and space as stipulated by the "independent" central bank model, is underdeveloped. "[T]rue central bank independence is a goal which can never be achieved within the conventional approach to centralized monetary institutions, with true independence, if desired, only feasible via different (and radical) institutional alternatives," Hartwell (2019: 63) argues. The central bank supposedly acts independently from the political system (this type of simplification of complex processes into neatly compartmentalized entities can be permitted for the benefit of the clarity of the argument), but de facto, it is simultaneously an economic *and* political institution, "staffed by political appointees and having chosen a political approach to overcome economic problems," Hartwell (2019: 71) says. In this way, the declared independence is a chimera as the central bank, Hartwell (2019: 71) continues, is "nested within one set of political institutions (government), nested within another set of economic institutions (the institutions of the marketplace), nested within the meta-institution of society, and then even further embedded into an international system." It should be noticed that, for example, Binder and Spindel (2017) suggest that the formal separation of Congress and the Federal Reserve in the United States is the outcome from Congress' efforts to distance itself from potentially unpopular economic policies, which suggests that it is primarily political rather than economic or financial interests that uphold the independent central bank doctrine. That is, Binder and Spindel (2017: 2) suggest that Congress and the Fed are *interdependent*: "From atop Capitol Hill, Congress depends on the Fed to both steer the economy and absorb public blame when the economy falters." They continue:

> [O]ver the Fed's first century, Congress has delegated increasing degrees of responsibility to the Fed for managing the nation's economy. But by centralizing power in the hands of the Fed, lawmakers can more credibly blame the Fed for poor economic outcomes, insulating themselves electorally and potentially diluting public anger at Congress.
>
> (Binder and Spindel, 2017: 2)

The semantic meaning of the term *independence* in everyday conversations cannot therefore be assumed to accurately describe these relations, and instead the term takes on alternative meanings that are poorly explained and communicated with, for example, non-expert audiences such as voters and citizens more widely. McNamara (2002: 47) more explicitly questions the democratic deficit of the current independent central bank model inasmuch as what she regards as the "insulation of central banks from the direct influence of elected officials" is a pre-eminent example of a form of delegation of key responsibilities to a "non-majoritarian institution." What is at stake, in the short as well as medium- to long-term views, is that the current central bank model fails to live up to declared standards regarding democratic accountability (McNamara, 2002: 48):

> The very act of granting a group of appointed (not elected) technocrats, independence form political power—that is, from elected representatives

or officials—reveals a fundamental tension in the way in which different kinds of issues are handled in modern societies [...] Especially monetary policy, have been socially and politically constructed as lying beyond the scope of democratic oversight and control.

(Polillo and Guillén, 2005: 1794)

Just like Hartwell (2019), McNamara (2002: 47) does not believe that it is possible to construe central bank responsibilities as a form of "apolitical" assignment. Proponents of central bank independence underline the need to "insulate monetary policy from politics" and the "severing [of] ties to democratic representatives" to better apply technocratic expertise to cases at hand. Still, this advocacy as such accomplishes little in terms of changing the factual role of central banks, that is, to act on a delegation from democratically (in the ideal case) elected political entities, such as parliaments and other legislative bodies. Major (2014: 207) straightforwardly states that to move regulatory and monetary policymaking authority to central banks and financial ministries is a way to insulate "monetary policy making from mass political pressure." At this point. McNamara (2002) introduces the idea that independent central banks are in fact in the service of a "culture of neoliberalism," which here denotes the political campaign to separate market activities and market actors from the legislative and regulatory control of the sovereign state, and instead to employ state capacities to create new markets and market-like conditions that further propel the market society. In this view, the ability to institutionalize the independent central bank as a central mechanism in the contemporary economy is one of the most significant accomplishments of proponents of liberal and market-based economies.

While neither endorsing nor using the term *neoliberalism*, both Kus (2012) and Wansleben (2018) suggest that the low interest rate policy is a matter of supporting finance industry interests: "Since inflation undermined banks' ability for borrowing money from customers and lending it to investors, and ultimately decreased bank profitability, these inflation targeting policies proved favourable to banks and were welcome by the larger finance community," Kus (2012: 485–486) writes. Wansleben (2018: 776) refers to "a symbiosis" between "inflation targeting" and "financialized capitalism," which indicates a model that De Grauwe (2013), who examines the eurozone policy, names the "Brussels–Frankfurt consensus." De Grauwe (2013: 159) argues that the Brussels–Frankfurt consensus is based on two theories, whereof the first is monetarist theory that stipulates that "the central bank cannot do much to stabilize the economy"; if a central bank "tries too hard to fine-tune the economy, it will end up with more inflation, so the best thing a central bank can do is to stabilize the price level." The second theory is the efficient market hypothesis, which straightforwardly disqualifies the very idea of bubbles and crises in markets on the basis of the superior capacity of market participants to process public information:

[B]ubbles and crashes would not be tolerated in efficient financial markets because rational agents would not allow prices to deviate from their underlying fundamentals. The implication of this view is that financial markets could be left to themselves. All they needed was a stability-oriented monetary policy that would allow these agents to create the best of all possible worlds.

(De Grauwe, 2013: 159)

In De Grauwe's view (2013), the Brussels–Frankfurt consensus is a puzzling historical phenomenon inasmuch as it is hard to understand how what De Grauwe (2013: 160) regards as "practical men" could pledge their belief in "such a fictional world for so long." In the end, still, it was not so much economic doctrines and stated theories that propelled the eurozone policies as, De Grauwe (2013: 160) writes, "European political leaders did not understand the economics of a monetary union." In the absence of a more comprehensive and robust analytical model (i.e. something else than the monetarist theory and the efficient market hypothesis), "European policy makers were driven by purely political objectives" (De Grauwe, 2013: 160).

One such political objective that arguably served as the key driver of this univocal spread of independent central banks in advanced economies is the signalling to all actors in the global market that the specific economy honours and holds a liberal and private business-based economic system in esteem, which attracts investment and creates the necessary confidence needed to commit resources to economic ventures and projects:

[I]n an increasingly globalised international financial market, central bank independence is one way of signalling to investors a government is truly 'modern,' ready to carry out extensive reforms to provide a setting conducive to business.

(McNamara, 2002: 60)

Regarding the empirical evidence of the welfare-generating consequences of an independent central bank, both Hartwell (2019) and McNamara (2002) provide data that fail to unambiguously support the current doctrine.

Empirical evidence challenging the central bank independence model

Two types of evidence are of interest when the independent central bank model is examined. First, the question is whether central banks actually do make independent decisions on the basis that the economies their board of directors monitor represent underlying specific or even idiosyncratic conditions such as geographical and meteorological conditions, of relevance for agriculture businesses, population growth, and the quality of the political institutions. Second, the question is whether, for example, a low inflation/low interest policy (i.e. a price stability policy) has been beneficial for economic welfare in countries with independent central banks.

Regarding the former question, Hartwell (2019: 76) provides evidence that suggests that central banks such as the Federal Reserve and the European Central Bank in fact make interest rate decisions that correlate to a significant degree, which renders the central idea of the "independence" of central banks dubitable:

> In fact, a simple Pearson correlation between the rates utilized by the Fed and the ECB over this time frame gives a result of 0.79, an incredibly strong positive correlation (which is significant well beyond the 1% level). At the time that central banks were assuming their highest levels of legal independence from domestic politics, they were suddenly beginning to move in lockstep with their peers, with the Fed taking the lead.

Even "transnational" central banks such as the ECB, which monitor economies as diverse as those of Greece, Germany, and Estonia, reveal a pattern of interest rate decision-making that correlates with that of the considerably older institution of the Federal Reserve (which still, in comparison to European states, is a relatively new constitutional creation, founded only in 1913; Block, 2010: 183). Independence from national political entities is apparently more highly prioritized than independence from other central banks.

The second question, whether a central bank's decision-making generates economic welfare is of course complicated to assess as it would demand some counterfactual benchmark to which net economic welfare effects can be compared. On the one hand, the world's most advanced economies, with the highest economic welfare, do host independent central banks, but these economies, primarily located in the industrialized West and a handful of Asian jurisdictions, had the institutional infrastructure and a historical track record in business venturing prior to the establishment of independent central banks, so that argument is essentially beside the point. However, the univocal emphasis on price stability as being the foremost argument in favour of independent central banks has been questioned on substantive grounds. This economic idea is essentially a monetarist doctrine that was advanced as a contestant to the dominant Keynesian economic policy that dominated in the post–World War II period until the mid-1970s, when the global economy was severely harmed by persistent inflation. For instance, McNamara (2002: 57) cites the work of Joseph Stiglitz, a leading economists and contributor to information economics theory in particular, to address the efficacy of price stability policy. According to McNamara, Stiglitz argues that the two basic assumptions in independent central bank policy, (1) that "[i]nflation will accelerate uncontrollably if left unchecked," and (2) that inflation "is costly to reverse," are not substantiated by empirical data (McNamara, 2002: 57). In fact,

Stiglitz finds no statistical evidence that "inflation builds on itself," but instead shows that "when it has been rising it is likely to reverse its course" (McNamara, 2002: 57). That is, the adjustment occurs in an economy "in more effective ways" than is generally assumed by proponents of price stability policy. This means that inflation is not so costly to curb once it has been decided that it is undesirable. Furthermore, McNamara (2002: 58) refers to empirical evidence from Germany that indicates that the Bundesbank, the federal central bank, has been successful in fighting inflation and in accomplishing price stability, not so much due the measures taken by the board of directors but because there is a widespread societal consensus among German economic agents that price stability is a desirable social good. In other words, social norms and social capital expressed in terms of trust in economic institutions are the factual drivers of the German economy's consistent price stability.

The works of Stiglitz and others does not suggest that inflation is a good thing, or that it should not have been prioritized during episodes of notoriously high inflation, such as in the late 1970s and early 1980s, propelled by the oil embargo initiated by the OPEC cartel as a response to political conditions. The question is instead why independent central banks prioritize price stability above all things and on a year-in, year-out basis? One explanation, already addressed, is that low inflation is supportive of finance industry interests, and central bank directors may treat an efficient capital formation process as being a prioritized goal among a variety of objectives. Jacobs and King (2016: 3) advocate this explanation and point at the close connections between Wall Street and the Federal Reserve:[3]

> [The Federal Reserve's] exercise of power consistently favours banks and investment firms not only in response to lobbying or the seduction of revolving doors, but also because thriving finance helps the Fed itself by generating revenues and pleasing its allies.

This explanation may appear conspicuously tendentious as the Federal Reserve is supposed to serve as the watchdog that barks whenever Wall Street (the metonymy *par préférence* to denote the American finance industry in its entirety) digresses from what are widely understood as prudential or sound business practices. In real life, that role is not of necessity always honoured by the Fed as its directors may either be uninformed about finance industry practice and the risks they induce (as suggested by Fligstein, Brundage, and Schultz, 2017), or more simply share a commitment to what free market theory refers to as market efficiency maximization. Leaving the issue of factual motivations to the side (after all, beliefs, preferences, and expectations are murky territories to explore in both theoretical and empirical terms; Davidson, 1963), and instead the direct consequences of the "zero-interest rate" policy, being the price stability policy outcome in the post-2008 period, needs to be examined.

The consequences of low interest rate policy

Maddaloni and Peydró (2011: 2124) examine the consequences of low interest rates in the eurozone, which is interesting to consider as "monetary policy rates are identical across countries," at the same time as there are "significant differences in terms of GDP and inflation." Maddaloni and Peydró's (2011: 2124) empirical data provide "robust evidence" that show how low short-term interest policy "soften[s] lending standards for both firms and households." This means that centrally imposed low-inflation policies result in low interest, which in turn promotes credit supply at low cost. Rational actors therefore assume that if credit supply is bountiful, then neither lenders nor borrowers have to worry about strictness regarding the creditworthiness of borrowers. Expressed differently, the price stability policy of independent central banks offers the finance industry the possibility to expand its balance sheets and to increase its turnover. Second, Maddaloni and Peydró (2011) examine whether the degree of securitization co-varies with low interest rates. In Europe, Maddaloni and Peydró, 2011: 2136) write, "[t]he coefficient of the interaction between securitization and short-term rates is positive and statistically significant (at 1% or 5%), implying that the impact of low short-term rates on the softening of lending standards is amplified by securitization activity." The independent central bank price stability policy and the financial innovation of securitization combined therefore results in less strict lending standards, which on the one hand are beneficial for the finance industry, which can expand its business operations and balance sheets, but on the other hand result in inflated housing prices and increased levels of household debt, a well-documented condition in the scholarly literature (Dwyer, 2018; Fuller, 2016; Zinman, 2015; Turner, 2015; Hyman, 2011; Peñaloza and Barnhart, 2011; Barba and Pivetti, 2009; Montgomerie, 2009). "All in all," Maddaloni and Peydró (2011: 2145) summarize, "the analysis suggests that the impact of low short-term rates on the softening of lending standards is amplified by securitization (i.e. high securitization activity and low monetary policy rates complement each other in the softening of standards)." Dell'Ariccia, Laeven, and Marquez (2014) report similar evidence, which indicates that low interest rates lead to an amplified leverage and higher risk-taking in banks. In this view, price stability policy is conducive to systemic risk growth that central banks are assigned the role to monitor and keep at a manageable level, but now actively contribute to leverage themselves.

The brew of low-interest rate policy and financial innovations has arguably increased the credit supply in European economies, but the question is whether the credit supply can per se be construed as evidence of increased economic welfare in all income strata. When considering the 2008 crisis, created on the basis of low-interest rates, the extensive securitization of assets, and an overoptimistic view of projected housing prices, Jacobs and King (2016: 9) would disconnect current independent central bank policy and economic welfare: "By the middle of 2013, median [US] household income was still 6 percent lower than it was before 2008" (for a more comprehensive overview of the consequences of the Great Recession, see, e.g., Redbird and Grusky, 2016). More generally, in the United States, which hosts the most advanced and expansive finance industry, access to banking services is unevenly distributed, primarily because low net-income households are unattractive clients for banks. What Karger (2005) refers to as the *fringe economy*, the economy that operates outside of the formal finance industry, is considerable in the United States. Baradaran (2015: 139) says that 70 million Americans do not even have a bank account or access to traditional financial services. This exclusion from traditional banking altogether is a costly affair for low net-worth households, and empirical evidence indicates that "the average unbanked family" spends "almost 10 percent of its income" on financial transactions (Baradaran, 2015: 94). Needless to say, this group is already economically vulnerable, so any additional fee-based expenses to access money further restrain household budgets. More generally speaking, the US population may benefit from a sizeable finance industry, but unequally so. Karger (2005: 18) says that no less than 43 per cent of Americans "spend more than they earn" annually, a growth of "debtfare" as receding social welfare is compensated by increased levels of household debt (Lavinas, 2018). In addition, Prasad (2012: 21) adds, "[t]he United States [has had] the highest relative poverty of all advanced industrial countries of the west for almost all combinations of household form and labor participation."

In the end, the purportedly independent central bank may do excellent work in supporting finance industry interests, but has been less vocal and active in terms of enforcing legislation and regulatory guidelines that assist net economic welfare in distributive terms. Such changes in governance objectives and in economic policy are consistent with the transnational governance model imposed by the World Bank and the IMF during the neoliberal era, Mehrpouya and Salles-Djelic (2019) argue. The catchphrase for this transnational governance regime was "transparency," and this quality was accomplished on the basis of the development and implementation of accounting standards. In contrast to previous transnational governance regimes, the transparency model served to (1) make the state itself become subject to the "disciplining power and 'intelligence' of financial markets" (Mehrpouya and Salles-Djelic, 2019: 22), and (2) completely marginalize the individual, either as a "carrier of economic rationality," or as "the beholder of political/legal rights" (Mehrpouya and Salles-Djelic, 2019: 22). That is, the transparency-driven transnational governance regime enacts the sovereign state and private actors as entities whose primary role is to submit standardized accounts "to imagined, mobile and invisible financial markets," but otherwise should remain passive to best take advantage of the many wonders of finance market pricing and transaction activities (Mehrpouya and Salles-Djelic, 2019: 22). This transnational governance regime undermines meaningful agency on the aggregated and the individual level, and thereby essentially erases the individual as "a beneficiary and an enabler of economic/market governance" (Mehrpouya and Salles-Djelic, 2019: 22). The term *transparency* is thus saturated with technocratic meaning as it is primarily operationalized in ways that benefit finance market actors' interests, and leave the issue of the distribution of net economic welfare as a secondary concern, at best.

Potentially, such goals are exactly the type of objectives that proponents of independent central banks want to downplay and marginalize as they are regarded as "political" issues (i.e. they presuppose political objectives and epistemic values such as "fairness" or "equality," and thus demand judgement), but that preference for finance industry support does not per se justify the central bank, which serves a finance industry support function of sorts, at least not as long as political entities, being the principal of central banks regardless of their declared independence, represent *all* voters' interests. Based on such concerns, Maddaloni and Peydró (2011: 2151) suggest that their results support new responsibilities for the ECB and the Federal Reserve to execute "macroprudential supervision to monitor systemic risk." Dell'Ariccia, Laeven, and Marquez (2014: 88) call for a broadening of the scope of central bank responsibilities, which clearly discounts the monetarist doctrine that central banks can do little more than to ensure price stability:

> Central banks should take these effects on financial stability into account when setting monetary policy, in addition to the traditional trade-off between employment and inflation, especially when they have a dual mandate that includes safeguarding financial stability.

To monitor the systemic risk derived from the low-interest policy and financial innovations being introduced is thus a key regulatory objective of central banks, and not only to singlehandedly target low inflation as some kind of "master-measure" that would generate a variety of benevolent outcomes. That model has been experimented on during the last three decades, and the outcome is arguably not as favourable as its original proponents claimed it would be at the beginning of the period.

Risk calculation as the basis of the financial economy: consequences and policy implications

The first three sections of this chapter have examined a number of components of the institutional logic of the finance-led economy:

1. *The influence of rentier interest.* The rentier economy is a complement to, or competitor of entrepreneurial activities (depending on theoretical assumptions; see, e.g., Hanson, 1958). As a consequence, overinvestment

in the one sector may harm the other as it reduces the incentive to accumulate finance capital, or overrates the market value of start-up businesses (in the case of entrepreneurs being overcompensated), or reduces incentives to create new businesses (in the case of rentiers being overcompensated).

2. *The continuous financial asset creation.* Specific financial asset classes (e.g. social impact bonds, SIBs) can, when certain minimal requirements regarding, for example, risk calculation and projected return are satisfied, be used to finance almost any kind of social activity, project, or welfare provision. Only professional norms and ethical beliefs impose limitations on how far finance assets can be taken in terms of funding, for example, welfare services. Whether this way of financing social welfare activities is efficient remains to be determined.

3. *The credit supply doctrine.* The sheer support of credit supply cannot solve underlying economic and financial dysfunctions, including stagnant real-wage growth and reduced job creation rates, as increased levels of debt must be repaid on the basis of future income.

4. *The regulatory framework.* Central banks, being the centrepiece of the regulatory framework stipulated by the legal theory of finance, are not "independent" in the conventional semantic meaning of the term but display evidence of convergence that indicates epistemic community norms and lower degrees of integrity than is commonly assumed in official declarations and formal speeches.

On the basis of these three scenarios, a more general explanation for the operations of the financial economy can be formulated. The financial economy is not primarily characterized by the risk-taking of finance capital owners as many entrepreneurial activities are not considered attractive investment options, given the irreducible presence of uncertainty in, for example, science-based development work. Nor is the finance-led economy determined by a tendency towards the "assetification" of everything under the sun (even though there is evidence of practices, including SIBs, which may suggest otherwise). Furthermore, it is not the case that the financial economy operates strictly on the basis of local and regional fluctuations in production factor prices (if that were the case, central banks would display more variety in their decision-making and the policies implemented). What characterizes the finance-led economy is the capacity to conduct adequate and functional risk calculations to determine what investment opportunities and assets are worthy of being targeted, given certain risk-aversion preferences. The taming of chance and the externalization of risks (more specifically, the costs derived from calculated, parametric risk) are at the very core of the finance-led economy. In this context, certain industries, such as the construction industry, are consistently thickly capitalized whereas other industries are thinly capitalized to a varying degree. In cases wherein risk cannot be calculated with good precision (e.g. in life science start-ups, where, e.g., clinical trials frequently reveal previously unknown properties of underlying assets, say, regarding the efficacy of an active compound in a candidate drug), the state either needs to provide subsidies and insurances against losses, or to take over the role as principal investor (as in the case, by and large, of life science venturing in Sweden).

Risk is by definition what can be calculated on the basis of parametric methods, whereas uncertainty falls to the side of what is known or knowable on the basis of calculative practices; therefore, uncertainty is anathema to all finance capital investors. At times, legal-regulatory devices such as insurances, subsidies, or tax exemptions provided by the state can convince private finance capital owners to commit their resources to high-risk ventures, but when risks are incalculable and uncertainty looms, there is no basis for the type of rational decisions that guide most finance capital investment. Individuals being critical of the finance industry and what Thorstein Veblen (1916: 16) spoke of as the "financial captains of industry" may believe that a profit motive (or even greed, some commentators suggest) is a defining mark of capital owners and money managers and their investment activities. Unfortunately, such derogatory views do not explain why, for example, venture capital investors are willing to continue their work despite having a track record of writing off circa 75 per cent of their finance capital investment as losses, and to make all their returns on the last ten successful per cent of their portfolio holdings. There may be evidence of strong profit motives (and greed, some propose) in the finance industry (as indicated by a number ethnographic studies, e.g., Omarova, 2013; Ho, 2009; Zaloom, 2006; Abolafia, 2001), but what external observers refer to as greed is merely a second-order description embedded in a normative view, derived from the core activities to calculate risks and returns and to make investments on the basis of such calculations. In the domain of finance capital investment activities, thickly capitalized industries provide good possibilities for calculating risks and negotiating packages of insurances and subsidies from the sovereign state. In contrast, in industries with limited possibilities for calculating risk and/or projecting income flows, business ventures become thinly capitalized as there are weak incentives to commit finance capital to such business ventures, given all other investment opportunities being provided. The finance-led economy is thus an aggregate of thickly, moderately, and thinly capitalized business activities that (on average) add to net economic welfare in their own specific ways.

Ludwig Wittgenstein (1974: 19) writes that "the task of philosophy is not to create an ideal language, but to clarify the use of existing language." A task in analogy with this stated intention of relevance for management studies scholars is to examine "the rules of the game" of the financial economy, but without conducting this scholarly work on the basis of too many assumptions regarding the beliefs, desires, and norms of finance industry agents and their regulators, or too heavy-handedly impose various stipulated ideals thereupon. The finance-led economy coexists with welfare states in most parts of the developed world, and it is plausible that the finance-led economy is an important contributor to economic and social welfare, despite all the concerns addressed in this volume. At the same time, evidence of imbalances in the finance-led economy (which translates into, e.g., soaring economic inequality, growing household debt, and increased rentier returns) calls for measures to be taken. The legal theory of finance provides a variety of mechanisms for pushing down risk-taking and promoting prudent investment behaviour, so worrying tendencies can arguably be handled effectively if policymakers believe they need to take action.

Summary and conclusion

The legal theory of finance view of the financial economy pursued in this volume proposes that finance markets (and by implication, all other markets that are dependent on functional finance markets for their capital supply) are rendered operational on the basis of a combination of legislative activities, state insurances and regulatory control, and risk management practices, including systematic risk assessment of asset holdings. In this theoretical model, the market is not so much a calculative device, or an apparatus of distributed cognition, as it is human accomplishment and institutional creation based on a complex legal and institutional framework wherein all market participants and market makers jointly determine the functionality of the market and its capacity to operate on the basis of expectations. As Morris and Shin (2012: 1–2) remark, "It is not enough that each market participant believes that the fundamentals are sound. Market confidence requires that the fundamental soundness is *commonly understood* among market participants" (emphasis in the original). The market can always include a number of naive investors and other uninformed traders that bias the market pricing process, but the majority of the participants need to be informed about the conditions under which markets operate. Morris and Shin (2012: 2) thus speak about "the self-referential nature of 'market confidence,'" which indicates that confidence (and its derivative terms, such as expectations, projected returns, etc.) is the single most important outcome from a market creation process as "[o]nly traders with market confidence participate in the market," Morris and Shin (2012: 2) contend.

One of the consequences of the centrality of market confidence is that, from an analytical point of view, some of the most intriguing questions regarding the functioning of financial markets are, in Riles' (2010) term, "epistemological." For instance, how do facts such as risk rating measures or market prices get constructed in markets? In this view, Riles (2010: 795) proposes, financial traders act "as analogs to scientists, who can be shown to be making, in the guise of merely discovering, market realities." When facts are produced within a technoscientific apparatus (in the case of scientists) or in a legal-calculative setting (in the case of finance traders), politics is never far away, Riles (2010) stipulates. However, unlike the more popular view of finance as some veiled and mystified practice that generates economic wealth on the basis of the deployment of an almost impenetrable apparatus that includes a variety of calculative devices and technical systems, Riles (2010: 797) recognizes that finance is "a realm of explicit politics." As opposed to being a "hidden politics," masked as "epistemological practice," the politics of finance reveals what Riles (2010: 797) characterizes as a "candid, pedestrian, and on-the-surface quality." Finance trade may appear esoteric and complex in its details to both experts and lay audiences, but its operations are oftentimes quite straightforward inasmuch as legal and regulatory rules are combined with calculative practices and the production of legal documents (see, e.g., Riles, 2011). That is, the complexity that finance traders encounters in their day-to-day work are not different in kind in relation to scientists, who operate in their laboratories on the basis of defined experimental systems and theoretical frameworks to be tested against empirical data. When penetrating the facade of financial institutions, in the back offices there are in many cases practices that are surprisingly tangible in nature (MacKenzie, 2018; MacKenzie and Spears, 2014; Callon, Millo, and Muniesa, 2007), as in the case of the production of the documents that serve as collateral in the over-the-counter derivatives trade and in repo markets—functional markets that maintain the liquidity of the finance market and hence keep the advanced economic system of competitive capitalism operational.

In financial markets, which are of necessity characterized by various degrees of systemic risks (see, e.g., Gubler, 2014: 225), it is difficult for market makers such as the state to uphold confidence in the market over the economic cycle, and during episodes of, for example, asset price drops and other dramatic events, the state might need to intervene in markets to restore its faith based on capital infusions (i.e. bailouts) and/or other insurances or regulatory changes. Markets are not informationally efficient, evidence indicates,[4] and consequently market actors cannot assess their risk exposure as, for example, systemic risks are not mirrored in the market pricing of assets (Ferrillo, Dunbar, and Tabak, 2004: 83). The foremost policy implication from this condition is that investors and other market participants cannot or do not rely on the "integrity of the market," if that integrity is at best "semi-strong efficient" (Ferrillo, Dunbar, and Tabak, 2004: 117).[5] This means that the market is essentially a matter of legal construction, law enforcement, and regulatory control, but only in collaboration with, and under the influence of the consent of informed market participants. If, and only if, the state and transnational market makers and market participants can agree on a series of issues, can finance markets be rendered operational and supportive of economic growth.

Where legislation determines operations, interests and politics are not too far away (or to put it differently, legislative practices are interests and politics pursued by other means). Ultimately, it is the policymakers (and in democratic societies, voters) that determine what industries and sectors of the economy to subsidize and support. If the political objective to support house ownership is a prioritized political issue vis-à-vis other objectives (say, full employment, a low statistical poverty rate), then there are a variety of measures to be taken so that tax money and regulatory efforts translate into affordable housing. If, in contrast, say, life science ventures and the development of new drugs, medical technologies, and diagnostic tools are rated higher vis-à-vis other objectives, then the state can choose to transfer economic resources in that direction. In the financial economy, the state still maintains a central role as the market maker, and in the end the economic welfare generated, including not the least the ability to assess the costs and benefits of economic equality/inequality, derived from these investment decisions, serves as hard-end data points. This is in principle no different from how, for example, states allocate, for instance, culture budgets to elite institutions such as opera houses and symphonic orchestras in relation to smaller events such as music festivals and poetry-reading nights. It still appears as an unambiguous fact that the middlemen of all activities benefit greatly from the state acting as a guarantor for economic stability over the economic cycle, and therefore policymakers should carefully consider to what extent, for example, industry subsidies and insurances actually result in benefits for taxpayers, either directly as in the form of a more generous supply of credit, or indirectly, as in the case of economic growth that generates jobs and real wage growth in various sectors. Unless tax money creates economic welfare in predefined terms (sweeping prophecies regarding "the tide raises all boats" are insufficient contributions), economic policies may be sub-optimal and should be subject to critical reflection and potentially reforms. In the end, the finance-led economy is and will remain a most complex human accomplishment and institutional creation that demands scholarly attention and public debate, or else it may only benefit certain market participants unduly, but with net losses in economic welfare. A first step towards this reflexivity is to sketch intelligible models of underlying economic transactions and to identify how the economic value created is distributed in society.

Postscript

This volume has examined the consequences of a finance-led economy wherein the sovereign state acts to provide financial institutions with business charters so that they can issue credit as private corporations, operating on the basis of a series of insurances, subsidies, and exemptions granted by the sovereign state. Already in this regime, the capacity of financial institutions to generate credit relations outside of the sovereign state's insurances, for example, in the shadowing banking system, is remarkable. This is indicative of credit relations as being a social relation predicated on the capacity of either business partner to fulfil their contractual obligations until the contract is terminated as stipulated by the terms. However, there is an entirely different financial economy on the rise that is still too vague in its contours and too subterranean to be fully explored in detail. For instance, by 2010, fintech companies (fintech is defined shortly) in the marketplace lending area "originated less than 1% of consumer loans" in the United States; in 2018, so-called person-to-person (P2P) lenders, for the most part owned by fintech companies and being a leniently regulated branch of the financial market, "originated 38% of all loans in the $138 billion U.S. consumer debt market" (Luther, 2020: 1020). "And there is no reason to believe that this growth will slow down," Luther (2020: 1020) adds. As a bridge towards the future, this postscript of the volume will examine some features of this new regime of credit formation and financial intermediation.

Recently, there is evidence of a sharp growth of the creation of new cryptocurrencies that generate new credit relations within the economic system. Cohney, Hofman, Sklarof, and Wishnick (2019) examine what they refer to as initial coin offering (ICO), which is a new approach to create a synthetic cryptocurrency that enables the issuer to access financial assets to run their operations and development work. "Old institutions like banks and venture capital firms are finding themselves supplanted by masses of individuals coordinating through new financial platforms," Cohney, Hofman, Sklarof, and Wishnick (2019: 593) write. ICOs represent an innovative, low-cost method to raise funds, and are consequently indicative of "the increasing financialization of internet-based peer production" (Cohney, Hofman, Sklarof, and Wishnick, 2019: 597). In 2017 alone, 453 ICOs raised an estimated $6.58 billion (Cohney, Hofman, Sklarof, and Wishnick, 2019: 595). In today's Internet-based business, the creation of a cryptoasset is a fairly standardized activity, and it currently requires only a "minimum of approximately fifty lines of code" and three "decision components": "the asset's name, its ticker symbol, and the number of units—or 'tokens'— to mint" (Cohney, Hofman, Sklarof, and Wishnick, 2019: 605). To mint a cryptoasset token demands an act of "founder fiat." This means that an actor, the issuer of the cryptoasset, generates a blockchain that presumptive buyers can interact with at a nominal cost.[6] For the issuer, the blockchain technology enables a rapid raise of capital "without the formalities required by corporate law and regulation" (Cohney, Hofman, Sklarof, and Wishnick, 2019: 620). Buyers, in turn, might be attracted by cryptoasset holdings simply because of the absence of strict regulatory control. That is, cryptoasset issuance is unfortunately frequently associated with illicit activities such as money laundering and fraud.

Despite these concerns, there are many cases of ICOs that have been hugely successful. The Silicon Valley company Kik Interactive, mostly known for its social media app Kik, managed to raise $98.8 million for a project, and brought home the total amount of almost $150 million when including the "private presale" (Cohney, Hofman, Sklarof, and Wishnick, 2019: 621). In some cases, the ICO targets specific segments of the market, as in the case of the company Paragon, which initiated an ICO that stated in its White

Paper that it served the end of "revolutionizing all things cannabis with blockchain" (cited in Cohney, Hofman, Sklarof, and Wishnick, 2019: 625):

> [T]he project does have a dedicated cryptoasset: an ERC-20 token called PRG. The whitepaper specifies that PRG holders will be able to interact with all of the project's many initiatives; holders will be able to vote on real estate investments, guide project governance decisions, purchase access to coworking services, and exchange tokens for local currency in cannabis-unfriendly jurisdictions.

The most widely known cryptoasset, bitcoin, at this stage being almost a household name as the soaring levels of value of bitcoins have attracted news media attention (see, e.g., Orrell and Chlupaty, 2016, chapter 9; Ferguson, 2019), operates like all other cryptocurrencies in the absence of "any single institution to keep the system secure" (Hockett and Omarova, 2016: 1208). "Bitcoin is the first significant digital currency system that needs no centralized intermediary to maintain proper books," Cohney, Hofman, Sklarof, and Wishnick (2019: 603) write.[7] In lieu of institutional support from, for example, the sovereign state and its regulatory agencies, the bitcoin system must maintain trust in the network and the blockchain technology itself, including "a trustworthy record of ownership rights" (Cohney, Hofman, Sklarof, and Wishnick, 2019: 603). Given that cryptocurrencies such as bitcoin operate in the absence of patronage from the sovereign state, the new financial model "[a]ppear[s] to threaten the very core of the finance franchise, the centrality of the sovereign's full faith and credit as the foundation of money," Hockett and Omarova (2016: 1208) write. At the same time, it is disputable whether a monetary system can operate strictly on the basis of private ordering principles, that is, outside of the patronage and proprietorship of a sovereign state. Lawson (2018: 1173) says that in principle and practically over time,

> [f]or something to work as money, it needs to be trusted as a stable liquid store of value, and very likely this requires something that was trusted as a store of relatively liquid value prior to, or independently of, its positioning.

However, as money is ultimately embedded in trust in the economic and social systems that back up the currency, it may be that money claims based on a private ordering system work for some time, but Lawson (2018: 1173) is still sceptical regarding the robustness of this model:

> *If* unbacked-up paper was so accepted, and trusted, and everyone else expected everyone else to keep using it, then it could serve the functions of money and so be money. But I am contending that that situation is not one that pertains. (Emphasis in the original)

At the same time, Lawson (2018) admits that his own doubt is not a solid argument against private ordering-backed monetary systems. That is, it could be the case that the centrality of the sovereign state as the principal of the monetary system and the credit formation process will diminish in the future:

> There remains, of course, the interesting question of whether the structures of capitalist society could be *transformed* in such a manner that forms of branded paper, with little or no intrinsic value, could be trusted enough in themselves to be capable of alone serving the functions of money (if appropriately positioned as money).
>
> (Lawson, 2018: 1173; emphasis in the original)

Although this issue is an empirical question to be determined on the basis of data currently generated, Lawson (2018: 1173) speculates that it is difficult to muster the resources that build sufficient trust in such a monetary system so that stability and fairness can be achieved; there is reason to doubt that "such a scenario is achievable in a system based on money accumulation, contestation and conflict, in which trust (which is always required) is hard won."

In addition to the constitutive weaknesses of cryptocurrencies, another major concern is that they may operate as intended, as a form of private ordering market model grounded in the advanced and innovative use of computer technology, and with the majority of the investors/participants acting prudently, but still attracting fraudsters and illegal activities. Substantial empirical evidence indicates that is the case: "[A]pproximately one half of bitcoin transactions are associated with illicit activity," Cohney, Hofman, Sklarof, and Wishnick (2019: 607, footnote 64) report. The heightened "transactional privacy and security" (Hockett and Omarova, 2016: 1209) make cryptocurrencies such as bitcoin "an attractive means of money laundering, terrorist financing, and illegal trading in online black markets." "This is a financial form ripe for fraud, and it has allegedly been used to that precise end," Cohney, Hofman, Sklarof, and Wishnick (2019: 594) observe. Furthermore, a recent study found that "approximately 20% of ICOs examined by the authors have red flags, including plagiarism in their whitepapers, false promises of returns, and fake founder profiles" (Cohney, Hofman, Sklarof, and Wishnick, 2019: 594, footnote 8). Omri (2013: 39) argues that cryptocurrencies possess "the traditional characteristics" of tax havens inasmuch as earnings are not subject to taxation and as taxpayers' anonymity is ensured. In addition, cryptocurrencies are not dependent on the existence of financial institutions. As opposed to traditional capital-market transactions that are "[h]eavily mediated by laws, regulations, contracts, and social norms," ICO transactions augment, and perhaps even replace, such mediators by "embedding controls within the smart contracts through which rules function," Cohney, Hofman, Sklarof, and Wishnick

(2019: 602) write (on smart contracts, see Buchwald, 2020; Young, 2018). In contrast to public equities such as stock or corporate bonds, traded in secondary markets such as the NYSE or NASDAQ, cryptoassets are changing hands (the metaphor here naturally reaches its outer limits and practical applicability) in hundreds of upstart markets, in many cases under light-to-nonexistent regulation (on the regulatory control of so-called fintech, which includes cryptocurrencies, see, for example, Brummer and Yadav, 2019; Magnuson, 2018; Arner, Barberis, and Buckley, 2015; Lin, 2014),[8] which also impairs investor protection:

> [T]he legal safeguards against ICO investor exploitation are, at present, significantly weaker than in other investment markets. It is easy for an issuer to set up shop in a low-regulation jurisdiction, and the architecture of the cryptoeconomy enables far more user and promoter anonymity than typical markets.
>
> (Cohney, Hofman, Sklarof, and Wishnick, 2019: 646)

Also Brummer and Yadav (2019: 242), speaking more broadly about fintech, call attention to the adverse consequences of cryptocurrencies and cryptoassets being developed on an industrial scale:

> [F]or some analysts, fintech represents nothing but a new iteration of the longstanding story of innovation in finance. We disagree and argue that in fact this time is different: fintech represents a phenomenon distinct from earlier eras of innovation. For one, much of today's innovation in the design and delivery of financial services utilizes not just more data, but qualitatively different forms of data—spanning social media, websites, or digital metadata—that have never before been available. Second, fintech tends to rely more than ever on not just online services, but also those underpinned by automated and increasingly self-learning operational systems. Finally, and critically, fintech is catalyzed by upstarts that identify and target discrete points in the supply chain for financial services—such as execution of financial transactions, surveillance and monitoring, payment and settlement, or a combination of all or any of these points.

Furthermore, fintech is not only problematic in terms of its design and possibilities, but also in the way that seemingly marginal errors and mistakes may generate considerable consequences in the global economy: "[B]y dint of poor programming, operational malfunctions, or hacking, [fintech] risk undermining core regulatory mandates such as financial stability and the protection of those who depend on financial markets for their economic security" (Brummer and Yadav, 2019: 243).

Evidence indicates that illicit activities increase the risk of more resolute legal and regulatory control, which per se makes, for example, bitcoin a less reliable store of value. By early 2019, US government agencies at both the federal and state levels had launched ICO investigations, resulting in several market actors being charged for being fraudulent or criminal enterprises. This ambition to regulate ICO activities was expected and is likely to expand in the future, Cohney, Hofman, Sklarof, and Wishnick (2019: 607) argue: "As the ICO market exploded so too did regulatory interest in its activities. Such scrutiny is no surprise: ICOs, like many internet-based phenomena before them, intentionally take place at the regulatory perimeter." Seen in this view, issuers of cryptoassets act as what Pollman and Barry (2017) refer to as "regulatory entrepreneurs," business promoters that actively challenge current legislation or regulatory practices as an integral component of their business model. Pollman and Barry (2017) count Uber, Airbnb, and Tesla in the category of regulatory entrepreneurs, high-profile companies that advance their business models despite being located in a legal grey zone and that actively engage, for example, clients to advocate legal and regulatory reforms being in the interest of the regulatory entrepreneur. In such situations, legal entities and regulatory agencies are likely to intervene to clarify market rules and to act as de facto and de jure market makers.

Regardless of such complications, the cryptoassets and cryptocurrencies emerging on the horizon of the financial economy are indicative of a social world and economy wherein credit relations can be generated quickly and virtually everywhere in a technology-mediated form. "It is increasingly clear that fintech is now an essential feature of the financial landscape," Magnuson (2018: 1173) writes. The domain of "regulated finance" (which some would regard as little more than a euphemism) has already proved to be complicated to uphold and to keep in balance despite the sharp growth in the number of agencies with specialized responsibilities, and if, for example, practices such as ICO spread rapidly, it will become increasingly difficult and costly for regulatory agencies to monitor credit supply. Needless to say, there has not yet been any major financial crisis resulting from an overheated cryptocurrency market—or rather, that is the conventional wisdom—and few experts and pundits would today be able to predict how such a situation would unfold and be handled on the basis of current political, legal, and regulatory devices and the resolution system at hand. In that situation, more detailed regulatory control and scholarly research would possibly deepen the understanding of how finance markets, cryptocurrencies, and the "real economy" (a term per se disputed on the basis of theoretical and substantive grounds) are interrelated and increasingly entangled.

Notes

1 Stock repurchase or stock repurchase announcements are debated in the scholarly literature. Some commentators regard stock repurchase as a legitimate mechanism as it enables insiders to signal to market actors that the market price of stock is

too low. Others argue that stock repurchases provide management with a device that enables a manipulation of stock market pricing, and that stock repurchases are theoretically inconsistent with the theory of strong or semi-strong market efficiency that otherwise justifies a number of governance practices. Furthermore, as an empirical fact, there is no evidence of companies making announcements that the stock is too *highly* valued, so the stock repurchase mechanism works "in one direction only"—to boost but not to moderate stock market evaluations. Despite these animated discussions in scholarly quarters, empirical evidence indicates a quite widespread use of the repurchase device. Data from 298 S&P Europe 500 companies reveal that stock repurchases tripled between 2000 and 2007, and in the 2009–2015 period, following the global finance industry meltdown, they again more than doubled (Dawid, Harting, and van der Hoog, 2019: 681). At the same time, the average "share-based component" (stock plus stock options) of CEO remuneration in S&P 500 companies increased from 36 to 60 per cent between 1992 and 2014 (Dawid, Harting, and van der Hoog, 2019: 681). That is, CEOs are increasingly compensated on the basis of their ability to increase the stock market evaluation of the firm's shares, and the growing popularity of this compensation package design coincides with active stock repurchases on the firm level. On average, "share-based pay" today accounts for 51 per cent of total CEO compensation, Dawid, Harting, and van der Hoog (2019: 691) write.

Dawid, Harting, and van der Hoog (2019) argue that stock repurchases and the increased return of residual cash to shareholders in terms of dividends harm the long-term competitiveness of the firm and reduce the compensation to labour. For instance, the above-mentioned study of 298 S&P Europe 500 companies shows that the total R&D expenditures were approximately €136 billion, whereas approximately €60 billion was used to repurchase stock. Furthermore, €268 billion was paid out to shareholders as dividends. That is, of the total amount of residual cash, roughly 70 per cent was returned to shareholders in the form of dividends and stock repurchases (whereof the latter raises the value of the stock for the benefit of shareholders who can either keep the asset in their portfolios or liquidize a certain proportion of their holdings to reinvest their return elsewhere). In conclusion, Dawid, Harting, and van der Hoog (2019: 700) argue that an "industry-wide adoption of a stronger orientation toward share-based remuneration" benefits shareholders, but that it would not increase "the speed of technological change and economic growth," and such shareholder benefits would come "at the expense of wage-earners' purchasing power." Expressed differently, Dawid, Harting, and van der Hoog (2019) do not regard stock repurchase programs in affirmative terms as some information-efficiency inducing device but as a zero-sum game wherein the shareholders' return comes at the cost of slower technological change and economic growth, and the wage-earners' loss.

2 Another class of social impact bonds are "health impact bonds," an investment device that "generate[s] income streams that are linked to reduced future uptake of health and welfare services, as well as anticipated increases in productivity" (Rowe and Stephenson, 2016: 1205). Similar to other SIBs, health impact bonds are designed to share the risk of future social problems between the state and private investors, and consequently, the efficacy of the investment device is dependent on a variety of underlying calculative practices, assumptions, and agreements, including the "stratification of risk exposure, outcome measurement strategies and use of population data to establish counterfactuals" (Rowe and Stephenson,

2016: 1205). In other words, to render health impact bonds attractive investment opportunities for private investors (say, pension funds or mutual funds), a great deal of the calculable risk and uncertainty must arguably be contained by the issuer, that is, the sovereign state or regional governments.

3 In fact, the institutional significance of the Federal Reserve in US policy is broader than is oftentimes recognized, Conti-Brown and Zaring (2019) argue. The Federal Reserve's primary role as a regulator and domestic guarantor of currency has been widely studied and debated, but its global reach and role in the financial system are comparably overlooked. In the US model, there is a "deep distinction" between "international and domestic monetary policy," Perry (2020: 748) writes. According to Stephen Axilrod, the former head of domestic monetary policy at the Federal Reserve Bank of New York (cited by Perry, 2020: 748), the Federal Reserve is "totally and utterly independent when making a domestic monetary policy decision," whereas the situation in the international arena is "more complicated": here, the Federal Reserve's independence is "unknown and has not been fully tested," and "the Treasury controls international finance." By design and in its effective role, the Federal Reserve needs to handle two sets of "tensions" (Conti-Brown and Zaring, 2019: 669): the first is the tension between "nationalism and cosmopolitanism," and the second is the Federal Reserve's "willingness to coordinate with other parts of government" and "its independence from the political branches" (Conti-Brown and Zaring, 2019: 669). In terms of the former issue, the historical record proves that the Federal Reserve is "cosmopolitan when it comes to regulating banks," whereas in the domain of monetary policy, it leans towards a nationalist credo. The second issue is perhaps more thorny from a constitutional and legal-political perspective as the American Constitution rests on the legal fiction of the president as being "the sole organ" through which the country's "foreign affairs are transmitted," thus being a "unitary voice" through which "executive policy is formulated" (Conti-Brown and Zaring, 2019: 672). But as with all legal fictions (defined in legal theory terms in Chapter 2), this vision of the presidency has both its conveniences and its limitations as it is more a figure of speech than a factual condition. In the modern bureaucratic administration, the diplomatic independence of the Federal Reserve is frequently glossed over. As a matter of fact, the diplomatic independence of the Federal Reserve actively supports the principal idea of the distribution of power into legal, political, and executive powers in the American Constitution inasmuch as the current situation wherein "a presidential election rises or falls on concepts of economic nationalism," the Federal Reserve may counterbalance such tendencies by supporting international standards for the financial system regardless of the (more short-term) policy of the current presidential administration.

In the end, the Federal Reserve carries a substantially larger regulatory burden than to simply regulate the financial system as the central bank acts with a great deal of independence to balance a variety of national and cosmopolitan objectives. This role cannot be abandoned as long as the United States enjoys what has been referred to as the "exorbitant privilege" to promote the US dollar as the dominant currency in the financial system and in global trade.

4 That is, markets are not perfectly informationally efficient as stipulated by the Efficient Market Hypothesis. At the same time, Bai, Philippon, and Savov (2016: 626) find that for the 1960–2014 period, so-called "price informativeness," defined as the ability of market prices to predict future returns, increased

dramatically over the medium- to long-term horizons, while remaining "relatively stable at short horizons (one year)." In fact, Bai, Philippon, and Savov (2016: 635) say, "[f]ive-year price informativeness is about 50% higher in the 2000s than in the 1960s." Documented improvements in price informativeness contribute to an increase in the "efficiency of capital allocation in the economy," Bai, Philippon, and Savov (2016: 626) propose, but they also recognize that "more informative prices do not necessarily imply that financial markets have generated an improvement in welfare." Market prices contain information produced independently by investors, but also include "information disclosed by firms." Only the "independent, market-based component of price informativeness" can contribute to the efficiency of capital allocation, Bai, Philippon, and Savov (2016: 626) remark, and therefore there is no straightforward causality between improved price informativeness and more efficient allocation of economic resources, nor the net economic welfare growth that is stipulated to follow from that condition.

5 One implication from such empirical evidence is that the fallacy that markets can price commodities in accordance with some "fundamental value" can be buried. For instance, Macey (2017) downplays the risk that hedge-fund activism would result in short-termism (i.e. a sub-optimization of the use of economic resources) as Macey believes "markets have become more efficient," which results in share prices more accurately and more quickly reflecting "market value," and that in turn undermines the value of "long-term investment." At this point Macey stipulates that the market pricing process is efficient (which Ferrillo, Dunbar, and Tabak, 2004, deny is the case on the basis of empirical evidence), which this does not prevent Macey from making the claim, a few pages later, that hedge fund activism serves a prophylactic role in terms of targeting "undervalued companies." But the very concept of "undervaluation" implies that the pricing process is not optimally efficient, because otherwise there would be no cases of undervalued companies to target, and "undervaluation" would be an oxymoron. In the first case, Macey claims, hedge fund activism is harmless simply because markets are stipulated to be informationally efficient, whereas in the second case, hedge funds do market participants the service of detecting and targeting companies whose shares are inaccurately priced. It is inconsistent to define market efficiency as it suits the argument: either markets are efficient (and hedge fund activism cannot do any harm in terms of reducing the value of long-term asset holding), or they are not (wherein hedge funds could do the service of detecting undervalued firms to discipline management to run them more effectively, given specific preferences), but the two conditions cannot coexist at the same time.

6 Cong and He (2019: 1754) define blockchain as a "distributed ledger technology typically managed in a decentralized manner." This ledger technology seeks to actively balance a "fundamental tension" between what Cong and He (2019: 1755) refer to as *decentralized consensus* and *information distribution*. Consequently, blockchain governance is based on an innovative and sophisticated technological governance model that scholars currently examine (e.g. Parkin, 2019).

7 Whereas Hockett and Omarova (2016) and Cohney, Hofman, Sklarof, and Wishnick (2019) emphasize that cryptocurrencies are in fact capable of operating outside of the central governance of a sovereign state on the basis of an innovative digital media-based private ordering model, Parkin (2019) stresses what he refers to as the "senatorial governance" of bitcoin currency. The bitcoin governance process is "[b]y no means a radical algocracy where automotive, decentralized code

is left alone to run economic transactions on behalf of society but, rather, is a structured hierarchy of disparate actors jostling for power to change the software design," Parkin (2019: 477) writes. This mode of governance includes a strict hierarchical authority that serves to render the cryptocurrency transparent and resilient, in Parkin's (2019) account. Blockchain-based currencies are consequently not as self-regulating and as self-enclosed as some commentators may believe, but include a fair share of traditional centralized monitoring and management. "The cost of collective action is hierarchy," Parkin (2019: 481) says.

8 Magnuson (2018: 1174) defines fintech broadly as "[t]he new breed of companies that specialize in providing financial services primarily through technologically enabled mobile and online platforms."

Bibliography

Abolafia, Michael, (2001), *Making markets: opportunism and restraints on Wall Street*, Cambridge, MA: Harvard University Press.

Abolafia, Mitchel Y., and Kilduff, Martin, (1988), Enacting market crisis: the social construction of a speculative bubble, *Administrative Science Quarterly*, 33(2): 177–193.

Acemoglu, Daron, and Restrepo, Pascual, (2017), Secular stagnation? The effect of aging on economic growth in the age of automation, *American Economic Review*, 107(5): 174–79.

Acharya, Viral, and Viswanathan, S. (2011), Leverage, moral hazard, and liquidity, *Journal of Finance*, 66: 99–138.

Adelino, Manuel, Schoar, Antoinette, and Severino, Felipe, (2018), The role of housing and mortgage markets in the financial crisis, *Annual Review of Financial Economics*, 15: 25–41.

Adrian, Tobias, and Ashcraft, Adam B., (2012), Shadow banking regulation, *Annual Review of Financial Economics*, 4: 99–140.

Adrian, Tobias, and Shin, Hyun Song, (2010), Liquidity and leverage, *Journal of Financial Intermediation*, 19(3): 418–437.

Adrian, Tobias, Fleming, Michael, Shachar, Or, and Vogt, Erik, (2017), Market liquidity after the financial crisis, *Annual Review of Financial Economic*, 9: 43–83.

Adrian, Tobias, Kiff, John, and Shin, Hyun Song, (2018), Liquidity, leverage, and regulation 10 years after the global financial crisis, *Annual Review of Financial Economics*, 15: 1–24.

Agarwal, Sumit, Amromin, Gene, Ben-David, Itzhak, Chomsisengphet, Souphala, and Evanoff, Douglas D., (2014), Predatory lending and the subprime crisis, *Journal of Financial. Economics*, 113(1): 29–52.

Akerlof, George, (1970), The market for "lemons": quality uncertainty and the market mechanism, *Quarterly Journal of Economics*, 84(3): 488–500.

Allen, Douglas W., (2012), *The institutional revolution: measurement and the economic emergence of the modern world*, Chicago & London: University of Chicago Press.

Allen, Franklin, and Gale, Douglas, (1994), Liquidity preference, market participation and asset price volatility, *American Economic Review*, 84(4): 933–955.

Allen, Franklin, Vayanos, Dimitri, and Vives, Xavier, (2014), Introduction to financial economics, *Journal of Economic Theory*, 149: 1–14.

Allen, Hilary J. (2018), The SEC as financial stability regulator, *Journal of Corporation Law*, 43(4): 715–774.

Almandoz, Juan, (2014), Founding teams as carriers of competing logics: when institutional forces predict banks' risk exposure, *Administrative Science Quarterly September*, 59(3): 442–473.

Alp, Aysun, (2013), Structural shifts in credit rating standards, *The Journal of Finance*, 68(6): 2435–2470.

Alstadsæter Annette, Johannesen Niels, and Zucman, Gabriel, (2019), Tax evasion and inequality, *American Economic Review*, 109(6): 2073–2103.

Ambrose, Brent W., Conklin, James, and Yoshida, Jiro, (2016), Credit rationing, income exaggeration, and adverse selection in the mortgage market, *Journal of Finance*, 71(6): 2637–2686.

Andrews, Edmund L., (2009), *Busted: life inside the great mortgage meltdown*, New York: W. W. Norton.

Ansell, Ben, (2014), The political economy of ownership: housing markets and the welfare state, *American Political Science Review*, 108(2): 383–402.

Arner, Douglas W., Barberis, Janos, and Buckley, Ross P., (2015), The evolution of fintech: a new post-crisis paradigm, *Georgetown Journal of International Law*, 47: 1271–1319.

Arnold, Patricia J., (2005), Disciplining domestic regulation: the World Trade Organization and the market for professional services, *Accounting, Organizations and Society*, 30(4): 299–330.

Atkinson, Abbye, (2019), Rethinking credit as social provision, *Stanford Law Review*, 71(5): 1093–1162.

Audretch, David B., (2007), *The entrepreneurial society*, Oxford: Oxford University Press.

Auvray, Tristan, and Rabinovich, Joel, (2019), The financialisation–offshoring nexus and the capital accumulation of US non-financial firms, *Cambridge Journal of Economics* 2019, 43(5): 1183–1218.

Awrey, Dan, (2012), Complexity, innovation, and the regulation of modern financial markets, *Harvard Business Law Review*, 2: 235–294.

Awrey, Dan, (2013), Toward a supply-side theory of financial innovation, *Journal of Comparative Economics*, 41(2): 401–419.

Babb, Sarah, (2013), The Washington Consensus as transnational policy paradigm: its origins, trajectory and likely successor, *Review of International Political Economy*, 20(2): 268–297.

Bai, Jennie, Philippon, Thomas, and Savov, Alexi, (2016), Have financial markets become more informative? *Journal of Financial Economics*, 122(3): 625–654.

Baker, H. Kent, Powell, Gary E., and Veit, E. Theodore, (2003), Why companies use open-market repurchases: a managerial perspective, *Quarterly Review of Economics and Finance*, 43(3): 483–504.

Ball, Laurence M., (2018), *The Fed and Lehman Brothers: setting the record straight on a financial disaster*, Cambridge: Cambridge University Press.

Banner, Stuart, (2017), *Speculation: a history of the elusive line between gambling and investment*, New York & Oxford: Oxford University Press.

Baradaran, Mehrsa, (2015), *How the other half banks: exclusion, exploitation, and the threat to democracy*, Cambridge, MA: Harvard University Press.

Barba, Aldo, and Pivetti, Massimo, (2009), Rising household debt: its causes and macroeconomic implications – a long-period analysis, *Cambridge Journal of Economics*, 33(1): 113–137.

Barker, Richard, and Schulte Sebastian, (2016), Representing the market perspective: fair value measurement for non-financial assets, *Accounting, Organizations, and Society*, 56: 55–67.

Baron, Robert A., (2008), The role of affect in the entrepreneurial process, *Academy of Management Review*, 33: 328–340.

Baumer, Eric P., Ranson, J. W. Andrew, Arnio, Ashley N., Fulmer, Ann, and De Zilwa, Shane (2017), Illuminating a dark side of the American dream: assessing the prevalence and predictors of mortgage fraud across U.S. counties, *American Journal of Sociology*, 123(2): 549–603.

Baumol, William J., (2002), *The free-market innovation machine: analyzing the growth miracle of capitalism*, Princeton: Princeton University Press.

Belinfanti, Tamara, and Stout, Lynn, (2018), Contested visions: the value of systems theory for corporate law, *University of Pennsylvania Law Review*, 166: 579–631.

Bell, Stephen, and Quiggin, John, (2006), Asset price instability and policy responses: the legacy of liberalization, *Journal of Economic Issues*, 60: 629–649.

Berman, Elizabeth Popp, (2012), Explaining the move toward the market in US academic science: how institutional logics can change without institutional entrepreneurs, *Theory and Society*, 41: 261–299.

Besedovsky, Natalia, (2018), Financialization as calculative practice: the rise of structured finance and the cultural and calculative transformation of credit rating agencies, *Socio-Economic Review*, 16(1): 61–84.

Beswick, Joe, and Penny, Joe, (2018), Demolishing the present to sell off the future? The emergence of "financialized municipal entrepreneurialism" in London, *International Journal of Urban and Regional Research*, 42(4): 612–632.

Bidwell, Matthew J., (2013), What happened to long-term employment? The role of worker power and environmental turbulence in explaining declines in worker tenure, *Organization Science*, 24(4): 1061–1082.

Bidwell, Matthew, Briscoe, Forrest, Fernandez-Mateo, Isabel, and Sterling, Adina, (2013), The employment relationship and inequality: how and why changes in employment practices are reshaping rewards in organizations, *Academy of Management Annals*, 7: 61–121.

Binder, Sarah, and Spindel, Mark, (2017), *The myth of independence: How congress governs the Federal Reserve*, Princeton & Oxford: Princeton University Press.

Birch, Kean, (2017), Rethinking value in the bio-economy: finance, assetization, and the management of value, *Science, Technology, & Human Values*, 42(3): 460–490.

Blair, Margaret M, (2013), Making money: Leverage and private sector money creation, *Seattle University Law Review*, 36: 417–454.

Blancheton, Bertrand, (2016), Central bank independence in a historical perspective: myth, lessons and a new model, *Economic Modelling*, 52: 101–107.

Blanchflower, David G., (2019), *Not working: where have all the good jobs gone?* Princeton & Oxford: Princeton University Press.

Block, Cheryl, (2010), Measuring the true cost of government bailout, *Washington University Law Review*, 88: 149–228.

Block, Fred, and Somers, Margaret R., (2014), *The power of market fundamentalism: Karl Polanyi's critique*, Cambridge & London: Harvard University Press.

Bluhm, Christian, and Wagner, Christoph, (2011), Valuation and risk management of collateralized debt obligations and related securities, *Annual Review in Financial Economics*, 3: 193–222.

Bohle, Dorothee, (2014). Post-socialist housing meets transnational finance: foreign banks, mortgage lending, and the privatization of welfare in Hungary and Estonia, *Review of International Political Economy*, 21(4): 913–948.

Bohle, Dorothee, (2018), Mortgaging Europe's periphery, *Studies in Comparative International Development*, 53(2): 196–217.

Bolton, Patrick, Freixas, Xavier, and Shapiro, Joel, (2012), The credit ratings game, *Journal of Finance*, 67(1): 85–112.

Bond, Philip, Musto, David K., and Yilmaz, Bilge, (2008), Predatory mortgage lending, *Journal of Financial Economics* 94: 412–427.

Botzem, Sebastian, and Dobusch Leonhard, (2017). Financialization as strategy: accounting for inter-organizational value creation in the European real estate industry, *Accounting, Organizations, and Society*, 59: 31–43.

Bougen, Philip D., and Young, Joni J., (2012), Fair value accounting: simulacra and simulation. *Critical Perspectives on Accounting*, 23(4): 390–402.

Boy, Nina, and Gabor, Daniela, (2019), Collateral times, *Economy and Society*, 48(3): 295–314.

Braudel, Fernand, (1977), *Afterthoughts on material civilization and capitalism*, trans. by Patricia M. Ranum, Baltimore: Johns Hopkins University Press.

Braun, Benjamin, (2016), Speaking to the people? Money, trust, and central bank legitimacy in the age of quantitative easing, *Review of International Political Economy*, 23(6): 1064–1092.

Briffault, Richard, (2010), The most popular tool: Tax increment financing and the political economy of local government. *University of Chicago Law Review*, 77: 65–95.

Brine, Kevin R., and Poovey, Mary, (2017), *Finance in America: an unfinished story*, Chicago & London: University of Chicago Press.

Brummer, Chris, (2015), *Soft law and the global financial system: rule-making in the 21st century*, 2nd ed., Cambridge: Cambridge University Press.

Brummer, Chris, and Yadav, Yesha, (2019), Fintech and the innovation trilemma, *Georgetown Law Journal*, 107: 235–307.

Bryan, D., Rafferty, M., Toner, P., and Wright, S. (2017), Financialisation and labour in the Australian commercial construction industry, *Economic and Labour Relations Review*, 28(4): 500–518.

Bryan, Dick, and Rafferty, Michael, (2013), Fundamental value: a category in transformation, *Economy and Society*, 42(1): 130–153.

Bryan, Dick, and Rafferty, Michael, (2014), Financial derivatives as social policy beyond crisis, *Sociology*, 48(5): 887–903.

Brynjolfsson, Erik, and Saunders, Adam, (2010), *Wired for innovation: how information technology is reshaping the economy*, Cambridge & London: MIT Press.

Bubb, Ryan, and Prasad, Krishnamurthy, (2014), Regulating against bubbles: how mortgage regulation can keep main street and Wall Street safe-from themselves, *University of Pennsylvania Law Review*, 163: 1539–1630.

Buchak, Greg, Matvos, Gregor, Piskorski, Tomasz, and Seru, Amit, (2018), Fintech, regulatory arbitrage, and the rise of shadow banks, *Journal of Financial Economics*, 130(3): 453–483.

Buchwald, Michael, (2020), Smart contract dispute resolution: the inescapable flaws of blockchain-based arbitration, *University of Pennsylvania Law Review*, 168(5): 1369–1423.

Bullough, Oliver, (2019), The financial black hole at the heart of America, *The Guardian Weekly*, 22 November. [URL: www.pressreader.com/uk/the-guardian-weekly/20191122/page/36. Accessed 3 December 2019]

Calder, Lendol, (2009), *Financing the American dream: a cultural history of consumer credit*, Princeton: Princeton University Press.

Callon, Michel, Millo, Yuval, and Muniesa, Fabian, eds., (2007), *Market devices*, Oxford & Malden: Blackwell.

Calomiris, Charles W., and Haber, Stephen H., (2014), *Fragile by design: the political origins of banking crises and scarce credit*, Princeton & Oxford: Princeton University Press.

Carnes, Nicholas, (2013), *White-collar government: the hidden role of class in economic policy making*, Chicago & London: University of Chicago Press.

Carruthers, Bruce, (2005), The sociology of money and credit, in Smelser, Neil J. & Swedberg, Richard, (2005), *The handbook of economic sociology*, 2nd ed., Princeton & London: Princeton University Press, pp. 355–378.

Carruthers, Bruce G., (2015), Financialization and the institutional foundations of the new capitalism, *Socio-Economic Review*, 13(2): 379–398.

Caverzasi, Eugenio, Botta, Alberto, and Capelli, Clara, (2019), Shadow banking and the financial side of financialisation, *Cambridge Journal of Economics*, 43(4): 1029–1051.

Cerulo, Karen A., (2006), *Never saw it coming: cultural challenges to envisioning the worst*, Chicago: University of Chicago Press.

Cestau, Dario, Green, Richard C., and Schürhoff, Norman, (2013), Tax-subsidized underpricing: the market for Build America bonds, *Journal of Monetary Economics*, 60(5): 593–608.

Cestau, Dario, Hollifield, Burton, Li, Dan, and Schürhoff, Norman, (2019), Municipal bond markets, *Annual Review of Financial Economics*, 11: 65–84.

Chaboud, Alain P., Chiquoine, Benjamin, Hjalmarsson, Erik, and Vega, Clara, (2014), Rise of the machines: algorithmic trading in the foreign exchange market. *The Journal of Finance*, 69(5): 2045–2084.

Chabrak, Nihel, (2012), Money talks: the language of the Rochester School, *Accounting, Auditing & Accountability Journal*, 25(3): 452–485.

Chan, Konan, Ikenberry, David L., Lee, Inmoo, and Wang, Yanzhi, (2010), Share repurchases as a potential tool to mislead investors, *Journal of Corporate Finance*, 16(2): 137–158.

Cheffins, Brian R., and Armour John, (2011), The past, present, and future of shareholder activism by hedge funds, *Journal of Corporation Law*, 37: 51–103.

Chorev, Nitsan, and Babb, Sarah, (2009), The crisis of neoliberalism and the future of international institutions: a comparison of the IMF and the WTO, *Theory and Society*, 38: 459–484.

Chwieroth, Jeffrey M., (2010), *Capital ideas: the IMF and the rise of financial liberalization*, Princeton & Oxford: Princeton University Press.

Cingano, Federico, Manaresi, Francesco, and Sette, Enrico, (2016), Does credit crunch investment down? New evidence on the real effects of the Bank-Lending channel, *Review of Financial Studies*, 29(10): 2737–2773.

Coffee, John C. Jr., (2011), Systemic risk after Dodd-Frank: contingent capital and the need for regulatory strategies beyond oversight, *Columbia Law Review*, 111(4): 795–847.

Coffee, John C. Jr., (2012), The political economy of Dodd-Frank: why financial reform tends to be frustrated and systemic risk perpetuated, *Cornell Law Review*, 97: 1019–1082.

Cohney, Shaanan, Hofman, David, Sklarof, Jeremy, and Wishnick, David, (2019), Coin-operated capitalism, *Columbia Law Review*, 119(3): 591–676.

Colyvas, Jeannette A., and Powell, Walter W., (2007), From vulnerable to venerated: the institutionalization of academic entrepreneurship in the life sciences, *Research in the Sociology of Organizations*, 25: 219–259.

Comte, Auguste, (1975), *Auguste Comte and positivism: essential writings*, ed. by Gertrud Lenzer, New York: Harper Torchbooks.

Cong, Lin William, and He, Zhiguo, (2019), Blockchain disruption and smart contracts, *Review of Financial Studies*, 32: 1754–1797.

Conley, Dalton, and Gifford, Brian, (2006), Home ownership, social insurance, and the welfare state, *Sociological Forum*, 21: 55–82.

Conti, Annamaria, (2018), Entrepreneurial finance and the effects of restrictions on government R&D subsidies, *Organization Science*, 29(1): 134–153.

Conti, Joseph A., (2010), Producing legitimacy at the World Trade Organization: the role of expertise and legal capacity, *Socio-Economic Review*, 8(1): 131–155.

Conti-Brown, Peter, and Zaring, David, (2019), The foreign affairs of the Federal Reserve, *Journal of Corporation Law*, 44: 665–712.

Cooper, Christine, Graham, Cameron, and Himick, Darlene, (2016), Social impact bonds: the securitization of the homeless, *Accounting, Organizations and Society*, 55: 63–82.

Cornaggia, Jess, and Cornaggia, Kimberly J., (2013), Estimating the costs of issuer-paid credit ratings, *Review of Financial Studies*, 26(9): 2229–2269.

Cornaggia, Jess, Cornaggia, Kimberly J., and Israelsen, Ryan D. (2017), Credit ratings and the cost of municipal financing, *Review of Financial Studies*, 31(6): 2038–2079.

Coval, Joshua, Jurek, Jakub, and Stafford, Erik, (2009), The economics of structured finance, *Journal of Economic Perspectives*, 23(1): 3–25.

Crawford, Kate, and Schultz, Jason, (2014), Big data and due process: toward a framework to redress predictive privacy harms, *Boston College Law Review*, 55: 93–128.

Crowston, Clare Haru, (2013), *Credit, fashion, sex: economies of regard in Old Regime France*, Durham: Duke University Press.

Dallas, Lynne L., (2011), Short-termism, the financial crisis, and corporate governance. *Journal of Corporation Law*, 37: 264–364.

Damanpour, Fariborz, (1992), Organization size and innovation, *Organization Studies*, 13(3): 375–402.

Darcillon, Thibault, (2015), How does finance affect labor market institutions? An empirical analysis in 16 OECD countries, *Socio-Economic Review*, 13(3): 477–504.

Dari-Mattiacci, Giuseppe, Gelderblom Oscar, Jonker, Joost, and Perotti, Enrico C., (2017), The emergence of the corporate form, *The Journal of Law, Economics, and Organization*, 33(2): 193–236.

Davidson, Donald, (1963), Actions, reasons, and causes, *The Journal of Philosophy*, 60(23): 685–700.

Davidson, Paul, (2014), Income inequality and hollowing out the middle class, *Journal of Post Keynesian Economics*, 36(2): 381–384.

Davis, Gerald F., and Kim, Suntae, (2015), Financialization of the economy, *Annual Review of Sociology*, 41: 203–221.

Davis-Blake, Alison, and Broschak, Joseph P., (2009), Outsourcing and the changing nature of work, *Annual Review of Sociology*, 35: 321–340.

Dawid, Herbert, Harting, Philipp, and van der Hoog, Sander (2019), Manager remuneration, share buybacks, and firm performance, *Industrial and Corporate Change*, 28(3): 681–706.

Decker, Ryan, Haltiwanger, John, Jarmin, Ron, and Miranda, Javie, (2014), The role of entrepreneurship in US job creation and economic dynamism. *The Journal of Economic Perspectives*, 28(3): 3–24.

Decker, Ryan A., Haltiwanger, John, Jarmin, Ron S., and Miranda, Javin, (2016), Where has all the skewness gone? The decline in high-growth (young) firms in the US, *European Economic Review*, 86: 4–23.

Decker, Ryan A., Haltiwanger, John, Jarmin, Ron S., and Miranda, Javin, (2017), Declining dynamism, allocative efficiency, and the productivity slowdown. *American Economic Review*, 107(5): 322–326.

Deeg, Richard, (2009), The rise of internal capitalist diversity? Changing patterns of finance and corporate governance in Europe, *Economy and Society*, 38(4): 552–579.

De Grauwe, Paul, (2013), The political economy of the euro, *Annual Review of Political Science*, 16: 153–170.

De la Mano, Miguel, and Padilla, Jorge, (2018), Big Tech banking, *Journal of Competition Law & Economics*, 14(4): 494–526.

Dell'Ariccia, Giovanni, Laeven, Luc, and Marquez, Robert, (2014), Real interest rates, leverage, and bank risk-taking, *Journal of Economic Theory*, 149: 65–99.

De Rassenfosse, Gaétan, and Thomson, Russell, (2019), R&D offshoring and home industry productivity, *Industrial and Corporate Change*, 28(6): 1497–1513.

Deringer, William, (2015), For what it's worth: historical financial bubbles and the boundaries of economic rationality, *Isis*, 106(3): 646–656.

Desmond, Matthew, (2012), Eviction and the reproduction of urban poverty. *American Journal of Sociology*, 118(1): 88–133.

Desmond, Matthew, and Wilmers, Nathan, (2019), Do the poor pay more for housing? Exploitation, profit, and risk in rental markets, *American Journal of Sociology*, 124(4): 1090–1124.

Deutschmann, Christoph, (2011), Limits of financialization: Sociological analyses of the financial crisis, *European Journal of Sociology*, 52(3): 347–389.

Diamond, Douglas W., and Dybvig, Philip H., (1983), Bank runs, deposit insurance, and liquidity, *Journal of Political Economy*, 91: 401–419.

Diogenes the Cynic, (2012), *Sayings and anecdotes*, trans. by Robin Holt, Oxford & New York: Oxford University Press.

Dodd, Nigel, (2014), *The social life of money*, Princeton & London: Princeton University Press.

Dore, Ronald, (2008), Financialization of the global economy, *Industrial and Corporate Change*, 17(6): 1097–1112.

Dow, Sheila, (2017), Central banking in the twenty-first century, *Cambridge Journal of Economics*, 41(6): 1539–1557.

Downer John, (2011), "737-Cabriolet": the limits of knowledge and the sociology of inevitable failure, *American Journal of Sociology*, 117(3): 725–762.

Drutman, Lee, (2015), *The business of America is lobbying: how corporations became politicized and politics became more corporate*, Oxford: Oxford University Press.

Dukeminier, Jesse, and Krier, James E., (2002), The rise of the perpetual trust. *UCLA Law Review*, 50: 1303–1343.

Dunn, Mary R., and Jones, Candace, (2010), Institutional logics and institutional pluralism: the contestation of care and science logics in medical education, 1967–2005, *Administrative Science Quarterly*, 55: 114–149.

Dwyer, Rachel E., (2018), Credit, debt, and inequality, *Annual Review of Sociology*, 44: 237–261.

Eggert, Kurt, (2002), Held up in due course: Ccodification and the victory of form over intent in negotiable instrument law, *Creighton Law Review*, 35: 503–640.

Eichengreen, Barry, (2015), *Hall of mirrors: the Great Depression, the Great Recession, and the uses – and misuses – of history*, New York & Oxford: Oxford University Press.

Eichenseht, Kristen E., (2019), Digital Switzerlands, *University of Pennsylvania Law Review*, 167(3): 665–732.

Eisenberg, Melvin Aron, (1975), Private ordering through negotiation: dispute-settlement and rulemaking, *Harvard Law Review*, 89: 637–681.

Elkin-Koren, Niva, (2005), What contracts cannot do: the limits of private ordering in facilitating a creative commons, *Fordham Law Review*, 74: 375–422.

Engel, Kathleen C., and McCoy, Patricia A., (2001), A tale of three markets: the law and economics of predatory lending, *Texas Law Review*, 80(6): 1255–1381.

Engel, Kathleen C., and McCoy, Patricia A., (2007), Turning a blind eye: Wall Street finance of predatory lending, *Fordham Law Review*, 75(4): 2039–2103.

Engelen, Ewald, (2017), Shadow banking after the crisis: the Dutch case, *Theory, Culture & Society*, 34(5–6): 53–75.

Englund, Peter, (1999), The Swedish banking crisis: roots and consequences, *Oxford Review of Economic Policy*, 15(3): 80–97.

Epstein, Gerald A., ed., (2005), *The financialization of the world economy*, Northampton: Edward Elgar.

Epstein, Rachel A., (2017), *Banking on markets: the transformation of bank-state ties in Europe & beyond*, New York: Oxford University Press.

Favara, Giovanni, and Imbs, Jean, (2015), Credit supply and the price of housing, *American Economic Review*, 105(3): 958–992.

Favilukıs, Jack, Ludvigson, Sydney C., and Van Nieuwerburgh, Stijn (2017) The macroeconomic effects of housing wealth, housing finance, and limited risk sharing in general equilibrium, *Journal of Political Economy*, 125(1): 140–223.

Ferguson, Frances, (2019), Bitcoin: a reader's guide (the beauty of the very idea), *Critical Inquiry*, 46(1): 140–166.

Fernandez, Rodrigo, and Wigger, Angela, (2016), Lehman Brothers in the Dutch off-shore financial centre: the role of shadow banking in increasing leverage and facilitating debt, *Economy and Society*, 45(3–4): 407–430.

Ferrillo, Paul A., Dunbar, Frederick C., and Tabak, David, (2004), The "less than" efficient capital markets hypothesis: requiring more proof from plaintiffs in fraud-on-the-market cases, *St. John's Law Review*, 78(1): 81–129.

Fields, Desiree, and Uffer, Sabina, (2016), The financialisation of rental housing: a comparative analysis of New York City and Berlin, *Urban Studies*, 53(7): 1486–1502.

Flaherty, Eoin, (2015), Top incomes under finance-driven capitalism, 1990–2010: Power resources and regulatory orders, *Socio-Economic Review*, 13(3), 417–447.

Fleming, Jonathan J., (2015), The decline of venture capital investment in early-stage life sciences poses a challenge to continued innovation, *Health Affairs*, 34(2): 271–276.

Fligstein Neil, and Roehrkasse, Alexander F., (2016), The causes of fraud in the financial crisis of 2007 to 2009: evidence from the mortgage-backed securities industry, *American Sociological Review*, 81(4): 617–643.

Fligstein, Neil, Brundage, Jonah Stuart, and Schultz, Michael, (2017), Seeing like the Fed: culture, cognition, and framing in the failure to anticipate the financial crisis of 2008, *American Sociological Review*, 82(5): 879–909.

Florida, Richard, (2002), *The rise of the creative class*, New York: Basic Books.

Forrest, Ray, and Hirayama, Yosuke, (2018), Late home ownership and social restratification, *Economy and Society*, 47(2): 257–279.

Fourcade, Marion, (2017), The fly and the cookie: alignment and unhingement in 21st-century capitalism, *Socio-Economic Review*, 15(3): 661–678.

Fourcade, Marion, and Healy, Kieran, (2013), Classification situations: life-chances in the neoliberal era, *Accounting, Organizations and Society* 38(8): 559–572.

Frame, W. Scott, and White, Lawrence J., (2004), Empirical studies of financial innovation: lots of talk, little action?, *Journal of Economic Literature*, 42(1): 116–144.

Frank, Robert H., (2007), *Falling behind: how rising inequality harms the middle class*, Berkeley: University of California Press.

Frieden, Jeffry, (2016), The governance of international finance, *Annual Review of Political Science*, 19: 33–48.

Friedlander, Roger, and Alford, Robert R., (1991), Bringing society back in: symbols, practices and institutional contradictions, in DiMaggio, Paul J., & Powell, Walter W., (1991), *The new institutionalism in organizational analysis*, Chicago: University of Chicago Press, pp. 232–263.

Froot, Kenneth A., Scharfstein, David S., and Stein, Jeremy C., (1992), Herd on the street: informational inefficiencies in a market with short-term speculation, *The Journal of Finance*, 47(4): 1461–1484.

Fuller, Gregory W., (2016), *The great debt transformation: households, financialization, and policy responses*, New York & Houndmills: Palgrave Macmillan.

Funk, Russell J., and Hirschman, Daniel, (2014), Derivatives and deregulation: financial innovation and the demise of Glass–Steagall, *Administrative Science Quarterly*, 59(4): 669–704.

Fuster, Andreas, Plosser, Matthew, Schnabl, Philipp, and Vickery, James, (2019), The role of technology in mortgage lending, *Review of Financial Studies*, 32(5): 1854–1899.

Gabor, Daniela, (2016), The (impossible) repo trinity: the political economy of repo markets, *Review of International Political Economy*, 23(6): 967–1000.

Garg, Sam, (2013), Venture boards: distinctive monitoring and implication for firm performance, *Academy of Management Review*, 38(1): 90–108.

Gelpern, Anna, and Gerding, Erik F., (2016), Inside safe assets, *Yale Journal on Regulation*, 33: 363–421.

Gerding, Erik F., (2005), Next epidemic: bubbles and the growth and decay of securities regulation, *Connecticut Law Review*, 38: 393–453.

Giebel, Marek, and Kraft, Kornelius, (2019), The impact of the financial crisis on capital investments in innovative firms, *Industrial and Corporate Change*, 28(5): 1079–1099.

Gielnik, Michael M., Spitzmuller, Matthias, Schmitt, Antje, Klemann, D. Katharina, and Frese, Michael. (2015), "I put in effort, therefore I am passionate": Investigating the path from effort to passion in entrepreneurship, *Academy of Management Journal*, 58(4): 1012–1031.

Gilens, Martin, (2005), Inequality and democratic responsiveness, *Public Opinion Quarterly*, 69(5): 778–796.

Gilens, Martin, (2012), *Affluence and influence: Economic inequality and political power in America*, Princeton & Oxford: Princeton University Press.

Gilens, Martin, and Page, Benjamin I., (2014), Testing theories of American politics: elites, interest groups, and average citizens, *Perspectives on Politics*, 12(3): 564–581.

Gilson, Ronald J., (2003), Engineering the venture capital market, *Stanford Law Review*, 55(4): 1067–1103.

Girdwood, John, (2007), Reforming the World Bank: from social-liberalism to neo-liberalism, *Comparative Education*, 43(3): 413–431.

Glaeser, Edward, and Gyourko, Joseph, (2018), The economic implications of housing supply. *Journal of Economic Perspectives*, 32(1): 3–30.

de Goede, M., (2005), *Virtue, fortune, and faith: a genealogy of finance*, Minneapolis & London: University of Minnesota Press.

Goldschlag, Nathan, and Tabarrok, Alex, (2018), Is regulation to blame for the decline in American entrepreneurship? *Economic Policy*, 33(93): 5–44.

Goldstein, Adam, (2018), The social ecology of speculation: Community organization and nonoccupancy investment in the U.S. housing bubble, *American Sociological Review*, 83(6): 1108–1143.

Goldstein, Adam, and Fligstein, Neil, (2017), Financial markets as production markets: the industrial roots of the mortgage meltdown, *Socio-Economic Review*, 15(3): 483–510.

Gompers, Paul, Gornall, Will, Kaplan, Steven N., and Strebulaev, Ilya A., (2019), How do venture capitalists make decisions? *Journal of Financial Economics*, 135(1): 169–190.

Goodrick, Elizabeth, and Reay, Trish, (2011), Constellations of institutional logics: changes in the professional work of pharmacists, *Work and Occupations*, 38(3): 372–416.

Gorton, Gary, (2017), The history and economics of safe assets, *Annual Review of Economics*, 9: 547–586.

Gorton, Gary, and Metrick, Andrew, (2012), Securitized banking and the run on repo, *Journal of Financial Economics*, 104: 425–451.

Gorton, Gary, and Pennacchi, George, (1990), Financial intermediaries and liquidity creation, *The Journal of Finance*, 45(1): 49–71.

Gorton, Gary, Lewellen, Stefan, and Metrick Andrew, (2012), The safe-asset share, *American Economic Review*, 102(3): 101–106.

Goshen, Zohar, and Parchomovsky, Gideon, (2006), The essential role of securities regulation, *Duke Law Journal*, 55: 711–782.

Greenberger, Michael, (2013), Closing Wall Street's commodity and swaps betting parlors, *George Washington Law Review*, 81(3): 707–748.

Greenwald, Bruce C., and Stiglitz, Joseph E., (1986), Externalities in economies with imperfect information and incomplete markets, *Quarterly Journal of Economics*, 101(2): 229–264.

Greenwood, Robin, and Scharfstein, David, (2013), The growth of finance, *Journal of Economic Perspectives*, 27(2): 3–28.

Griffin, John M., and Maturana, Gonzalo, (2016), Who facilitated misreporting in securitized loans? *Review of Financial Studies*, 29(2): 384–419.

Griffin, John M., Lowery, Richard Lowery, and Saretto, Alessio, (2014), Complex securities and underwriter reputation: do reputable underwriters produce better securities? *Review of Financial Studies* 27: 2872–2925.

Grossman, Sanford J., and Stiglitz, Joseph E., (1980), On the impossibility of informationally efficient markets, *American Economic Review*, 70(3): 393–408.

Grullon, Gustavo, and Ikenberry, David L., (2000), What do we know about stock repurchases? *Journal of Applied Corporate Finance*, 13(1): 31–51.

Gubler, Zachary J., (2014), Regulating in the shadows: systemic moral hazard and the problem of the twenty-first century bank run, *Alabama Law Review*, 63: 221–273.

Guerrieri, Veronica, and Shimer, Robert, (2014), Dynamic adverse selection: a theory of illiquidity, fire sales, and flight to quality, *American Economic Review*, 104(7): 1875–1908.

Guironnet, Antoine, Attuyer, Katia, and Halbert, Ludovic, (2016), Building cities on financial assets: the financialisation of property markets and its implications for city governments in the Paris city-region, *Urban Studies*, 53(7): 1442–1464.

Gupta, Priya S., (2019), The entwined futures of financialisation and cities, *Cambridge Journal of Economics*, 43(4): 1123–1148.

Hacker, Jacob S., and Pierson, Paul, (2016), *American amnesia: how the war on government led us to forget what made America prosper*, New York: Simon and Schuster.

Haiven, Max, (2014), *Cultures of financialization: fictitious capital in popular culture and everyday life*, Basingstoke: Palgrave Macmillan.

Hall, Bronwyn H., (1993), The stock market's valuation of R&D investment during the 1980's. *The American Economic Review*, 83(2): 259–264.

Hall, Peter A., and Thelen, Kathleen, (2009), Institutional change in varieties of capitalism, *Socio-Economic Review*, 7: 7–34.

Hanson, Norwood Russell, (1958), *Patterns of discovery: an inquiry into the conceptual foundations of science*, Cambridge: Cambridge University Press.

Harris, Robert S., Jenkinson, Tim, and Kaplan, Steven N., (2014), Private equity performance: What do we know? *The Journal of Finance*, 69(5): 1851–1882.

Hartwell, Christopher A., (2019), On the impossibility of central bank independence: four decades of time- (and intellectual) inconsistency, *Cambridge Journal of Economics*, 43(1): 61–84.

Haskel, Jonathan, and Westlake, Stian, (2017), *Capitalism without capital: the rise of the intangible economy*, Princeton: Princeton University Press.

Ho, Karen, (2009), *Liquidated: an ethnography of Wall Street*, Durham & London: Duke University Press.

Hockett, Robert, (2015), The macroprudential turn: from institutional "safety and soundness" to systematic "financial stability" in financial supervision, *Virginia Law & Business Review*, 9(2): 201–256.

Hockett, Robert C., and Omarova, Saule T., (2016), The finance franchise, *Cornell Law Review*, 102(5): 1143–1218.

Hoffman, Philip T., Postel-Vinay, Gilles, and Rosenthal, Jean-Laurent, (2000), *Priceless markets: the political economy of credit in Paris, 1660–1870*, Chicago: University of Chicago Press.

Houle, Jason N., and Berger, Lawrence, (2015), Is student loan debt discouraging homeownership among young adults? *Social Service Review*, 89(4): 589–621.

Howell, Sabrina T., (2017), Financing innovation: evidence from R&D grants. *American Economic Review*, 107(4): 1136–1164.

Huang, Laura, (2018), The role of investor gut feel in managing complexity and extreme risk, *Academy of Management Journal*, 61(5): 1821–1847.

Huang, Laura, and Knight, Andrew P., (2017), Resources and relationships in entrepreneurship: an exchange theory of the development and effects of the entrepreneurs-investor relationship, *Academy of Management Review*, 42(1): 80–102.

Hume, David, (1996), *Selected essays*, Oxford & New York: Oxford University Press.

Hunt, John Patrick, (2009), Credit rating agencies and the worldwide credit crisis: the limits of reputation, the insufficiency of reform, and a proposal for improvement, *Columbia Business Law Review*, 109(1): 109–209.

Hyman, Louis, (2011), *Debtor nation: the history of America in red ink*, Princeton: Princeton University Press.

Ireland, Paddy, (2010), Limited liability, shareholder rights and the problem of corporate irresponsibility, *Cambridge Journal of Economics*, 34: 837–856.

Ivanova, Maria N., (2019), Inequality, financialization, and the US current account deficit, *Industrial and Corporate Change*, 28(4): 707–724.

Jacobides, Michael G., (2005), Industry change through vertical disintegration: how and why markets emerged in mortgage banking, *Academy of Management Journal*, 48(3): 465–498.

Jacobs, David, and Myers, Lindsey, (2014), Union strength, neoliberalism, and inequality: contingent political analyses of U.S. income differences since 1950, *American Sociological Review*, 79(4): 752–774.

Jacobs, Lawrence R., and King, Desmond S., (2016), *Fed power: how finance wins*, New York: Oxford University Press.

Johnson, Kristin N., (2017), Regulating innovation: high frequency trading in dark pools, *Journal of Corporation Law*, 42: 833–886.

Jones, Daniel Stedman, (2012), *Masters of the universe: Hayek, Friedman, and the birth of neoliberal politics*, Princeton & Oxford: Princeton University Press.

Jordà, Òscar, Schularick, Moritz, and Taylor, Alan M., (2016), The great mortgaging: housing finance, crises and business cycles, *Economic Policy*, 31(85): 107–152.

Judge, Kathryn, (2017), Information gaps and shadow banking, *Virginia Law Review*, 103(3): 411–482.

Jung, Jiwook, (2016), Through the contested terrain: implementation of downsizing announcements by large U.S. firms, 1984 to 2005, *American Sociological Review*, 81(2): 347–373.

Kahle, Kathleen M., (2002), When a buyback isn't a buyback: open market repurchases and employee options, *Journal of Financial Economics*, 63(2): 235–261.

Kalecki, Michał, (1971), *Selected essays on the dynamics of the capitalist economy 1933–1970*. Cambridge: Cambridge University Press.

Kang, Karam, (2015). Policy influence and private returns from lobbying in the energy sector, *The Review of Economic Studies*, 83(1): 269–305.

Karger, Howard, (2005). *Shortchanged: life and debt in the fringe economy*. Oakland: Berrett-Koehler Publishers.

Katz, Avery, (1996), Taking private ordering seriously, *University of Pennsylvania Law Review*. 144: 1745–1763.

Keller, Matthew R., and Block, Fred, (2013), Explaining the transformation in the US innovation system: the impact of a small government program, *Socio-Economic Review*, 11(4): 629–656.

Kentikelenis, Alexander E., and Babb, Sarah, (2019), The making of neoliberal globalization: norm substitution and the politics of clandestine institutional change, *American Journal of Sociology*, 124(5): 1720–1762.

Kerr, William R., Nanda, Ramana, and Rhodes-Kropf, Matthew, (2014). Entrepreneurship as experimentation, *Journal of Economic Perspectives*, 28(3): 25–48.

Keynes, John Maynard, (1953), *The general theory of employment, interest and money*, New York & London: Harcourt.

Keys, Benjamin J., Mukherjee, Tanmoy, Seru, Amit, and Vig, Vikrant, (2009), Did securitization lead to lax screening? Evidence from subprime loans, *Quarterly Journal of Economics*, 125: 307–362.

Killewald, Alexandra, Pfeffer, Fabian T., and Schachner, Jared N., (2017), Wealth inequality and accumulation, *Annual Review of Sociology*, 43: 379–404.

Kindleberger, Charles P., (2007), *A financial history of Western Europe*, New York & London: Routledge.

Kornberger, Martin, and Carter, Chris, (2010), Manufacturing competition: how accounting practices shape strategy making in cities, *Accounting, Auditing & Accountability Journal*, 23(3): 325–349.

Krawiec, Kimberly D., (2013), Don't "screw Joe the Plumber": the sausage-making of financial reform, *Arizona Law Review*, 55: 53–103.

Krippner, Greta R., (2017), Democracy of credit: ownership and the politics of credit access in late twentieth-century America, *American Journal of Sociology*, 123(1): 1–47.

Kroll, Joshua A., Huey, Joanna, Barocas, Solon, Felten, Edward W., Reidenberg, Joel R., Robinson, Dvadi G., and Yu, Harlan, (2017), Accountable algorithms, *University of Pennsylvania Law Review*, 165(3): 633–705.

Kumhof, Michael, Rancière, Romain, and Winant, Pablo, (2015), Inequality, leverage, and crises, *American Economic Review*, 105(3): 1217–1245.

Kus, Basak, (2012), Financialisation and income inequality in OECD nations: 1995–2007, *Economic and Social Review*, 43(4): 477–495.

Lander, Michel W., Koene, Bas A. S., Linssen, Shelly N., (2013), Committed to professionalism: organizational responses of mid-tier accounting firms to conflicting institutional logics, *Accounting, Organizations and Society*, 38: 130–148.

Langley, Paul, Anderson, Ben, Ash, James, and Gordon, Rachel, (2019), Indebted life and money culture: payday lending in the United Kingdom, *Economy and Society*, 48(1): 30–51,

Lavinas, Lena, (2018), The collateralization of social policy under financialized capitalism, *Development and Change*, 49(2): 502–517.

Lawson, Tony, (2018), Debt as money, *Cambridge Journal of Economics*, 42(4): 1165–1181.

Lazonick, William, and Mazzucato, Mariana, (2013), The risk-reward nexus in the innovation-inequality relationship: who takes the risks? who gets the rewards?, *Industrial and Corporate Change*, 22(4): 1093–1128.

Lazonick, William, and O'Sullivan, Mary, (2000), Maximizing shareholder value: a new ideology for corporate governance, *Economy and Society*, 29(1): 13–35.

Lefcoe, George, (2010), Competing for the next hundred million Americans: The uses and abuses of tax increment financing, *The Urban Lawyer*, 43(2): 427–482.

Lépinay, Vincent Antonin, (2011), *Codes of finance: engineering derivatives in a global bank*, Princeton: Princeton University Press.

Lerner, Josh, (2009), *Boulevard of broken dreams: why public efforts to boost entrepreneurship and venture capital have failed and what to do about it*, Princeton & London: Princeton University Press.

Levitin, Adam, and Wachter, Susan M., (2020), *The great American housing bubble: what went wrong and how we can protect ourselves in the future*, Cambridge, MA: Harvard University Press.

Levitin, Adam J., (2011), In defense of bailouts, *Georgetown University Law Review*, 99: 435–514.

Levitin, Adam J., (2014), The politics of financial regulation and the regulation of financial politics: a review essay, *Harvard Law Review*, 127(7): 1991–2068.

Levitin, Adam J., (2016), Safe banking: finance and democracy, *The University of Chicago Law Review*, 83(1): 357–455.

Lin, Tom C.W., (2014), The new financial industry, *Alabama Law Review*, 65: 567–623.

Linton, Oliver, and Mahmoodzadeh, Soheil, (2018), Implications of high-frequency trading for security markets, *Annual Review of Economics*, 10: 237–259.

Lipson, Jonathan C., (2011), Re: Defining Securitization, *Southern California Law Review*, 85: 1229–1281.

Listokin, Yair, (2019), *Law and macroeconomics: legal remedies to recessions*, Cambridge, MA, & London: Harvard University Press.

Listokin, Yair, and Murphy, Daniel, (2019), Macroeconomics and the law, *Annual Review of Law and Social Science*, 15: 377–396.

Livne, Roi, and Yonay, Yuval P., (2016), Performing neoliberal governmentality: an ethnography of financialized sovereign debt management practices, *Socio-Economic Review*, 14(2): 339–362.

Lockwood, Erin, (2015), Predicting the unpredictable: Value-at-risk, performativity, and the politics of financial uncertainty, *Review of International Political Economy*, 22: 719–756.

Lok, Jaco, (2011), Institutional logics as identity projects, *Academy of Management Journal*, 53(6): 1305–1335.

LoPucki, Lynn M., (1996), The death of liability, *Yale Law Journal*, 106(1): 1–92.

Lupo-Pasini, Federico, (2017), *The logic of financial nationalism: the challenges of cooperation and the role of international law*, New York: Oxford University Press.

Luther, Jeffrey, (2020), Twenty-first century financial regulation: P2P lending, fintech, and the argument for a special purpose fintech charter approach, *University of Pennsylvania Law Review*, 168(4): 1013–1059.

Lysandrou, Photis, (2011), Global inequality as one of the root causes of the financial crisis: a suggested explanation. *Economy and Society*, 40(3): 323–344.

Lysandrou, Photis, and Nesvetailova, Anastasia, (2015), The role of shadow banking entities in the financial crisis: a disaggregated view, *Review of International Political Economy*, 22(2): 257–279.

MacKenzie, Donald, (2006), *An engine, not a camera: how financial models shape markets*, Cambridge, MA, & London, MIT Press.

MacKenzie, Donald, (2018), "Making," "taking" and the material political economy of algorithmic trading, *Economy and Society*, 47(4): 501–523.

MacKenzie, Donald, and Spears, Taylor, (2014), "A device for being able to book P&L": the organizational embedding of the Gaussian copula, *Social Studies of Science*, 44(3): 418–440.

Macey, Jonathan, (2017), Their bark is bigger than their bite: an essay on *Who bleeds when the wolves bite*, *Yale Law Journal Forum*, 126: 526–537.

Macey, Joshua, and Salovaara, Jackson, (2019), Bankruptcy as bailout: coal company insolvency and the erosion of federal law, *Stanford Law Review*, 71(4): 879–962.

Maddaloni, Angela, and Peydró, José-Luis, (2011), Bank risk taking, securitization, supervision, and low interest rates: evidence from the euro-area and the U.S. lending standards, *Review of Financial Studies*, 24(6): 2121–2165.

Magnuson, William, (2018), Regulating fintech, *Vanderbilt Law Review*, 71: 1167–1126.

Major, Aaron, (2014), Architects of austerity: international finance and the politics of growth, Redwood City: Stanford University Press.

Mallaby, Sebastian, (2016), *The man who knew: the life and times of Alan Greenspan*, London: Penguin Press.

Manzo, Lidia K. C., Druta, Oana, and Ronald, Richard, (2019), Supported home ownership and adult independence in Milan: the gilded cage of family housing gifts and transfers, *Sociology*, 53(3): 519–537.

Marshall, Wesley C., and Concha, Elizabeth, (2012), Fannie Mae and Freddie Mac: a bailout for the people? *Journal of Economic Issues*, 46(2): 557–564.

Marti, Emilio, and Scherer, Andreas G., (2015), Financial regulation and social welfare: the critical contribution of management theory, *Academy of Management Review*, 41(2), 298–323.

Martin, Andrew W., (2008), The institutional logic of union organizing and the effectiveness of social movement repertoires, *American Journal of Sociology*, 113(4): 1067–1103.

Martin, Antoine, Skeie, David, and von Thadden, Ernst-Ludwig (2014), The fragility of short-term secured funding markets, *Journal of Economic Theory*, 149: 15–42.

Mathis, Jérmôme, McAndrews, James, Rochet, Jean-Charles, (2009), Rating the raters: are reputation concerns powerful enough to discipline rating agencies? *Journal of Monetary Economics*, 56(5): 657–674.

Mayer, Christopher, (2011), Housing bubbles: a survey, *Annual Review of Economics*, 3: 559–577.

Mayer, Jörg, (2012), The growing financialization of commodity markets: divergences between index investors and money managers, *Journal of Development Studies*, 48(6): 751–767.

McConnell, John J., and Buser, Stephen A., (2011), The origins and evolution of the market for mortgage-backed securities, *Annual Review in Financial Economics*, 3: 173–192.

McCrain, Joshua, (2018), Revolving door lobbyists and the value of congressional staff connections, *Journal of Politics*, 80(4): 1369–1383.

McDonald, L. G. and Robinson, P., (2009), *A colossal failure of common sense: the inside story of the collapse of Lehman Brothers*, London: Ebury Press.

Mcfall, Liz, (2014), *Devising consumption: cultural economies of insurance, credit and spending*, London & New York: Routledge.

McKay, Amy Melissa, (2018). Fundraising for favors? Linking lobbyist-hosted fundraisers to legislative benefits, *Political Research Quarterly*, 71(4): 869–880.

McNamara, Kathleen R., (2002), Rational fictions: central bank independence and the social logic of delegation, *West European Politics*, 25(1): 47–76.

Mehrpouya, Afshin, and Salles-Djelic, Marie-Laure, (2019), Seeing like the market: exploring the mutual rise of transparency and accounting in transnational economic and market governance, *Accounting, Organizations, and Society*, 76: 12–31.

Meyer, Renate E., and Hammerschmid, Gerhard, (2006), Changing institutional logics and executive identities: a managerial challenge to public administration in Austria, *American Behavioral Scientist*, 49(7): 1000–1014.

Mian, Atif, and Sufi, Amir, (2014), *House of debt*, Chicago & London: University of Chicago Press.

Mian, Atif, and Sufi, Amir, (2018). Finance and business cycles: the credit-driven household demand channel, *Journal of Economic Perspectives*, 32(3): 31–58.

Mian, Atif, Sufi, Amir, and Verner, Emil, (2017), Household debt and business cycles worldwide, *The Quarterly Journal of Economics*, 132(4): 1755–1817.

Milberg, William, (2008), Shifting sources and uses of profits: sustaining US financialization with global value chains, *Economy and Society*, 37(3): 420–451.

Miller, Merton H., (1986), Financial innovation: the last twenty years and the next, *Journal of Finance Theory and Quantitative Analysis*, 21: 459–471.

Min, David, (2018), Housing finance reform and the shadow money supply, *Journal of Corporation Law*, 43(4): 899–937.

Merton, Robert C., (1987), A simple model of capital market equilibrium with incomplete information, *Journal of Finance*, 42(3): 483–510.

Modigliani, Franco, and Miller, Merton H., (1958), The cost of capital, corporation finance and the theory of investment, *American Economic Review*, 48(3): 261–297.

Molotch, Harvey, (1976), The city as a growth machine: toward a political economy of place, *American Journal of Sociology*, 82(2): 309–332.

Montesquieu, Charles-Louis de Secondat, ([1748] 1788a), *De l'esprit des lois: Oeuvres de Montesquieu*, Tome Deuxième. Paris: Jean-Françoise Bastien.

Montesquieu, Charles-Louis de Secondat, ([1748] 1788b), *De l'esprit des lois: Oeuvres de Montesquieu*, Tome Troisième. Paris: Jean-Françoise Bastien.

Montgomerie, Johnna, (2009), The pursuit of (past) happiness? Middle-class indebtedness and American financialisation, *New Political Economy*, 14(1): 1–24.

Morris, Stephen, and Shin, Hyun Song, (2012), Contagious adverse selection, *American Economic Journal: Macroeconomics*, 4(1): 1–21.

Muldrew, Craig, (1998), *The economy of obligation: the culture of credit and social relations in early modern England*, Basingstoke: Macmillan.

Müller, Julian, (2014), An accounting revolution? The financialisation of standard setting, *Critical Perspectives on Accounting*, 25(7): 539–557.

Murdock, Charles W., (2012), The big banks: background, deregulation, financial innovation, and "too big to fail,: *Denver University Law Review*, 90: 505–558.

Naciri, Ahmed, (2015), *Credit rating governance: global credit gatekeepers*, Abingdon & New York: Routledge.

Neff, Gina, (2013), *Venture labor: work and the burden of risk in innovative industries*, Cambridge & London: MIT Press.

Neu, Dean, Gomez, Elizabeth Ocampo, Graham, Cameron, and Heincke, Monica, (2006), "Informing" technologies and the World Bank, *Accounting, Organizations and Society*, 31(7): 635–662.

Nigam, Amit, and Ocasio, William, (2010), Even attention, environmental sensemaking, and change in institutional logics: an inductive analysis of the effects of public attention to Clinton's health care reform initiative, *Organization Science*, 21(4): 823–841.

Nissanke, Machiko, (2012), Commodity market linkages in the global financial crisis: excess volatility and development impacts, *Journal of Development Studies*, 48(6): 732–750.

Omarova, Saule T., (2013), The merchants of Wall Street: banking, commerce, and commodities, *Minnesota Law Review*, 98: 265–355.

Omri, Marian, (2013), Are cryptocurrencies super tax havens? *Michigan Law Review First Impressions*, 112: 38–48.

Onaran, Özlem, Stockhammer Engelbert, and Grafl, Lucas, (2011), Financialisation, income distribution and aggregate demand in the USA, *Cambridge Journal of Economics*, 35(4): 637–661.

Orhangazi, Özgür, (2019), The role of intangible assets in explaining the investment–profit puzzle, *Cambridge Journal of Economics*, 43(5): 1251–1285.

Orrell, David, and Chlupaty, Roman, (2016), *The evolution of money*, New York & London: Columbia University Press.

Pacewicz, Josh, (2012), Tax increment financing, economic development professionals and the financialization of urban politics, *Socio-Economic Review*, 11(3): 413–440.

Pache, Anne-Claire, and Santos, Filipe, (2013), Embedded in a hybrid context: how individuals in organizations respond to competing institutional logics, *Research in the Sociology of Organizations*, 37: 3–35.

Pagano, Udo, (2014), The crisis of intellectual monopoly capitalism, *Cambridge Journal of Economics*, 38(6): 1409–1429.

Pagano, Ugo, and Rossi, Maria Alessandra, (2009), The crash of the knowledge economy, *Cambridge Journal of Economics*, 33(4): 665–683.

Palan, Ronen, Murphy, Richard, and Chavagneux, Christian, (2010), *Tax havens: how globalization really works*, Ithaca: Cornell University Press.

Palma, José Gabriel, (2009), The revenge of the market on the rentiers: why neo-liberal reports of the end of history turned out to be premature, *Cambridge Journal of Economics*, 33(4): 829–869.

Pargendler, Mariana, (2016), The corporate governance obsession, *Journal of Corporation Law*, 42(2): 359–403.

Parkin, Jack, (2019), The senatorial governance of Bitcoin: making (de)centralized money, *Economy and Society*, 48(4): 463–487.

Pattillo, Mary, (2013), Housing: commodity versus right, *Annual Review of Sociology*, 39: 509–531.

Pauly, Mark V., and Swanson, Ashley, (2017), Social impact bonds: new product or new package?, *The Journal of Law, Economics, and Organization*, 33(4): 718–760.

Peck, Jamie, and Whiteside, Heather, (2016), Financializing Detroit, *Economic Geography*, 92(3): 235–268.

Peñaloza, Lisa, and Barnhart, Michelle, (2011), Living U.S. capitalism: the normal-ization of credit/debt, *Journal of Consumer Research*, 38(4): S111–S130.

Perrow, Charles, (1984), *Normal accidents*, New York: Basic Books.

Perry, Alexander R., (2020), The Federal Reserve's questionable legal basis for foreign bank liquidity swaps, *Columbia Law Review*, 120(3): 729–767.

Peterson, Christopher L., (2007), Predatory structured finance, *Cardozo Law Review*, 28(5): 2185–2282.

Philippon, Thomas, (2019), *The great reversal: how America gave up on free markets*, Cambridge, MA: Belknap Press.

Pierce, Justin R., and Schott, Peter K., (2016), The surprisingly swift decline of US manufacturing employment, *American Economic Review*, 106(7): 1632–1662.

Piskorski, Tomasz, Seru, Amit, and Vig, Vikrant, (2010), Securitization and distressed loan renegotiation: evidence from the subprime mortgage crisis, *Journal of Financial Economics*, 97(3): 369–397.

Pistor, Katharina, (2013), A legal theory of finance, *Journal of Comparative Economics*, 41(2): 315–330.

Pistor, Katharina, (2020), The value of law, *Theory and Society*, 49(1): 165–186.

Polillo, Simone, (2011), Money, moral authority, and the politics of creditworthiness, *American Sociological Review*, 76(3): 437–464.

Polillo, Simone, and Guillén, Mauro F., (2005), Globalization pressures and the state: the worldwide spread of central bank independence, *American Journal of Sociology*, 110(6): 1764–1802.

Pollman, Elizabeth, and Barry, Jordan M., (2017), Regulatory entrepreneurship, *Southern California Law Review*, 90: 383–448.

Polanyi-Levitt, Kari, (2013a), From mercantilism to neoliberalism and the financial crisis of 2008, in Kari Polanyi-Levitt (2013), *From the Great Transformation to the Great Financialization: on Karl Polanyi and other essays*, New York: Zed Books, pp. 137–179.

Posner, Eric A., and Weyl, E. Glen, (2012), An FDA for financial innovation: applying the insurable interest doctrine to 21st century financial markets, *Northwestern University Law Review*, 107(3): 1307–1358.

Power, Michael, (2010), Fair value accounting, financial economics and the transformation of reliability, *Accounting and Business Research*, 40(3): 197–210.

Prasad, Monica, (2012), *The land of too much: American abundance and the paradox of poverty*, Cambridge, MA, & London: Harvard University Press.

Pressman, Steven, (2007), The decline of the middle class: an international perspective, *Journal of Economic Issues*, 41(1): 181–200.

Punwani, A. (1997) A study of the growth-investment-financing nexus of the major UK construction groups, *Construction Management & Economics*, 15(4): 349–361.

Puri, M., and Zarutskie, R., (2012), On the life-cycle dynamics of venture-capital- and non-venture-capital-financed firms, *Journal of Finance*, 67(6): 2247–2293.

Quinn, Sarah L., (2017), "The miracles of bookkeeping": How budget politics link fiscal policies and financial markets, *American Journal of Sociology*, 123(1): 48–85.

Rajan, Raghuram G., and Zingales, Luigi, (2003), The great reversals: the politics of financial development in the twentieth century, *Journal of Financial Economics*, 69: 5–50.

Rajan, Uday, Seru, Amit, and Vig, Vikrant, (2015), The failure of models that predict failure: distance, incentives, and defaults, *Journal of Financial Economics*, 115: 237–260.

Reay, Trish, and Hinings, C. Robert, (2009), Managing the rivalry of competing institutional logics, *Organization Studies*, 30(6): 629–652.

Redbird, Beth, and Grusky, David B., (2016), Distributional effects of the Great Recession: where has all the sociology gone? *Annual Review of Sociology*, 42: 185–215.

Revest, Valérie, and Sapios, Alessandro, (2012), Financing technology-based small firms in Europe: what do we know? *Small Business Economics*, 39: 179–205.

Richardson, Matthew, Schoenholtz, Kermit L., and White, Lawrence J., (2015), Deregulating Wall Street, *Annual Review of Financial Economics*, 15: 199–217.

Richardson, Matthew P., Nieuwerburgh Stijn Van, and White, Lawrence J., (2017), What to do about the GSEs? *Annual Review of Financial Economics*, 9: 21–41.

Ricks, Morgan, (2011), Regulating money creation after the crisis, *Harvard Business Law Review*, 1: 75–143.

Ricks, Morgan, (2018), Money as infrastructure, *Columbia Business Law*, 3: 757–851.

Riles, Annelise, (2010), Collateral expertise, *Current Anthropology*, 51(6): 795–818.

Riles, Annelise, (2011), *Collateral knowledge: legal reasoning in the global financial markets*, Chicago: University of Chicago Press.

Roberts, Anthony, and Kwon, Roy (2017), Finance, Inequality and the varieties of capitalism in post-industrial democracies, *Socio-Economic Review*, 15(3): 511–538.

Robinson, Joan, (1966), *The accumulation of capital*, 2nd ed., London: Macmillan.

Robinson, John N. III, (2020), Making markets on the margins: housing finance agencies and the racial politics of credit expansion, *American Journal of Sociology*, 125(4): 974–1029.

Roe, Mark J., (2018), Stock market's short-termism's impact, *University of Pennsylvania Law Review*, 167(1): 71–121.

Rom, Mark Carl, (2009), The credit rating agencies and the subprime mess: greedy, ignorant, and stressed? *Public Administration Review*, 69(4): 640–650.

Rona-Tas, A., and Hiss, S., (2010), The role of ratings in the subprime mortgage crisis: the art of corporate and the science of consumer credit rating, *Research in the Sociology of Organizations*, 30A: 115–155.

Rona-Tas, Akos, (2017), The off-label use of consumer credit ratings, *Historical Social Research*, 42(1): 52–76.

Rosas, Guillermo, (2006), Bagehot or bailout? An analysis of government responses to banking crises, *American Journal of Political Science*, 50(1): 175–191.

Rowe, Rachel, and Stephenson, Niamh, (2016), Speculating on health: public health meets finance in "health impact bonds," *Sociology of Health & Illness*, 38(8): 1203–1216.

Saez, Emmanuel, and Zucman, Gabriel, (2019), *The triumph of injustice: how the rich dodge taxes and how to make them pay*, New York: Norton.

Scannell, Kara, and Houlder, Vanessa, (2016), US tax havens: the new Switzerland. *Financial Times*, 9 May [URL: http://bcrdc.com/BZ-FT-USTaxHavens_TheNewSwitzerland.pdf Accessed 3 December 2019]

Scheidel, Walter, (2017), *The great leveler: violence and the history of inequality from the Stone Age to the twenty-first century*, Princeton: Princeton University Press.

Schragger, Richard C., (2009), Mobile capital, local economic regulation, and the democratic city, *Harvard Law Review*, 123: 482–540.

Schragger, Richard C., (2010). Rethinking the theory and practice of local economic development, *University of Chicago Law Review*, 77: 311–339.

Schumpeter, J. A., (1928), The instability of capitalism, *Economic Journal*, 38: 361–386.

Schumpeter, Joseph A., ([1928] 1991), Capitalism, in Schumpeter, Joseph A., ([1928] 1991), *Essays: On entrepreneurs, innovations, business cycles, and the evolution of capitalism*, ed. by Clemence, Richard V., New Brunswick and London: Transaction Publishers, pp. 189–210.

Schwarcz, Steven L. L. (2002). Private ordering. *Northwestern University Law Review*, 97(1): 319–349.

Schwartz, Herman, (2012), Housing, the welfare state, and the global financial crisis: what is the connection? *Politics & Society*, 40(1): 35–58.

Schwartz, Herman Mark, (2016), Wealth and secular stagnation: the role of industrial organization and intellectual property rights. *RSF: The Russell Sage Foundation Journal of the Social Sciences*, 2(6): 226–249.

Schwert, Michael, (2017), Municipal bond liquidity and default risk, *Journal of Finance*, 72(4): 1683–1722.

Scott, Robert H., and Pressman, Steven, (2011), A double squeeze on the middle class, *Journal of Economic Issues*, 45(2): 333–342.

Searle, Llerena Guiu, (2018), The contradictions of mediation: intermediaries and the financialization of urban production, *Economy and Society*, 47(4): 524–546.

Sgambati, Stefano, (2016), Rethinking banking: debt discounting and the making of modern money as liquidity, *New Political Economy*, 21(3): 274–290.

Shane, Scott, (2017), *Is entrepreneurship dead? The truth about startups in America*, New Haven & London: Yale University Press.

Shapiro, Carl, (2018), Antitrust in a time of populism, *International Journal of Industrial Organization*, 61: 714–748.

Sheppard, Eric, and Leitner, Helga, (2010), Quo vadis neoliberalism? The remaking of global capitalist governance after the Washington Consensus, *Geoforum*, 41(2): 185–194.

Shin, Hyun Song, (2009), Securitization and financial stability. *The Economic Journal*, 119(536): 309–332.

Simon, Herbert A., ([1947] 1976), *Administrative behavior*, 3rd. ed., New York: Free Press.

Sissoko, Carolyn, (2019), Repurchase agreements and the (de)construction of financial markets, *Economy and Society*, 48(3): 315–341.

Smith, Adam, ([1776] 1986), *The wealth of nations*, London: Penguin.

Smith, Matthew, Yagan, Danny, Zidar, Owen, and Zwick, Eric, (2019), Capitalists in the twenty-first century, *Quarterly Journal of Economics*, 134(4): 1675–1745.

Sockin, Michael, and Xiong, Wei, (2015), Informational frictions and commodity markets, *Journal of Finance*, 70(5): 2063–2098.

Soener, Matthew, (2015), Why do firms financialize? Meso-level evidence from the US apparel and footwear industry, 1991–2005, *Socio-Economic Review*, 13(3): 549–573.

Sørensen, Morten, (2007), How smart is smart money? A two-sided matching model of venture capital, *Journal of Finance* 62(6): 2725–2762.

Souleles, Daniel, (2019), The distribution of ignorance on financial markets, *Economy and Society*, 48(4): 510–531.

Spears, Taylor, (2019), Discounting collateral: quants, derivatives and the reconstruction of the "risk-free rate" after the financial crisis, *Economy and Society*, 48(3): 342–370.

Stein, Samuel, (2019), *Capital city: gentrification and the real estate state*, London: Verso.

Stinchcombe, Arthur L., (1965), Social structure and organization, in March, J. G., ed., (1965), *Handbook of organizations*, Chicago: Rand McNally, pp. 142–155.

Stockhammer, Engelbert, (2013), Financialization and the global economy, in Wolfson, Martin H. and Epstein, Gerald, A., eds., (2013), *Handbook of the political economy of financial crises*, New York & Oxford: Oxford University Press, pp. 512–525.

Strahan, Philip E., (2013), Too big to fail: causes, consequences, and policy responses, *Annual Review in Financial Economics*, 5: 43–61.

Styhre, Alexander, (2019), *Venture work: employees in thinly capitalized firms*, Basingstoke & New York: Palgrave Macmillan.

Summers, Larry H., (2014), US economic prospects: secular stagnation, hysteresis, and the zero lower bound, *Business Economics*, 49(2): 65–73.

Summers, Nicole, (2020), The limits of good law: a study of outcomes in housing court, *The University of Chicago Law Review*, 87: 145–221.

Swedberg, Richard, (2010), The structure of confidence and the collapse of Lehman Brothers, *Research in the Sociology of Organizations*, 30A: 71–114.

Tang, Ke, and Xiong, Wei, (2012), Index investment and the financialization of commodities, *Financial Analysts Journal*, 68(6): 54–74.

Temin, Peter, (2017), *The vanishing middle class: Prejudice and power in a dual economy*, Cambridge, MA: MIT Press.

Thornton, Patricia H., (2002), The rise of the corporation in a craft industry: conflict and conformity in institutional logics, *Academy of Management Journal*, 45(1): 81–101.

Tillman, Joseph A., (2012). Beyond the crisis: Dodd-Frank and private equity. *New York University Law Review*, 87: 1602–1640.

Tomaskovic-Devey, Donald, Lin, Ken-Hou, and Meyers, Nathan, (2015), Did financialization reduce economic growth? *Socio-Economic Review*, 13(3): 525–548.

Tori, Daniele, and Onaran, Özlem, (2018), The effects of financialization on investment: evidence from firm-level data for the UK, *Cambridge Journal of Economics*, 42(5): 1393–1416.

Travis, Adam, (2019), The organization of neglect: Limited liability companies and housing disinvestment, *American Sociological Review*, 84(1): 142–170.

Tsui, Anne S., Enderle, Georges, and Jiang, Kaifeng, (2018), Income inequality in the United States: reflections on the role of corporations, *Academy of Management Review*, 43(1): 156–168.

Tucker, Paul, (2018), *Unelected power: the quest for legitimacy in central banking and the regulatory state*, Princeton: Princeton University Press.

Turner, Adair, (2015), *Between debt and the devil: money, credit, and fixing global finance*, Princeton: Princeton University Press.

Vallas, Steven, and Angèle Christin, (2018), Work and identity in an era of precarious employment: how workers respond to "personal branding" discourse, *Work and Occupations*, 45(1): 3–37.

Van Arnum, Bradford M., and Naples Michele I., (2013), Financialization and income inequality in the United States, 1967–2010, *American Journal of Economics and Sociology*, 72(5): 1158–1182.

Van der Zwan, Natascha, (2014), Making sense of financialization, *Socio-Economic Review*, 12(1): 99–129.

Veblen, Thorstein, (1916), *The industry systems and the captains of industry*, New York: Oriole Chapbooks.

Vives, Xavier, (2019), Digital disruption in banking, *Annual Review of Financial Economics*, 11: 243–272.

Vogel, Steven Kent (2018), *Marketcraft: How governments make markets work*, New York: Oxford University Press.

Waldron, Richard, (2016), The "unrevealed casualties" of the Irish mortgage crisis: analysing the broader impacts of mortgage market financialisation, *Geoforum*, 69: 53–66.

Wansleben, Leon, (2018), How expectations became governable: institutional change and the performative power of central banks, *Theory and Society*, 47(6): 773–803.

Wansleben, Leon, (2020), Formal institution building in financialized capitalism: the case of repo markets, *Theory and Society*, 49(1): 187–213.

Warner, Mildred E., (2013), Private finance for public goods: social impact bonds. *Journal of Economic Policy Reform*, 16(4): 303–319.

Webber, David, (2018), *The rise of the working-class shareholder: labor's last best weapon*, Cambridge, MA, & London: Harvard University Press.

Weiss, Marc A., (1989), Real estate history: an overview and research agenda, *Business History Review*, 63(2): 241–282.

Westphal, James, and Zajac, Edward, (2001), Decoupling policy from practice: the case of stock repurchase programs, *Administrative Science Quarterly*, 46(2): 202–228.

Wezel, Filippo Carlo, and Ruef, Martin, (2017), Agents with principles: The control of labor in the Dutch East India Company, 1700 to 1796, *American Sociological Review*, 82(5): 1009–1036.

White, Lawrence J., (2013), Credit rating agencies: an overview, *Annual Review in Financial Economics*, 5: 93–122.

Williams, James W., and Cook, Nikolai M., (2016), Econometrics as evidence? Examining the "causal" connections between financial speculation and commodities prices, *Social Studies of Science*, 46(5): 701–724.

Williamson, Oliver E., (2002), The lens of contract: private ordering, *American Economic Review*, 92(2): 438–443.

Willmott, Hugh, (2010), Creating "value" beyond the point of production: Branding, financialization and market capitalization, *Organization*, 17: 517–542.

Wilmarth, Arthur E. Jr., (2013), Turning a blind eye: why Washington keeps giving in to Wall Street, *University of Cincinnati Law Review*, 8(4): 1283–1445.

Wittgenstein, Ludwig, (1974), *Philosophical grammar*, ed. by Russ Rhees, trans. by Anthony Kenny, Oxford: Blackwell.

Wright, Mike, Lockett, Andy, Clarysse, Bart, and Binks, Martin, (2006), University spin-out companies and venture capital, *Research Policy*, 35(4): 481–501.

Yadav, Yesha, (2015), How algorithmic trading undermines efficiency in capital markets, *Vanderbilt Law Review*, 68(6), 1607–1671.

Yan, Shipeng, Ferraro, Fabrizio, and Almandoz, Juan (John), (2019), The rise of socially responsible investment funds: the paradoxical role of the financial logic, *Administrative Science Quarterly*, 64(2): 466–501.

Young, Charlotte R., (2018), A lawyer's divorce: will decentralized ledgers and smart contracts succeed in cutting out the middleman, *Washington University Law Review*, 96: 649–679.

Zaloom, Caitlin, (2006), *Out of the pits: trading and technology from Chicago to London*, Durham & London: Duke University Press.

Zhou, Xueguang, (2005), The institutional logic of occupational prestige ranking: reconceptualization and reanalyses, *American Journal of Sociology*, 111(1): 90–140.

Zingales, Luigi, (2017), Towards a political theory of the firm, *Journal of Economic Perspectives*, 31(3): 113–130.

Zinman, Jonathan, (2015), Household debt: facts, puzzles, theories, and policies, *Annual Review of Economics*, 7: 251–276.

Zucman, Gabriel, (2015), *The hidden wealth of nations: the scourge of tax havens*, trans. by Teresa Lavender Fagan, Chicago: University of Chicago Press.

Index

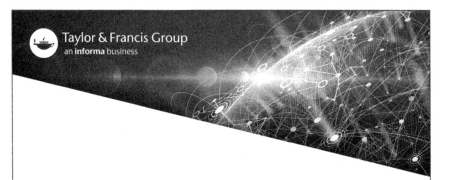

Printed in the United States
By Bookmasters